HOW
TO
SURVIVE
ON
LAND
&
SEA

The United States Naval Institute
Physical Education Series

Originating as a feature of the U. S. Navy's V-Five
Program during World War II, this series, comprising
a comprehensive library of sports and physical education,
has been continued by the U. S. Naval Institute, in support
of the belief that a high standard of physical fitness in
the youth of our nation is a prerequisite to national
preparedness. In preparing revisions of these works, every
effort is made to satisfy the need for adequate military
indoctrination while at the same time producing instructional
material compatible with civilian education interests.

HOW
TO
SURVIVE
ON
LAND
&
SEA

prepared by

FRANK C. CRAIGHEAD, JR., Ph.D.

and

JOHN J. CRAIGHEAD, Ph.D.

Wildlife Biologists
United States Fish and Wildlife Service

Illustrated by

ENSIGN ELIZABETH BUNKER, W-VS, U.S.N.R.

UNITED STATES NAVAL INSTITUTE

Annapolis, Maryland

Printed in the United States of America

by

GEORGE BANTA CO., INC., MENASHA, WISCONSIN

Preface

The first edition of this book was prepared from material used by numerous coaches and instructors in the U. S. Navy's V-Five Program during World War II, in order to provide the best possible standardized instruction in survival techniques for combat naval pilots, both on land and at sea.

Since World War II, the book has been widely used in the civilian field of instruction and reference. It is of interest and value to yachtsmen, hunters, explorers, sportsmen, Boy Scouts, and others interested in activities involving and dependent upon natural phenomena, in tropical, temperate or polar regions.

T. J. HAMILTON
Rear Admiral, U.S.N. (Ret.)

Executive Director
Athletic Association of Western Universities
San Francisco, California

Introduction

This text has been prepared to meet the need for essential yet comprehensive information on the techniques of survival under unusual conditions. It treats of survival on a global basis, emphasizing principles that can be grasped quickly and easily and practiced to the benefit of any person subjected to the hazards of nature.

This manual has been made as complete as is practical in the realization that a thorough knowledge of this subject gives confidence, aids in conquering fears of the unknown, and will serve as the foundation for making sound decisions. General and universally applicable principles formulated out of man's contact with nature throughout the ages have been set down and organized so as to enable the individual to make the maximum use of this knowledge at a time when survival may depend on the ability to apply it.

Much of the material included in this book is based on an actual survival survey by the authors of the Pacific areas during World War II.

In preparing such a text, it is impossible to rely upon information from any one source. A general acknowledgment is made to those individuals and institutions who throughout the years have recorded even the remotest of facts in order that such information might be available for the benefit of mankind. Various governmental agencies have furnished illustrations and their scientists have constructively reviewed this text. Among them are the Smithsonian Institution, the Bureau of Entomology and Plant Quarantine, the Bureau of Plant Industry, the Fish and Wildlife Service, the Special Forces Section O.Q.M.G., and the Emergency Rescue Equipment Section. The Library of Congress and the Department of Agriculture Library have also been most helpful.

Especial thanks are due O. Paul Carmi of the Training Section of the Navy Department's Bureau of Naval Personnel for preparing Chapter X.

Thanks are expressed to E. D. Merrill, Vilhjalmur Stefansson, and P. K. Emory whose published works were of value in preparing this book.

The sources of some of the plates were: *Wild Food Plants of the Philippines, Minor Products of Philippine Forests* by W. H. Brown; *Manual of the Trees of North America* by C. S. Sargent; and *An Illustrated Flora of the Northern United States, Canada, and the British Possessions* by Britton and Brown. Artwork opposite page 280 and on pages 343 and 345 is reproduced through the courtesy of Belmore Browne.

Acknowledgment is also made to the fine work of G. Donald Kepler in conducting the first Survival Training Course at the Navy Pre-Flight School, University of North Carolina.

Table of Contents

HOW
TO
SURVIVE
ON
LAND
&
SEA

A hastily-built camp which provided shelter for eleven fliers who were marooned for twelve days in northern Labrador.

CHAPTER I
Survival Hints

In a world-wide war of movement, you may suddenly find yourself stranded in unfamiliar conditions and surroundings in the Arctic, on the ocean, on a coral island, or in the jungle, or desert. You may tend to magnify the hazards of these strange places because of this unfamiliarity. Fear of the unknown weakens you by reducing your ability to think and plan. If you are armed with knowledge acquired beforehand, no part of the world will be completely strange or frightening to you. You will be capable of coping with the new surroundings and returning to your base in good physical and mental trim.

Survival in the jungle, desert, and arctic country depends largely on resourcefulness. Your chances of success will be greatly increased *if you are physically fit, if you are dressed and equipped for an emergency, if you know fundamental woodcraft principles and can to some extent apply them, and if you have at least a limited skill in a number of outdoor technics.* To feel at home in the wilderness you must learn to know it just as you have learned to know your home or city. You must learn what can be used for food, where to look for it, and how to prepare it. You must know how to care for your body, how to conserve energy, where to sleep, how to take shelter, and how to tell where you are at all times. Likewise, you must familiarize yourself with those things in the environment that will harm you. It is not an easy task, but you can do it.

Many forces will be operating against you to reduce the length of time you can survive. Food and water are always critical, but other factors such as warmth, shelter, and disease may also be hazardous, depending upon the conditions.

So many different emergency situations may confront you in a global war that it is impossible to lay out any definite survival formulae. The best assurance, therefore, that you can overcome all such adverse factors when on your own is to possess basic information on survival.

With even an elementary knowledge of fundamental woodcraft principles, you would not worry, for example, about a tiger being the cause of an unfamiliar night noise in our North American woods because you would know that tigers "can't happen here." Likewise, you would not waste valuable time and effort attempting to catch fish with a hook if you know that it is almost impossible to hook that particular species of fish because of its feeding habits.

3

FIG. 1. Individual Survival Equipment. A. Sheath Knife; B. Pocket Fishing Kit; C. Wrist Compass; D. Waterproof Matches and Case; E. Pencil Flashlight; F. Mosquito Head Net.

You may remember that a net or spear will do the trick, and know the method of making one from materials at hand. You may be covered with mosquito bites, but you are not concerned about contracting malaria in the North when you know that malaria is a disease of warm climates. Such elementary knowledge will enable you to eliminate many needless fears and absurd possibilities. Your survival time will be in direct proportion to the knowledge and skill you have at your immediate command, your ability to improvise successfully, and intelligently to apply specific information in supplying your immediate needs.

Be Prepared with Emergency Equipment

Well-considered preparation, made while you have time to prepare, will help you when an emergency comes. Every airman should take care to be dressed to cope with the physical conditions of the area over which he must fly and fight. He should have proper gear aboard his plane or on his person before he starts on a flight. The best kit is useless to a pilot who has crash-landed if the kit is on his bunk on the carrier or at the base 400 miles away. Planes *must* be checked before takeoff to see that necessary items are aboard.

The following items in your pockets or attached to your belt at all times will be excellent insurance, regardless of whether or not you also are carrying emergency and first-aid kits:

1. A strong pocket *knife* or sheath knife, preferably the latter.
2. *Waterproof matches* or matches in a waterproof container.
3. A small *waterproof compass.*
4. A *pencil flashlight* in a waterproof container.
5. A *shirt-pocket fishing kit.* This should consist of a dark lightweight fishing line, cadmium plated hooks (especially small sizes as most of the easily available food fish are small) and a small gold spinner with red and white streamer fly.
6. A *mosquito head net* is of great importance in jungle or arctic country, or wherever insect pests are numerous. Such a net will fold up no larger than a handkerchief.

This list is by no means exhaustive. The emergency kit should be carefully examined and additions made depending upon the type of country over which you must operate. Keep in mind, then, that a magnifying glass, a light harpoon-type spearhead, a side arm with shot shells (or shot shells that will fit your regular side arm) a light jungle hammock, a pocket size, one-burner gasoline stove, a first aid kit, rations, canteen, a small signalling mirror, a light down sleeping bag, a machete, and so on, are all of value.

Think Before Acting

When you are forced down on land in strange country, stick by your plane if there is a chance of rescue. It is easy to see, and may furnish a good shelter and base of operations. If you are in enemy territory, abandon the plane, first salvaging anything that can be of value to you in your trek to your own territory. Then sabotage the plane. Make a pack out of your parachute harness, cut a section of Nylon for a tent and hammock, save the shroud lines for a rope, and, if necessary, the rest of the Nylon for a blanket.

Over any considerable period you must have food, but remember that if water is available, if the body is not overexerted, and if the climate is warm, you can live off your muscle and fat for weeks. Don't eat if you lack water as eating uses up the body's water reserves. Determine a course to follow, and travel slowly. Don't exhaust yourself by pushing blindly and hurriedly on with a single objective in mind—to get out. Rather, your first consideration must be to keep physically and mentally fit. Start looking for food and water before you become too tired or exhausted to do so effectively. Prepare a bed and sleep when you become tired. Conserve your strength, and remember to observe and think so that when you act, you act intelligently.

Seeking Food

All food is either plant or animal, and is interrelated and distributed according to definite laws. There is order underlying the diversity in nature and this order will help you in searching for food. Since animals depend on plants for food, animal life is usually scarce where plant life is scarce.

Remember that climate is the greatest single factor affecting the abundance and distribution of plant and animal life. *Certain vegetative regions may be found throughout the world in more than one zone (Arctic, Temperate or Tropic) but wherever these regions occur they will have essentially the same appearance and will contain similar types of plants and animals.* Map I shows the distribution of these world vegetative regions where the problems of surviving and living off the land will be basically similar.

Within these regions are still smaller areas such as streams, lakes, marshes, swamps and various types of forests and grasslands, in which live specific characteristic forms of life. These areas are still further subdivided, and each subdivision has animals and plants peculiar to itself and all interrelated. Such areas are known as habitats.

This distribution greatly simplifies the search for food. If you know the edible animals and plants of North America and their habitat you can safely find and eat similar animals and plants in other parts of the world. Likewise your knowledge of one jungle or desert region may help you out of a similar spot on the other side of the earth.

Every climate and area will have some forms of life which are familiar to you, and some which are new but usable. Look for edible plants and animals in distant countries in the same type of places that you found them at home. If you hunted squirrels at home, you will know where to look for squirrel-like animals in other parts of the world. If you know where and how to look for crayfish, clams, rabbits or various birds at home, remember that similar regions abroad will have similar forms of life which you can seek in the same way.

More than half the task of obtaining food lies in knowing what to expect in a given area and where and how to look for it. You would not, for example, expect to find the coconut palm at high altitudes or in a dense forest, but in low, sandy, sea shore areas or on river flood plains. In an emergency, you might not start out to look for a particular type of food, but you will have a general idea of what to look for as you travel through different types of country, and can plan your course so as to enter areas where you can expect to find certain plants or animals.

Every animal is closely associated with a number of other animals living near it. A bird or animal beyond reach may still be a means of getting food if you make use of its presence intelligently. The fact that the bird or animal is there, indicates that its food source probably also is nearby, and it may be a source of food for you, too. If, for example, you see several hawks flying up at your approach, a careful search of the ground may disclose traces of mice, rabbits, or lizards, all sources of emergency food. On the arctic tundra a great snowy owl flitting ahead of you tells more plainly than words that you can expect to find mice or lemming beneath the snow or vegetation. A snake dropping into a jungle stream may startle you, but it should also let you know that a careful search may reveal an available source of food. Snakes are themselves edible, and they live exclusively on animal food. Water snakes live largely on fish, frogs, tadpoles and crayfish. These are all good eating for you, too, and are usually abundant where water snakes are found. Swarming bees may lead you to honey or to the bee grubs which natives consider a delicacy. Squirrels and related animals may be far out of reach, but their food supply of nuts, fruits, buds, seeds or leaves should be where you can get it. Diving terns, boobies, kingfishers or pelicans often indicate a good fishing spot. These are only a few examples of how plants or animals may point the way to food sources because all are intricately related by food chains. There are many more which you can use.

Testing Food

Never eat large quantities of a strange food without first testing it. If other foods are not available, eat a little of the strange one, and then wait a while. A small quantity of even a poisonous food is not likely to prove fatal or even dangerous, whereas a large quantity may be. In general it is safe to try foods that you observe being eaten by birds and mammals, but there are some exceptions. Food eaten by rodents (mice, rats, rabbits, beavers, squirrels, muskrats) or by monkeys, baboons, bears, racoons and various other omnivorous animals usually will be safe for you to try. Unknown plant foods with milky juices should be avoided. Any plant parts with an unusually bitter or otherwise disagreeable taste are not only unpleasant to eat but may be definitely harmful.

Throughout the world there are almost endless sources of food.

Plants, whether water or land, furnish edible:

Fruits	Buds	Nuts
Seeds	Leaves	Stems
Bark	Flowers	Roots
Tubers	Sap	Shoots
	Pods	

Edible animals vary infinitely:

1. Land mammals are easily recognized by their covering of hair. All are edible.
2. All birds and birds' eggs can be eaten.
3. Amphibians and reptiles (frogs, salamanders, toads, snakes, lizards and turtles) are good sources of edible meat.
4. Various other smaller forms of animal life may be the most available foods at a specific time and place. They include:
   Shellfish—clams, mussels, snails.
   Crustaceans—crayfish, crabs, shrimps, pawns.
   Insects—ants, termites, grasshoppers, locusts are numerous and are worldwide in distribution.
5. Animal byproducts include:
   Eggs—of birds, turtles.
   Honey—It can be found during most of the year, and is made by various types of bees.
   Caches—Fruits, nuts, seeds and roots are stored by mice, lemmings, squirrels, chipmunks.

CHAPTER II

Orientation and Traveling

One of your first problems when isolated in strange country is to determine approximately where you are and what direction you must travel in order to reach a base. The best insurance against getting lost in the event of a forced landing is to know the country over which you are going to fly. You can learn a great deal by studying maps, charts and photographs at every opportunity. Notice the general direction of flow of the larger rivers, the direction in which mountains or prominent ridges run, features of the shore line, the location of outstanding landmarks, *and their relationship to your base.*

If you're abandoning ship or plane at sea and have time, a notation of course and direction to the nearest land and of the latitude and longitude, will be most useful. If your watch is running and protected against crash or water damage it will help. Previously note the direction of prevailing winds and the flow of ocean currents, as these will determine the movement of your raft to a large extent. One may be favorable, the other unfavorable. With a favorable current and unfavorable wind, you can get farther by keeping the raft and yourself as low in the water as possible. Use of a sea anchor or drogue will increase the effect of the current. In a favorable wind, ride high by lightening the raft as much as is practical and hoist a makeshift sail.

If you find yourself lost on land, sit down, think the situation through, and don't be in a hurry to do anything. Try to avoid panic by divorcing from your mind any worry of the future. When you are calm and thinking clearly, see if you can recall to mind landmarks you saw from the air. Climb a high tree or hill and attempt to get your bearings.

If this does not give you a clue, you may experience a sense of utter isolation. Don't despair; restrain your impulse to push on, force yourself to observe, and remember that the worst fears are those of the imagination, and your greatest enemy is not the wilderness, but yourself.

Before you go anywhere, determine the cardinal directions from sun or stars and lay a course of travel. If you have a map or chart, it will be less difficult for you to establish where you are and where you wish to go.

The first step is to orient the map—with a compass if you have one, or if not, by the sun or the stars. Orienting a map consists simply of making north on the map coincide with true north. To orient with a compass, lay the map out flat, place the compass on it, and turn the map until the north-south grid lines are parallel to the compass needle, with map north coinciding with the

Fig. 2. Get a Clear View, Determine Your Course and Follow Your Compass

Fig. 3. Orient Map, Then Lay a Course of Travel

compass north. Then rotate the map and the compass together until the needle indicates the amount of magnetic declination (variation) for that area. The map is then oriented, and all directions on the map coincide with those on the ground. To determine the bearing you must follow to reach your destination, place the center of the compass over your own position on the oriented map. This is determined by an approximation or through the recognition of landmarks. A line from the center of the compass to your proposed destination will give you the bearing to follow. Remember that "compass north" is *magnetic* north, and that in most areas it is not the same as *geographic* north. The North Star gives you *geographic* north. Take heed of metal objects near your compass that may affect the reading.

If you are lost to such an extent that you do not know in which direction to travel in order to reach familiar territory, then a compass will only enable you to continue in a straight line along any course you choose.

CELESTIAL GUIDES

On land or sea, the sun and stars will guide you.

Sun

You can determine direction from the sun's position at any time of day, as well as in early morning and late evening.

The zenith is the point in the sky directly overhead. In the northern hemisphere, the path of the sun is distinctly south of the zenith in winter, and almost overhead during summer. At noon in winter the sun will be due south of you. In the southern hemisphere the situation is reversed.

In the tropics, the noon sun will be roughly either east or west of you, or directly overhead.

Notice where the sun strikes you when facing in the direction you want to travel. Relate its position to your direction frequently, and use it to help average your detours if you must follow a winding course.

In the northern hemisphere, a watch set by local sun time can be used to determine direction. Point the hour hand toward the sun. South will be half way between the hour hand and 12:00.

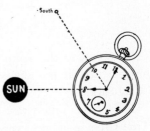

FIG. 4. Direction by Watch

On cloudy days, if the watch is held so that the shadow of a stick held upright at the center falls along the hour hand, North will be one half the distance between the shadow and 12:00 on the watch. These will give you only a rough approximation, and are not useful near the poles.

Stars

In the northern hemisphere, the two end stars on the bowl of the Big Dipper point to the North Star (Polaris) which is the last star in the handle of the Little Dipper. You can make a rough determination of your latitude by use of the fact that it is approximately the same number of degrees as the height of the North Star above the horizon.

In the southern hemisphere, a line through the long axis of the Southern

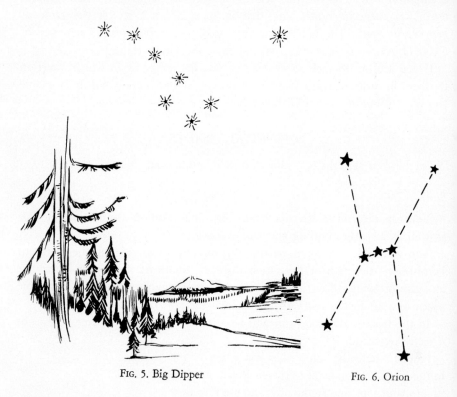

FIG. 5. Big Dipper   FIG. 6. Orion

Cross points to the south pole. There is no guiding star above it—only a blank space in the sky so dark by comparison that it is known as the "Coal Sack."

East of the True Cross are two very bright stars. By using these and the True Cross as guides, you can locate a spot within the Coal Sack which is approximately above the south pole. (See Figure 7.)

Extend a line along the long axis of the Southern Cross, to the south. Join the two bright stars east of the Cross by a line. Bisect this line with one at right angles. The point at which this line intersects the line through the Cross is approximately above the south pole.

Orion, an old friend of starry nights at home, is visible in most latitudes and will help you locate other familiar stars.

Near the equator, a star rising directly east of you will pass directly overhead and set directly west. In the northern hemisphere, that part of the horizon where the low stars move horizontally across the sky is the southern horizon. In the southern hemisphere, it is the northern horizon.

FIG. 7. Stars of Southern Cross That Point Due South

FIG. 8. Southern Cross

KEEPING A COURSE

The sun by day and the stars by night are valuable guides for maintaining a course, but they are not always visible, and you may in any case need to use additional methods. In strange country, observe outstanding features of the landscape and concentrate on keeping your course.

Observation from a high point, whether tree or ridge, will permit you to note the drainage patterns, the trend of ridges or mountains, and the character of the vegetation in an area.

If possible, choose a prominent landmark in the desired direction of travel that can be seen en route. Relate the position of the sun to yourself and the distant landmark. As you approach this landmark, line up another farther away. In dense forests where distant landmarks can't be seen, you can hold a course by lining up three trees. As soon as you pass one of these, line up another beyond the next two. Look back occasionally to note the relative positions of landmarks, slope and contour of the ground; for country looks entirely different when viewed from different observation points.

Streams, ridges, trees and bluffs will generally guide you in open country and enable you to retrace your route if it should be necessary. On cloudy days, in dense vegetation, or wherever the country presents a sameness of appearance, mark your trail with blazes, bent bushes, overturned logs, or rocks. Bushmarks are easily made, and should be cut or bent in such a manner that the under and lighter side of the leaves are uppermost. Such a sign is conspicuous in dense country.

Utilize trails when they are going in your general direction. You must look carefully for them as they may be well hidden, particularly in tropical rain forests and dense jungle country. At a fork, take the most traveled path and keep a lookout for traps and pitfalls on game trails.

If you lose your course or trail, stop and try to remember how long it has been since you were sure of your position. Mark the spot where you are with a pile of rocks, a bent bush, or blazes on four sides of a tree—marks you can see from some distance and any direction. Then you can start hunting or "back tracking" for your trail with the assurance that you can at least recognize the spot from which you started should you circle or choose the wrong direction. Don't travel by night in strange wooded country except in an emergency. In open or desert country, with the aid of the moon or stars, it is fairly simple and convenient. It may be the *only time* to travel in desert areas.

A light should be used at night only to read a map or compass, or in particularly rough or dangerous spots. Your eyes will adjust to darkness in a short time, while with a light you are blinded to everything outside the small area of illumination.

In open country you can hold a reasonably accurate course at night by selecting a fairly bright star near the horizon in your direct line of travel, and continuously lining it up with trees and other skyline landmarks ahead. Since stars appear to move from east to west due to the earth's rotation, you should check your direction frequently by the North Star or Southern Cross, and choose a new guide star when the old one moves out of position.

If you have a compass, check the magnetic bearing of your guide star every 15 minutes if the star is in the general direction of north or south, or every 30 minutes if it is east or west.

Detours

In rough country frequent detours must be made, and you should know how to compensate for them to get back on your course. Methods of doing this include:

1. In short detours, estimate the distance and average the angle of departure. On your return, gauge the angle and distance so as to strike your line again. For greater accuracy count paces and use a compass.

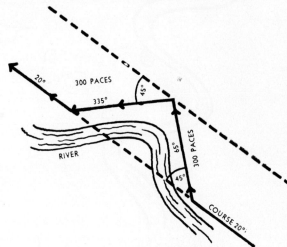

FIG. 9. Averaging Angle of Departure and Angle of Return

2. Select a prominent landmark ahead of you and one behind you on your line of travel. On returning from your detour, walk until you are again "lined up" on the two landmarks, then follow your original course.

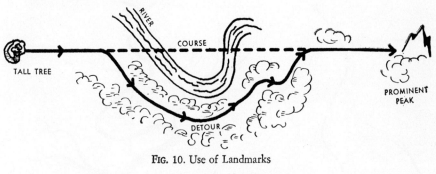

FIG. 10. Use of Landmarks

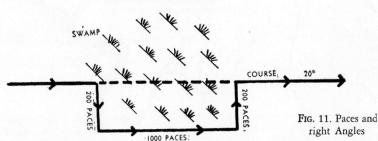

FIG. 11. Paces and right Angles

3. An easy way to compensate is by paces and right angles, although it requires more walking. (See Figure 11.)

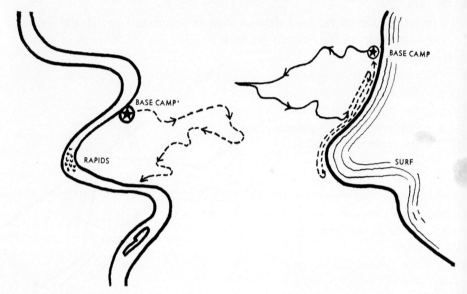

FIG. 12. Stream Base Line   FIG. 13. Shore Base Line

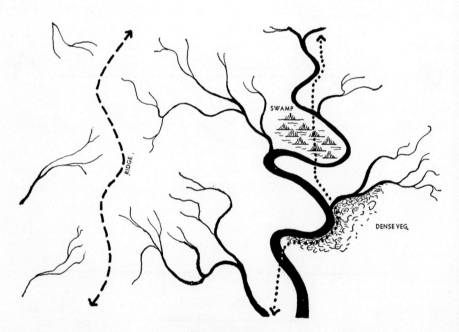

FIG. 14. Divide

Base Lines

If you have a more or less permanent camp site and want to explore unknown country, establish a base line at right angles to your intended reconnaissance direction. Any continuous line such as ridge, escarpment, range of hills, streams, seashore, or line of blazed trees or bushmarks will serve.

Explore the base line for several miles in each direction, noting characteristics you can remember so that you will know your approximate location on it when you strike it again. With a base line established, you can leave camp in search of food or water with reasonable assurance that you can return. As an example, let's assume that you are camped on a seashore. You leave camp, headed west in search of food or water. You know you have to go east to get back, but on your return you may veer from your course and strike the beach well above or below your camp.

If you have explored the beach for several miles each way from camp, you'll *know* whether you're above or below camp, and can travel back in the right direction. If you haven't established a base line, you may go several miles in the wrong direction, hunting camp, and then have to retrace your steps. You may cover 10 or 15 miles in getting to a camp only three miles away. (See Figures 12 and 13.)

TRAVEL HINTS

Whether you'll choose to travel on ridges and divides or follow valleys or streams; whether you'll follow trails or cut across country—these and many other questions will be determined by the situation in which you find yourself and the vegetation and topography of the area.

Ridges and Divides

Traveling on a ridge or divide is often easier than hiking in a valley or along a stream. Vegetation is usually less dense, the ridge itself serves as a guide, outlooks are frequent, and there will be few tributary streams or swamps to cross. On divides, be careful not to stray off on an intersecting ridge going the wrong direction.

Streams and Valleys

Following a stream generally requires much fording, detouring and penetration of thick vegetation. In mountain country there will be falls, cliffs, and side canyons. In flat country, the stream will meander, the vegetation will be dense, outlooks will be rare, and swamps common. Even so, it presents many advantages in strange country. It gives you a definite course which may lead to inhabited areas, and will also be a source of food, water, and a means of travel by boat or raft.

Shore Lines

A shore area may be easy or difficult to travel, but is almost always long and circuitous. Nevertheless, it is an excellent base line and food area, and a good place to "stick to" until you can orient yourself and lay a course for a known objective.

Jungle Brush or Dense Woods

Move through dense vegetation in one direction, but not in a straight line. Turn your shoulders, shift your hips, bend your body and shorten or lengthen, slow or speed your pace, as the situation requires. Avoid obstructions instead of fighting them. Keep alert, watching your surroundings generally and the ground in front of you closely. Stop and remain motionless now and then. You can thus hear or see an enemy, check your bearings, and locate animals. Rest frequently. A slow, steady rate of travel with rest as needed will get you much farther in the long run than a rate which will exhaust you in a short time.

Care of the Feet

Be sure your shoes fit well and that your feet are always in shape for a long walk. Heavy wool socks are best for hiking even in a warm climate, since they prevent chafing and absorb perspiration. Spare socks are a help, but if you can't change, you can at least wash those you have on, since dirty ones chafe and increase the danger of infection.

Attend to blisters or sprains at once.—Remove pressure on blisters by cutting your shoes or improvising footgear from canvas, plant fibers, or parachute silk. Don't break a blister. Prick the edge of it with a knife blade or thorn made sterile by flame or boiling. Then press out the fluid and keep the blister clean and dry, using a disinfectant if you have one. If infection develops, a day's rest may be well worth while. If you have salt, soaking an infected foot in hot salt water will help.

Wet shoes make the feet tender. Stop and dry them out if practicable.

A sprained ankle doesn't always swell or hurt immediately. If you give an ankle a bad wrench, bandage at once. Cold applications and rest will reduce the swelling and pain.

Concealment

In enemy territory, make use of natural cover and be sure that you have nothing on you that will reflect light or otherwise attract attention. Stop often to look and listen. Move quickly if crossing an exposed spot, and avoid silhouetting yourself against a contrasting background or the skyline. Conceal your trail by traveling on hard ground or in water. Avoid disturbing animal

FIG. 15. Signalling in the Snow with Evergreen Branches (Coast Guard)

life. Always look from the *dark* into the *light*. When danger threatens, never peer into the dark from a camp fire. By putting your head close to the ground and looking up you can see silhouettes against the night sky and remain unseen.

Signalling

Methods of making your whereabouts and needs known to rescuers include:

Signs—In snow you can tramp out letters or make them with evergreen branches. Against sand you can use shells, stones, or vegetation.

Smoke and Fire—You can produce heavy smoke by making a large fire and smothering it with damp vegetation, or by throwing engine oil on a fire.

FIG. 16. Signalling with Mirror

Flags—Parachutes spread against a dark background, or white clothing waving in the wind, will attract attention over moderate distances.

Mirrors—An aimed beam of light from a mirror made of any shiny material may be effective up to 10 miles on clear days. (See Figure 16)

Make a mirror from a food tin, or something else that is shiny on both sides. Punch a cross-hole in the center of the mirror and sight through the cross at the ship or plane with the mirror held about three inches in front of the face. The spot of light coming through the hole onto your face can be seen in the back mirror. Move the mirror so the cross of light on your face *disappears in the hole in the mirror, at the same time keeping a sight on the plane or ship.* The beam from the front of the mirror will then be aimed properly. With practice, you can signal down sun; the requirement is an angle between survivors, sun, and rescue party.

WATER TRAVEL

Streams, small and large, may present special hazards to you when trying to get back to your base.

FIG. 17. Use a Pole to Cross Swift Shallow Currents—Note Parachute Pack on Back

A stout pole, for use as a brace, will help you cross a shallow, swift stream. If the current is slow and the bottom rocky, keeping your body submerged will take most of the weight off your feet and reduce the danger from bruises. Cross deep, swift currents by swimming diagonally downstream.

In flat country the outsides of river bends generally have steeper banks and

Fig. 18. Swim Down Shallow Rapids Feet First on Your Back

Fig. 19. Inflate Trousers to Keep Your Feet Up

FIG. 20. Go Head First, on Your Belly in Deep Rapids

deeper and swifter water than inner curves. Cross diagonally and strike the inside of a bend where the water is apt to be slack and shallow. Often the current is slow and shallow at the widest part of a stream. Just above a riffle water is generally shallow. Use a log or small raft if the stream is wide, or you are a poor swimmer.

Rapids or swift water usually are not as dangerous as they look or sound. Never fight the current. Always swim *with* it and try to keep horizontal, to reduce the chance of being pulled under. *Go feet first, on your back, down fast, shallow rapids,* and "fin" your hands alongside your hips for buoyancy and as fenders against submerged rocks. Keep your feet *up* to avoid getting them bruised or caught by rocks. *Go head first, on your belly, down deep rapids* and angle toward shore as opportunity offers. Breathe between wave

FIG. 21. Don't Get Broadside to a Current

troughs. Be careful of backwater eddys and converging currents; they often contain dangerous swirls. Avoid bubbly water under falls as it has little buoyancy.

Don't take a chance in cold water, as your limbs will numb rapidly. Get something to hang onto, even if you are a strong swimmer.

If you must cross thin ice, distribute your weight even to the extent of lying down and pushing yourself along. When pulling yourself out of a hole in ice, place your hands on the ice, kick your feet until your body is level, then swim onto the ice and roll to a safe place. Don't stand up.

Canoes, Dugouts, Rafts

The easiest way to follow the course of a stream frequently will be to use it as a highway by means of a canoe, dugout, or raft.

If you can find a friendly native with a dugout, your travel troubles will be over. Since you may find the canoe and not the native, a little practice in canoe-handling will be useful. If there are no native craft available, you'll have to make and pole a raft.

Assuming that you're lucky enough to find a canoe or dugout but haven't handled one before, here are a few tips:

1. Keep your weight low, to reduce the chance of turning over.
2. Kneel amidships on one knee and paddle from this position. Paddle from the bow in a strong wind.
3. If you turn over, stay with the canoe. Climb into it over the bow or stern.
4. To paddle a straight course, pull your strokes straight back instead of following the contour of the canoe. Toward the end of each stroke turn the blade so that the inside edge is up. A short pull or shove with the turned paddle at the end of the stroke will turn the bow in the desired direction. The end of the canoe in which you are sitting will always move in the direction opposite to that of your paddle stroke.
5. Put the weight of your body behind each stroke. Don't paddle with your arms alone.

FIG. 22. Pick Your Course Before Starting Through Rapids

FIG. 23. Build a Raft and Follow a Stream to the Sea

Going *downstream* takes caution and quick action if the water is swift, particularly in rapids. Never enter rapids without first looking them over. Choose a course that will avoid rough water as much as possible. Locate submerged rocks. A split current indicates a rock close to the surface, a wave, a deeper rock. Don't get broadside to the current and don't hesitate too long in selecting a channel between rocks.

Going *upstream,* don't fight the current. Use eddies and back currents on the downstream side of rocks and shore projections. Paddle up in the lee of these projections, bucking the current only when necessary to shoot across the channel from one relatively calm spot to another. Hug the inside of bends, and cross fast water at an angle.

Poling a canoe or dugout is more efficient than paddling for going either up or down shallow rapids, or along a shallow protected coastline.

To pole a canoe or dugout, stand amidships, facing to one side. Drop the pole to the bottom so that it strikes directly below you. Slide your hands down and immediately lean forward, applying your weight backward against the pole while your hands alternately change position on the pole, "climbing" toward its upper end hand over hand.

If you can't find a canoe or dugout, two or more logs bound together will

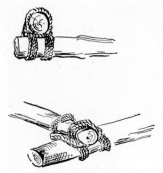

FIG. 24. Raft Lashing

serve as a raft for crossing or navigating a river. *Many tropical trees will sink even when the wood is dead, so be sure the wood you choose for a raft will float.* Stranded drift logs are the most readily available material. Float several such logs to a convenient spot and lash them together with bark. Dry and soft woods make better rafts than green or hard woods. Bundles of bamboo bound together with vines and lashed to cross pieces make an excellent raft. Palms do not float well.

Swimming in Aquatic Vegetation

While underwater and floating plants make swimming difficult, it is perfectly possible to swim through relatively dense vegetation. Keep calm, don't thrash about, and remove the plants as you would clothing, staying as near to the surface as possible, and swimming the breast stroke, with shallow arm or leg motion. Deep powerful strokes will entangle you. When you get tired, float or swim on your back.

Bogs, Quagmires, Muskeg, Quicksand

Swim, instead of attempting to walk, in any medium that won't support your weight. Muck, mud or sand will support your weight better than water, and you can float in water. The difference is that struggling or lifting your feet *while in a standing position* in muck or sand will only make you sink deeper. *If you feel yourself sinking, fall forward on your face, spread your arms, and start to swim or pull your way along, keeping your body horizontal.* In swampy areas, emergent vegetation usually indicates the ground is firm enough to support your weight. It probably will not be in areas of open mud or water, but if you are even a moderate swimmer you can swim, crawl, or pull your way through miles of bog or swamp.

You can get added buoyancy (as in water) by tying your pants at the ankles and forming air-pockets in the legs. You can also form air pockets over your shoulders by blowing your breath inside the front opening of your collar. Such a sack will keep your head from going under if you get caught in a vertical position, or need a rest.

Quicksand is sand held in suspension by water. It varies in depth and is usually, though not always, localized in area. Quicksands usually resemble ordinary sands and generally occur on flat shores, in silt-choked rivers with shifting water courses, and near the mouths of large rivers. Pebbles on sand are usually an indication the sand is not "quick" and you can test sand

FIG. 25. Flatten Out in Bog or Muck

FIG. 26. Forty Feet of Muck, but You Can Swim Through It

about which you are doubtful by tossing a small stone on it. The stone will sink in quicksand. In quicksand, as in a bog, flatten out, keep your lungs full of air, and move slowly. Quicksand exerts greater pressure than mud or muck.

Mangrove Swamps

Mangrove swamps occur along coastlines throughout the tropics. Wait for low tide before going through one. If you are on the shoreward side, look for a narrow area of trees and work seaward through these or follow the bed of a waterway or creek. In shallow water there is danger from crocodiles. Leave the water and scramble over the mangrove roots, or follow the soft mud banks. From the seaward side work inland along streams or channels. A raft is the best means of crossing a large swamp area.

Swimming in Surf and Currents

Knowledge of the action of the tides, currents, and surf will help you should you ever have to swim through them. In unknown waters, use the side or breast stroke to keep a reserve of strength for emergencies.

As waves break, they become higher, shorter, and the shoreward side curves to form a breaker. The water in a breaker, unlike that in an unbroken wave, actually moves forward instead of just seeming to do so. Small waves break in shallow water, large waves farther out.

If the surf is moderate, you can ride a small wave in by swimming forward with it as the crest picks you up, then surface-dive to end your ride just before the wave breaks. *If the surf is high, swim shoreward while in the trough between waves. As the next wave approaches, face the incoming breaker, submerge, and then work shoreward after it passes over.* Waves may break on reefs and bars miles from shore. Look for a channel or opening (indicated by the waves continuing shoreward unbroken). When swimming out through surf, wade as far as possible before swimming, dive under the breakers as they roll toward you and shove forward off the bottom as you come up.

Wave backwash or undertow is an outbound current set up by the seaward escape of water piled up on shore by breaking waves, and may be quite dangerous in the case of large waves. If you are caught in the backwash of a large wave, push off the bottom or swim to the surface, and ride shoreward on an incoming wave.

There are several types of dangerous marine currents which should be avoided if possible. *If you do get caught in a current, don't fight it. Swim parallel to the shore or diagonally across it as you would in a river current, heading shoreward only after you are out of the current.*

Rip currents are formed by the seaward escape of the water from waves which have broken over offshore bars or barrier reefs; runback occurs at the lowest point of the bar or reef. A similar outward current occurs where the backwash or the outgoing tide is confined to a narrow channel between rocks or shore projections. The water in a current is often murky or sandy in appearance, and usually will be deeper than adjacent waters. At ebb tide the waves in these currents are choppy and appear to be going out to sea instead of shoreward.

Strong tidal currents occur along many coasts and may carry you out to sea if you are caught in them. Tides on open, exposed coasts may average six

FIG. 27. Rip Current—Swim Across It to Calm Water and Then Shoreward

to eight feet, but may run to 30 or 40 feet and higher in narrow estuaries. In general, *high powerful tides* can be expected off rocky irregular shorelines, with alternating bays and promontories and *surf and rip currents* can be expected off low coastlines fringed with sandy bars, or coral reefs.

Fringing Coral Reefs

Fringing coral reefs extend out from the shore, forming shallow platforms. Coral is sharp, and severe cuts will result from swimming in a surf breaking over reefs. Go through a break in the reef, or go ashore opposite the mouth of a stream or wherever you see a depression or valley in the shore line, since coral cannot live in fresh water. This however, may involve going against a

current unless the tide is with you. Openings in the reefs may also be dis-
covered by the action of the breakers. Waves that do not break on the reef,
but continue their run toward shore, indicate a channel or area clear of coral.

Heavy Seas

In heavy seas, swim with the wind at your back, keeping as much of your

FIG. 28. In a Rough Sea Swim with Your Back to the Wind

body submerged as possible to avoid wave slap. Plunge through breaking
waves; don't attempt to swim over them.

Cramps

Stomach cramps can be avoided almost entirely by not entering the water
too soon after eating and by relaxing while swimming. Muscle cramps generally occur in very cold water or when the muscles are fatigued. At the first
indication of muscle cramp, try not to use the muscle involved. Continued
pressure and kneading of the knotted muscle will release the cramp.

Running a Boat Shoreward Through Surf

The greatest danger in running shoreward before a broken sea or in surf is that the boat may either be caught and thrown end over end or be turned broadside to the waves and capsized. A surf or roller overtaking the boat throws up the stern and depresses the bow. The forward motion of the boat must be sufficiently retarded to allow the surf to pass.

A sea anchor will check the boat's way and keep it end-on to the waves, reducing the danger of capsizing. A make-shift sea anchor can be made from a canvas bucket, a bundle of clothing, driftwood, a life jacket, or any object which can be fastened to a line and made to float, partially submerged, from the stern. Be liberal with the amount of line used.

If the surf is running high, go inshore against a current; the water will be deeper and the waves smaller there.

The surf will be less dangerous on a lee shore than on a windward shore.

Working a Boat Seaward Through Surf

Against a strong wind and heavy surf, a boat must have all possible speed as it approaches the crest of a wave, so as to pass through the crest as rapidly as possible and avoid being turned broadside or thrown end-over-end. Avoid meeting a large wave at the moment of breaking. If there is only medium surf, and no wind or an offshore wind, the boat must not be allowed to pass so rapidly through a wave that it falls suddenly after topping the crest.

If a boat turns over in the surf, fall out on the *seaward* side and grab hold of the boat.

TRAVEL IN MOUNTAINOUS OR OTHER ROUGH TERRAIN

Mountainous or deeply eroded country offers special difficulties. What appears as a single ridge and valley from a distance may prove to be numerous ridges and canyons, all of which must be crossed before reaching the main ridge. Snow fields which drop off in a sheer cliff may blend with those beyond to give the appearance of a continuous line of easy travel.

Your best bet in the mountains is to follow valleys or ridges; do not try to go at right angles to them. If you strike a blind canyon with nearly perpendicular walls, start over and try another route. Game trails may show you the best path.

If you must climb or descend a cliff, first attempt to choose a route that appears to offer hand and footholds, cracks, and ledges that offer an unbroken path from top to bottom. Chimneys are vertical cracks or troughs in a wall, and offer a variety of holds.

In climbing cliffs:

1. Test every hold carefully before trusting your weight to it.
2. Distribute your weight on two or more spots, particularly on loose rock. When standing, keep your feet apart.

3. Be cautious of getting into tight spots where you can't go either direction without danger.
4. Don't climb on loose or rotten rock. Remove loose stones as you descend, so they won't fall on you from above.
5. Keep your balance and keep moving, as a continuous movement from one hold to the other conserves strength. Use your legs as lifting power and your hands mainly for balance.
6. Use a rope, if possible, for descending steep cliffs or slopes. (See rappelling below.)
7. Keep your face, not your back, to the cliff, on a vertical descent.

Descending Cliffs

A rope for use in descending a cliff can be made by twisting four to six parachute shroud lines together.

Rappelling is a technic of using the friction of a rope against the body

Fig. 29. Keep Constantly Alert in Mountainous Country

in making a steep or vertical descent. (It is good for abandoning ship, as well as descending a cliff.) It combines a maximum of safety with a minimum of effort. If you're too weak to climb down a rope, you can still rappell down, rest on the way, and save the rope for future use.

To rappell, pass the rope around a tree or rock where it will not bind. Straddle both ropes and wrap them around one thigh, across the chest, over

FIG. 30. Rappelling

the opposite shoulder, and down across the back to be grasped by one hand. Grasp the rope in front of the body with the other hand. The arm that reaches forward is on the opposite side of the body from the encircled thigh. (See Figure 30.) Ease the grip of the hands and drop down in spurts, keeping the body more or less perpendicular to the cliff. The feet should be apart and against the cliff when possible. Slow or stop your drop by tightening your grip. After you get down, retrieve your rope. If there is no necessity

FIG. 31. Rappelling

FIG. 32. Climbing in a Spanish Bowline

for reuse of the rope, it can be tied single instead of double. Rappelling requires a heavy shirt and trousers to avoid rope burns.

When two people are present, one of the safest methods of descent is for one man to lower the other in a seat formed from a Spanish bowline. Use two ropes if possible. Secure one rope firmly to a tree and drop it over the cliff. Give the other rope a turn around the tree, get into the Spanish bowline, and let your comrade pay it out as you descend. The last man will have to rappell down.

Talus Slopes

A talus is a steep slope composed of loose rock at the base of a cliff. If it is of fine material, turn slightly sideways, keep

FIG. 33. Spanish Bowline

Fig. 34. Avoid Getting Caught on a High Peak in a Storm

Fig. 35. Glissading Down a Snowfield

your joints loose and go down on a diagonal course, taking long steps or jumps. If the talus is of coarse materials or large rocks, go more carefully, as a loose rock may roll under your weight.

Mountain Snowfields and Glaciers

The easiest and quickest method of getting down a steep snowfield may be to slide or glissade down, standing, using a short, tough stick which can

FIG. 36. Apply Pressure Gradually   FIG. 37. Snow Cornice

be dug into the snow to slow or stop your descent if you should fall. Beware of crevasses which are lightly covered with snow, or invisible from a distance.

Ice crevasses are particularly apt to occur on glaciers at right angles to the glacier flow. They seldom go all the way across the glacier, and thus may be detoured. Test a snow bridge across a glacier with a long pole before attempting to cross.

Kick or cut steps in a steep snow slope if you must cross it. Be on the lookout for avalanches of snow or rock, especially during thaws or in cold weather after a fresh snow. Rock falls are frequent in rugged mountains. Avoid traveling at the base of slopes or cliffs where you may be struck by them.

In topping a snow-covered ridge from the windward side, you may pass

FIG. 38. Climbing Coconut Palm   FIG. 39. Shinnying

FIG. 40. Right Way   FIG. 41. Wrong Way

the sound part of the ridge and walk out on a snow cornice that will break under your weight. From the leeward side, you can see such a cornice. Follow the ridge just below it.

Mountain Sickness

Lack of oxygen at high altitudes on the ground will have the same effect as lack of oxygen in a plane, except that the effect is intensified by physical exertion. Set a slow pace and make frequent short stops. Altitude or mountain sickness will be intensified by heavy exertion or by chilling, drinking cold water, or eating snow when you are tired and hot. An intense headache, weakness, and nausea are symptoms. Descent to lower altitudes and rest will effect a cure.

Climbing Trees

If you want to go up a palm tree after coconuts, do it native-style. Make a small loop from a rope of braided palm fibers or vines, and slip it around your ankles. Then grasp the trunk of the tree with your hands and climb. Hold with your hands as you draw up your feet, then straighten your body, using the friction of the rope and your feet against the tree to keep yourself from slipping. Another method is to loop the rope around the tree and the ankles. As you pull yourself up, the loop lifts with your feet and then binds on the tree.

FIG. 42. Use Low Limbs

As for tree climbing in general, remember to test all limbs before you put your weight on them; don't try to shinny up a tree so big that you can't reach around it or so high you'll be exhausted and fall before reaching the first branch. Dead limbs are notoriously untrustworthy and *any* limb is strongest next to the trunk. You can get badly burned from attempting to climb with little or no clothing. Seldom trust your entire weigh on one limb. Distribute it in two or three places. Be careful in climbing wet trees. When climbing large trees, utilize low-hanging branches, smaller trees and vines.

CHAPTER III

Water

Water is the most important single factor in determining survival. Without it, the presence or absence of food is of little importance. You can survive many days without food if you have water.

Under average conditions an individual needs at least a quart of water a day, but the amount essential under widely varying conditions of weather, climate and surroundings may be a great deal more or less. A man who knows how to use water intelligently may come through in reasonably good condition with a supply on which another man might die of thirst.

If you are extremely thirsty, sip slowly and don't take an excessive amount of water. Likewise, if you are hot from sun or from exercise, avoid drinking

FIG. 43. You Can Safely Drink from Streams Whose Upstream Portions or Sources Are Devoid of Human Habitations

cold water, or an excessive amount of water. If only cold water, snow, or ice is available, warm it in the mouth before swallowing.

If water is scarce, and you are exercising you will lose less through sweating if you drink a small amount at fairly frequent intervals than by taking a lot at a time. However, when the body is dehydrated there seems to be little difference.

FINDING WATER

The water table is the surface below which the rocks of the earth are saturated with water. Its level tends to follow the contours of the land surface,

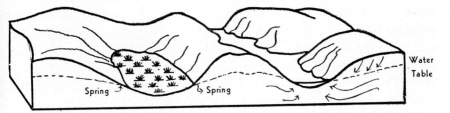

FIG. 44. Water Table

rising somewhat beneath hills, and in some places intersecting the surface to form springs and seepage areas or to merge with streams, swamps, lakes and oceans.

Water lying below the water table is termed ground water and in general is pure. Water lying above the table is runoff water and is much more likely to be contaminated. Water is an excellent germ-carrier and is almost always polluted near human habitations, particularly in the tropics. In inhabited areas it should be boiled. Streams, rivers and lakes usually are supplied by both ground and runoff water. Water from large lakes is generally safe if taken some distance from human habitation.

While running water tends to purify itself, it is not necessarily pure, nor is still water necessarily impure. A stagnant hole in the wilderness far from human habitation may be safe for drinking, and a running stream near a native village extremely dangerous. Water in swamps, bogs, and in pockets on the forest floor may be acid and dark from decaying vegetation, but it is not impure unless there is some outside source of pollution. Of course it should always be purified if it is near any human habitation.

A spring issuing from a rock usually is safe. Rain water is pure. *When looking for water remember that the water table is usually close to the surface and can be reached with little digging in low forested areas, along the seashore, and in the flood plains of large rivers.*

Along the Seashore

Rain water absorbed by the ground gradually seeps seaward, meeting the salt water at the shore. Drinking water usually can be obtained along the seashore by scooping out holes in the beach at low tide, or by digging a shallow well some distance from the shore. Water obtained away from the shore is generally fresher, but more labor is required in getting it. The best spot for digging is in a low basin where drainage from the land is concentrated.

Fresh water will be found first when you dig since it is lighter than salt water.

Water from any hole dug near the sea is apt to be brackish, but is safe to drink as it is found. Water too brackish to drink frequently can be made palatable by running it through a sand filter several times. Brackish water, although salty in taste, doesn't have a high enough salt concentration to be harmful. *Drinking sea water in any quantity when the body is dehydrated is extremely dangerous. The concentration of sodium and magnesium salts in it is so high that fluid must be drawn from the body to eliminate the salts, and eventually the kidneys cease to function.*

Desert or Arid Lands

In all arid parts of the world there are numerous indicators of the presence of water.

These include converging game trails, the presence and direction of flight of some birds, and the presence of certain plants.

Pigeons or parrots are always within reach of water. They may feed in the desert, but they will fly to water in the late morning and late afternoon. Water can be found by following their direction of flight. This rule may be of use in places as widely separated as our own Southwest, in Australia, and in desert regions of Asia and Africa. The sand grouse of arid parts of Asia are pigeon-like birds that fly many miles to congregate at water holes, for they must drink at least once a day. Crested larks and desert species of weaver birds and coursers may fly regularly to nearby water in the evening. Presence of diamond or zebra birds in the dry country of Australia is an almost infallible indication of

FIG. 45. Sand Grouse

the nearness of water. Many desert bats visit water regularly at the beginning of their evening flight.

Some plants grow only where ground water is close to the surface. Salt grass, rushes, sedges, cattails, greasewood, willows and elderberry are examples with which you may be familiar. Desert palms usually indicate surface water.

In dry regions, dig for water where vegetation appears to be greener or larger or markedly different from surrounding types, or where the sand is damp in dry river beds or other low areas. Brackish desert water should be filtered using soil a foot or so below the surface. The surface soil may itself be saturated with salts.

Dew can be collected in useful quantities during a clear night. Go abroad before daylight and gather it in a cup by tapping vegetation, or sponge it up with a handful of soft grass or a cloth. Australian natives sometimes mop up as much as a quart an hour in this way.

As a last resort, water may be obtained by breaking off a young desert tree at the base, and then removing the top. Turn the broken trunk upside down, and collect water from the drippings. (Methods of getting water from other plants are discussed on pages 44 through 48.

Mountains

On a clear day, mountain snow can be melted by placing a shallow container on a sunny exposure out of the wind. Apparently dry mountain stream beds often will contain water beneath the gravel stream bottom. Put your ear to the ground and listen for the trickle.

Finding Water in Cold Weather

In cold weather, springs and spring-fed streams remain open when other water courses are frozen.

Water can be obtained by cutting through the ice of a stream or lake. To obtain water by melting, use fresh ice or granular snow in preference to new spongy snow, as a smaller bulk will make more water and take less fuel and time. Eating snow and ice will quench thirst, but tends to chill the stomach and reduce body temperature.

In the Arctic Sea the most widely available water source is *old* salt-water ice, which can be distinguished from salt-ice by its bluish color and smooth, rounded corners. (Salt ice is grey and milky.) In summer, depressions on icebergs and floes contain fresh water. In bays or inlets protected from wind and current, water from melting snow and ice accumulates on the surface of the denser salt water and may remain fresh and unmixed with ocean water for long periods.

WATER FROM PLANTS

Sap is chiefly water and from many plants it is both fit to drink and readily available.

In an emergency, a water-yielding plant may save your life, or save valuable time by eliminating the necessity of purifying water from questionable sources. Some tropical lianas and palms have a steady flow of water in their stems. The fruits, growing tips, leaves, stems and buds of many plants contain small quantities of water.

Water from Succulent Plant Tissues

Many desert and other plants store water in their fleshy leaves or stems. In an emergency, such sources should be tried anywhere you happen to be.

The barrel cactus of the southwestern United States is well known as a source of water. Cut off the top of the plant, mash the pulp within against the inner sides, and the water will ooze out and collect in the bowl. The fruits and roasted pads or stems of very young prickly pears taste somewhat like asparagus and will help quench thirst.

Water from the Roots of Desert Plants

Water may be obtained from the roots of some desert plants that have their roots near the surface. The "water trees" of arid Australia are a part of the

Fig. 46. Getting Water from a Barrel Cactus

FIG. 47. Water from Grapevine

mallee scrub, one of the largest and most distinctive plant formations of Southern Australia. Roots of these "water trees" run out 40 to 80 feet at a depth of two to nine inches under the surface.

To get water from them, locate the root four or five feet from the tree trunk, pry it out of the ground, cut it into two- or three-foot lengths, and peel off the bark. Drain each section into a container, or suck out the water. One large mallee root usually will supply the water needs of two or three thirsty men.

Trees growing in hollows between ridges will have the most water, and roots one to two inches thick are ideal in size. Water can be carried in these roots by plugging one end with clay.

Water from the roots of all water producing plants is obtained in a manner similar to that described above. These plants include the Australian needle bush, desert oak, bottle tree, bloodwood, and several varieties of Acacia. The "water tree" or vine of Africa and South America is utilized in the same way.

Water from Vines, Stems, and Fruits

Vines.—Many large vines or lianas found in tropic rain forests contain a pure watery sap with a slightly acid flavor. Since not all of them will yield water, and the fluid from some is more palatable than others, it will be desirable for you to experiment with various species. Try any grapevine. The method of tapping them is the same for all:

Reach as high as you can and cut a deep notch in the vine or cut it off, keeping the severed end elevated. Then cut the vine close to the ground; this

FIG. 48. Make the Second Cut below the First One

should give you a water tube six to seven feet long. When water stops dripping from the lower end, cut another section off the top and more water will drain out. If the bottom of the vine is cut first, part or all of the water will be lost, as the water will ascend. (Grape vines found in the United States will yield water in this manner in the summer and fall.)

Many species of rattan palms produce good drinking water. They are vine-like palms with long, slender, segmented stems and sharp, downward curving thorns, and are widespread in tropical jungles and virgin forests.

Palms.—A drinkable sugary sap can be obtained in quantities from the buri, nipa, coconut, sugar and other palms. To start coconut sap flowing, bend the flower stalk downward and cut off the tip. Every 12 to 24 hours cut off a thin slice to renew the flow, which may reach a quart or more daily. The flow of sap can also be started by first bruising a lower frond and then pulling it down so the tree will "bleed" at the injury. The sap will run down the trough-like frond and can easily be collected.

On any one coconut palm, the nuts will be in varying stages of maturity. Contrary to your usual experience, the green nuts are the best. They are more easily opened with a knife or machete, have more fluid, and the fluid can be taken in quantity without harmful effects. The delicious juice of the ripened coconut will act as a violent physic if taken in quantities of more than three or four cups daily.

To get to the edible part of a coconut, slice off the stemless end of the outer husk to form a point, then cut off the point so as to sever the end of the inside shell. To husk a coconut without a knife, drive it on a sharp stick stuck in the ground, then crack the hard inner shell.

Banana and bamboo.—The slightly astringent water from the trunk of young banana trees is suitable for drinking. Water also can be obtained from the stems of some bamboos. (Shake them to see if water is inside.)

Plants That Catch and Hold Water

Many plants catch and store rain water in natural receptacles or decayed hollows.

The traveler's tree of Madagascar and Reunion has a cup-like sheath at the base of its vertical, fan-like leaves, in which quantities of drinkable water collect. Water can be obtained from both the leaf bases and roots of the umbrella tree of western tropical Africa.

The bottle-like trunk of the baobab tree of the sandy plains of northern Australia and Africa in the wet season collects water which frequently is found fresh and clear after weeks of dry weather.

Fig. 49. Bromelias

The air plants which affix themselves to jungle trees are good water reservoirs. Leaves of the pineapple-like Bromelias in particular form regular basins which may catch and hold several pints of rain water.

MUDDY, STAGNANT AND POLLUTED WATER

It is often necessary to use muddy, stagnant, or polluted water. Water polluted by mud or animals is unpleasant *but harmless if it is boiled*.

FIG. 50. Bamboo-sand
Water Filter

FIG. 51. Reed
Water Filter

Muddy water can be partially cleared by allowing it to stand overnight. It can be cleared more quickly, however, by passing it through a filter such as a sand-filled cloth, a length of bamboo filled with sand and clogged with grass or clothing to keep the sand in, or by using a grass or reed cone. For the latter, tie a handful of grass in the shape of a cone, six to eight inches long. Dip the cone into the puddle, then flick it upward and out. Water will trickle down through the small end of the cone.

Split cactus or Opuntia stems or "pads" placed in muddy water tend to clear it by gathering much of the sediment on their gelatinous tissues. These cacti are natives to the Americas but are also found in North Africa, Australia and India. (The best method of water clarification is by the use of ammonium alum, which forms a precipitate and settles to the bottom.)

Water with a disagreeable odor should be boiled and the odor neutralized by adding charcoal and ash from the fire.

Water that has merely had the sediment cleared out of it is not purified.

To be safe it must be boiled at least three minutes or longer. Halazone tablets, or three or four drops of iodine to a quart of water will help to

ourify unboiled water. Let it stand for a half hour before drinking. If there
s a slight chlorine smell, the water is safe to drink.

DANGERS OF DRINKING IMPURE WATER

Don't try to short-cut on water purification. Water-borne diseases are one
f the worst hazards of tropical
nd subtropical countries, particularly
vhere there are native populations. An
"untouched" wilderness is relatively
afe.

If you boil or chemically purify all
drinking water thoroughly you will
educe greatly the dangers of contract-
ng dysentery, cholera, typhoid fever
nd some of the parasitic infections.

Dysentery

Dysentery is the most common of
he water-borne diseases. The most
noticeable symptoms of both the
amoebic and bacillary dysentery are
evere and persistent diarrhea accompanied by mucus and blood mixed with
he stools. There is fever and general
veakness. If drugs are available, first

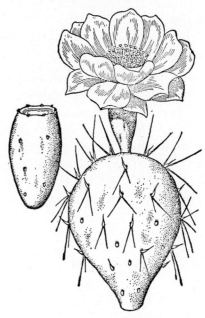

FIG. 52. Cactus (Opuntia)

ry bismuth subnitrate (one teaspoon every few hours in a little water until
disturbance stops). If this does not help, take 1 capsule of carbarsone (0.25
gm.) after each meal for five days and see a doctor as soon as possible.

Cholera and Typhoid

You will be given inoculations as a preventive against contracting these
wo diseases, but nevertheless don't take chances when they are prevalent.

Flukes and Worms

Blood flukes that parasitize man and cause painful and often fatal diseases
can be picked up through drinking sluggish, contaminated water in tropical
regions.

Some small crustaceans act as intermediate hosts to human parasites such
as the guinea worm, and are swallowed in drinking water. The guinea worm
larvae penetrate the walls of the intestines and migrate through the tissues,
lodging finally just beneath the skin. They produce blister-like lesions on the
lower extremities through which the young worms are discharged. If the

victim submerges himself in water, the worm protrudes its tail to eject egg
or larvae. Then it can be pinched and cautiously drawn out. Guinea worm
disease is found in large areas of Africa, India, Persia, Turkestan, West Indie
and Northern South America.

Prophylaxis consists in drinking only boiled water.

Leeches

In some areas, particularly in Africa, small leeches may be swallowed wit
the drinking water. They will attach themselves to the throat and nasal pas
sages, sucking blood and creating wounds which will continue to bleed afte
the leeches shift to new positions. The leeches can be removed with forcep
or by sniffing highly concentrated salt water.

The list of tropical diseases is impressive, but so is the list of those yo
might acquire at home if you didn't take normal precautions against them. Yo
have been immunized against some of them, and can greatly reduce th
chance of your getting any others by following recommended safety practice:
and using medical facilities whenever they are available.

CHAPTER IV

Wild Plant Food

Food follows water in the order of its importance in survival, and plants will be one of your most valuable food sources. To use them intelligently in an emergency you must have some practical knowledge of what they look like and where they grow.

RECOGNITION AND USE OF PLANTS

There are thousands of edible plants distributed throughout the world. Descriptions and pictures will help you identify them, but *the best way to familiarize yourself with the appearance and use of edible plants is to have someone point them out to you. Each time you are shown a plant, make a mental note of the kind of place (the habitat) in which you find it*. Without any particular effort you may soon find that you know just where to look for the best food plants of a region; for coconuts, breadfruit and plantains in the Tropics; for cranberries, salmon berries and crowberries in the Arctic.

Mastery of a few general facts and principles that you can learn before-hand will help you to find and recognize food plants in any part of the world.

Many groups of plants found at home are widespread throughout the world. Some of those found in North America also grow in the Philippines, in Malaya, Africa, India, China, Europe, the Arctic and other remote places. Although the different kinds or species which compose a group may be limited in distribution and habitat and may vary in minor details, all are similar in general appearance. When a plant appears to be familiar, use it as you would that kind of plant at home. The persimmons of the Philippines or China, for example, differ somewhat from our American ones, but they have character-istics by which you will recognize them as persimmons. (See Figures 53 and 95.)

Almost everyone has picked and eaten

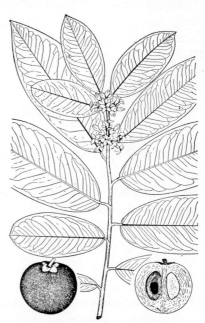

Fig. 53. Philippine Persimmon
(*Diospyros*)

51

raspberries or blackberries from thorny brambles near the edges of woods
fences, roads and trails. They will look the same when found in the Philip
pines, Pacific Islands, Africa, Australia, Siberia, Alaska, the Arctic, and othe
areas.

Most Americans have picked and eaten the round, dark blueberries, tha
grow on low bushes in areas where the
soil is acid, such as the borders of bogs
and swamps or sandy mountain or
coastal plain areas. Blueberries and
their close relatives are found in practically all parts of the world except
Australia. (See Figures 54 and 101.)

In Temperate zones fruit of some
kind can be found the year around,
though most of them are available only
in summer or fall.

In the Tropics some plants flower
and fruit continuously, and some fruits
are available at all times.

Arctic fruits ripen only during a
short summer period.

Edible portions of plants vary greatly in their food value. A diet of leaves
alone is at best like eating only spinach.
Select young, tender leaves in preference to old ones, and boil them.

FIG. 54. Philippine Blueberry (Vaccinium)

Change the water if they are bitter.
Buds are still more nourishing. The stems of some plants are excellent, fur
nishing starch, sugar, oils and greens. (See pages 72-74.)

Roots and Other Underground Parts

Many plants store food (starch) in underground parts. This is especially tru
of aquatic plants. Tubers are a source of food in all parts of the world and ar
often available throughout the year. In cold climates when plant food appear
completely absent, bulbs and roots can be found by digging where the drie
plant stalks remain. (See pages 63-67.)

FERNS

*The roots and young curled fronds of many ferns are edible and none ar
known to be poisonous.* The food value is not great, but it will help sustain lif
The brake fern is eaten by natives all over the world. A fern called Pakó fur
nishes edible young fronds which are eaten either raw or cooked by Philippin
natives. It grows in wet ground, on gravel bars, and along the banks of stream

FIG. 55. Gathering Tubers of Solomon's Seal

FIG. 56. Pulling Up Cattail Roots

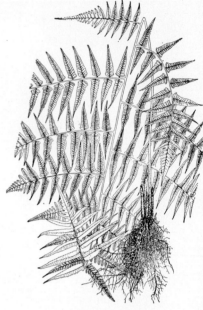

FIG. 57. High Climbing Fern
(Stenochlaena palustris)

FIG. 58. Pakó Fern
(Athyrium esculentum)

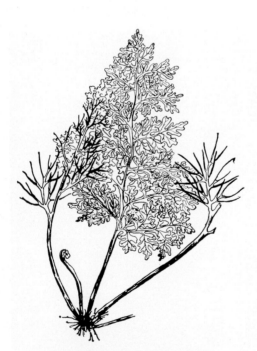

FIG. 59. Swamp Fern *(Ceratopteris)*

FIG. 60. Tree Fern *(Cyathea)*

The young shoots of a high climbing fern are eaten cooked or raw by natives of the South Pacific area and India. This fern grows in thickets in the vicinity of brackish or salt water. The young leaves and terminal buds of tree ferns are edible. These huge ferns may be 20 or more feet high and are found in wet jungle areas. The succulent foliage of the common swamp fern is boiled and eaten as a vegetable. It is found either floating or attached to the soil in shallow, still, or slightly moving fresh water in the subtropical and tropical regions of Asia, Africa, America and Australasia.

WIDELY DISTRIBUTED NUTS

Edible nuts are the most sustaining of all raw forest foods and are found throughout the world. Many American nut trees are found throughout the North Temperate zone and closely related trees of similar appearance grow in the Tropic and South Temperate zones. Familiarity with some of the common North American nut trees will help you to recognize and locate nut-bearing trees in other regions. *Pine trees, for example, grow throughout the North Temperate zone and seeds from the cones of many of them are edible and very sustaining.* They are a principle article in the winter diet of the Indians of our Southwest and of the peasants in remote regions of Siberia.

FIG. 61. Single Leaf Nut Pine
(*Pinus monophylla*)

The single leaf pine, the sugar pine, the limber pine, the nut or pinon pine and the Coulter pine of our American West produce cones containing seeds or nuts that are both tasty and nourishing. The seeds from the Nepal nut pine and the Emodi pine of the Himalayas, the Swiss stone pine of Europe and Asia, the Korean pine of China, Japan, Korea and Kamchatka, all produce edible nuts. *It is not necessary to be able to differentiate between pines.* Shake or break seeds out of the cones and try eating them.

Recognizable members of the pine family bearing edible seeds also grow in the tropical and South Temperate zones. Nuts from the Araucarias of Australia and New Zealand, Brazil, Chile, Norfolk Island and New Caledonia furnish excellent food. These are lofty evergreens bearing globular cones containing large chestnut-like nuts which may be eaten raw just before ripening, or may be either boiled or roasted. (See Figure 62.)

Nut-producing members of the beech family, represented in North America by the oaks, beechnuts and chestnuts, are found in many parts of the world.

Chestnuts, hazelnuts and walnuts are found in North America, the West Indies, Europe and all of Asia including the Philippines and the East Indies.

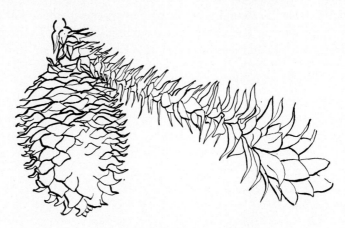

FIG. 62. Bunya Pine *(Araucaria)*

SOME NUT TREES WITH WIDE DISTRIBUTION

Beech.

Characteristics: Large forest trees producing triangular nuts. Bark smooth varying from light to dark gray.

Distribution: North temperate zone.

Eaten: Raw.

FIG. 63. Beech Nut *(Fagus grandifolia)*

Oak.

Characteristics: Trees and shrubs producing acorns; leaves either evergreen or deciduous (falling).

Distribution: Edible species found in Java, India, China, Mexico, North and South America, northern Africa, Mediterranean area.

FIG. 64. Oak *(Quercus alba)*

Eaten: Sweet acorns raw. Bitter acorns boiled in changes of water, or dried and roasted; or ground into flour, soaked in water, and baked or roasted in cakes.

FIG. 65. Chinquapin
(*Castanea pumila*)

Chestnut and Chinquapin.

Characteristics: Oak-like trees or shrubs containing nuts in burrs lined with soft, leathery covering.

Distribution: North America, West Indies, Europe, Asia including Philippines and East Indies.

Eaten: Raw, boiled, roasted.

FIG. 66. Bush chinquapin
(*Castanopsis sempervirens*)

Walnuts and Butternuts.

Characteristics: Large trees with alternate compound leaves. Nuts with fleshy husks which do not split into regular divisions when ripe.

Distribution: See Chestnuts and Hazelnuts.

Eaten: Raw.

FIG. 67. Walnut
(*Juglans nigra*)

Hazelnut.

Characteristics: Small trees or bushes with nuts in clusters and covered by leaf-like husk.

Distribution: See chestnut and chinquapin.

Eaten: Raw.

FIG. 68. Hazelnut (*Corylus americana*)
(*Corylus cornuta*)

Nuts Restricted in Distribution

Many nut trees, relatively restricted in range as are the hickory nuts and pecans of North America, will furnish food in certain areas of the world.

Australian nut trees.

Characteristics: Grow 25 to 30 feet tall, hard-shelled nuts grow in bunches and encased in husks like hickory nuts.

Distribution: Australian jungles.

Eaten: Raw.

Panama nut tree.

Characteristics: Immense forest tree with thick trunk of buttressed roots and huge crown with large hand-shaped leaves. Fruits in five pods containing black, peanut-like seeds, covered with irritating hairs.

Distribution: Central and South America, with other species in various parts of the Tropics.

Eaten: Raw or roasted.

FIG. 69. Panama Nut Tree
(Sterculia apetela)

African walnut or gabon.

Characteristics: Desert nut resembling a walnut.

Distribution: Liberia and adjacent regions.

Eaten: Raw, boiled, roasted.

Pili nut.

Characteristics: Large forest trees. Hard inner nuts are triangular in cross section and pointed at each end.

Distribution: Philippines, other Pacific islands, and Malaya.

Eaten: Raw, but much improved by roasting.

FIG. 70. Pili Nut *(Canarium)*

Brazil nut.

Characteristics: Grows in immense forests with trees attaining 150 feet in height and 4 feet in diameter.

Distribution: Brazil, the Guianas, Venezuela.

Eaten: Raw.

GRASSES

By far the largest part of human food comes from such grasses as oats, wheat, corn, and rice; and the seeds of all grasses are edible. Grasses are distinguished by their joined and usually hollow stems.

FIG. 71. Brazil Nut *(Bertholletia excelsa)*

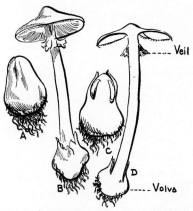

FIG. 73. Amanita Mushroom (Poisonous). a. Young Amanita; c. Cross Section of Young Amanita; b, d. Mature Mushroom.

FIG. 72. All Grass Seeds Are Edible

Wild rice, one of the staple foods of the American Indians, is distributed widely, with both wild and cultivated rice particularly abundant throughout the tropics. Many kinds of sorghums and millets are found in the tropics. Wild oats grow in Europe, Asia, North America, Australia, and the upland regions of South America. Their grains can be eaten raw, parched, or pounded into flour and roasted. At long intervals bamboo produces edible seeds, and the young shoots of most varieties may be eaten safely.

MUSHROOMS

Many mushrooms are edible and may furnish a source of food, particularly in temperate regions; but no species should be tried unless you are sure of its identity, for some species are deadly poisonous. The most widespread among the dangerously poisonous mushrooms are the Amanitas which have a frill or ring (veil) around the upper part of the stem, a bag (volva) at the bottom, and a white spore deposit which drops out of the gills. Don't try eating any mushroom that possesses these three characteristics. Amanitas almost always grow on the ground in the woods or shade. No poisonous mushrooms have ever been reported from the Northwest Canadian territories, and the only poisonous mushroom in Alaska is the Amanita. (See Figure 73.)

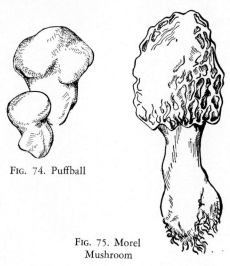

FIG. 74. Puffball

FIG. 75. Morel
Mushroom

Puffballs are more or less globular bodies that develop their spores inside and have a solid white interior when young. *All are edible when fresh.* An inexperienced person might at first mistake them for the young Amanita, but he can distinguish them readily by cutting them open. The young Amanita has all the characterstics of a mature mushroom, though reduced and compressed, while the puffballs do not. Avoid eating all fungi in the button or unexpanded stage. *Morel mushrooms are easily recognized and all are edible.*

BEVERAGES FROM PLANTS

Some plants which have little food value can be used for making refreshing beverages. The bark from sassafras roots, spicebushes, black birch, sumach berries, the leaves of wintergreen, Laborador tea, spruce, hemlock, many of the mints, and other plants produce palatable drinks when steeped or boiled.

BARK AS FOOD

The inner barks from numerous trees can be eaten raw or cooked. In famine areas people make bread from flour derived from the bark of trees. The thin, green, outer bark and white, innermost bark are those normally useable for food since brown bark ordinarily contains too much tannin. Among trees whose bark is used as sources of food are the poplars (including the cottonwoods and aspens) birches, willows, and the inner bark of a few species of pine, including the Scotch pine of northern Europe and Asia and the lodgepole or shore pine of western North America. Outer bark of these pines is scraped away and the inner bark stripped from the trunk and eaten fresh, dried or cooked. It is most palatable when newly formed in the spring.

POISONOUS AND IRRITATING SUBSTANCES

Some plants may be eaten only after poisonous or irritating substances are removed. Among these are a large group known as the Aroids, of which the taro root, a staple food of the Polynesians, is a good example. It is pungent and bitter when raw, but perfectly palatable after cooking. Jack-in-the-pulpit, found in the United States, and Badu or Coco of the West Indies or Central America are edible when the roots are cooked, but even prolonged cooking may not make elephant ear or skunk cabbage edible.

When eaten raw, the needle-shaped crystals of calcium oxalate puncture the tongue and cause a stinging sensation. Drying (roasting) so rearranges the crystals of some of them as to make them harmless. One taste of skunk cabbage or jack-in-the-pulpit will enable you to recognize this irritating principle when found in other plants.

Roots of the bitter manioc of South America contain small quantities of the poison, hydrocyanic acid. The root is prepared as food by crushing, pressing and washing the juice containing the poison and then heating to drive out the last traces.

Some fruits and seeds are poisonous at certain stages of growth but not at others; while many plants contain some edible and some poisonous parts. An example is the poke weed, whose young shoots and leaves are edible, but whose root is poisonous.

SOME COMMON EDIBLE WILD PLANTS OF THE UNITED STATES FOUND ELSEWHERE IN THE WORLD

The following groups or genera of food plants are widely distributed. Some contain numerous edible species. By learning a few plants from each group you will be better able to recognize and use the same or related species in any area of the world. Instead of attempting to learn them all in a short time, learn a few well, adding to the list from time to time.

FIG. 76. Digging Arrowhead Tubers

Along all streams, swamps or open water areas hunt for plant food by digging for roots and
tubers. The best time for gathering arrowhead tubers in the United States is the fall of the
year. Note the arrow-shaped leaves and pile of bulbs in the foreground. Roots that angle or go
straight down are more likely to terminate in a tuber than are the shallow lateral roots. (See
Arrowhead, page 65.)

Roots and Other Underground Parts

Wild onion.

Found: Small plants, North America, Asia, Europe. Year round but difficult to locate in winter.

Eaten: Bulb, boiled or raw.

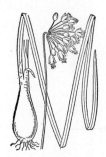

FIG. 77. Wild Onion
(Allium cernuum)

FIG. 78. Spring Beauty
(Claytonia virginica)

Spring beauty.

Found: Small plants, Africa, Europe, Australia, southern Asia, North America. Year round but difficult to find in winter. Common in moist woods of North America.

Eaten: Bulb raw or cooked.

Note: Leaves only of some species are eaten.

Nut grass.

Found: Sedge, worldwide, common in open ground and along river banks. Available in U.S. during summer, fall, winter.

Eaten: Small hard nut-like tubers, raw or cooked.

FIG. 78. Nut Grass
(Cyperus esculentus)

FIG. 80. Water Chestnut
(Eleocharis tuberosa)

Water chestnut.

Found: Many parts of world, particularly in southern Asia and Pacific Islands. Plant grows wild in some fresh water swamps of U.S.

Eaten: Tubers, raw or cooked.

Water lilies, lotus.

Found: Worldwide, year round.

Eaten: Fleshy rootstock, tubers and seeds, raw or cooked, but rootstock of bitter varieties require long cooking.

FIG. 81. Water Lilies *(Nymphaea, Nelumbo)*

FIG. 82. Wild Potato
(Ipomoea pandurata)

Wild and sweet potatoes.

Found: Trailing plants, in all warm climates of the world.

Eaten: Large tuberous roots, chiefly cooked (baked, roasted, boiled.) Leaves and stems as greens.

Solomon's seal.

Found: Small plants, North America, Europe, northern Asia, Jamaica. Available U.S. in spring or summer.

Eaten: Fleshy roots boiled or roasted taste like parsnips. Young shoots also edible.

FIG. 83. Solomon's seal *(Polygonatum commutatum)*

FIG. 84. Brake Fern *(Pteris aquilina)*

Brake fern.

Found: Nearly all temperate and tropical regions, year around.

Eaten: Preferably roast and chew starch out of roots, raw if necessary. Stalks and coiled young fronds as greens, in U.S. in spring or summer, but first remove wool-like covering.

Arrowhead.

Found: Small plants, North America, Europe, Asia. In U.S. year around. Follow thread-like root down to the bulb. Grows in wet ground and shallow water.

Eaten: Boil or roast. Tastes like a potato.

FIG. 85. Arrowhead *(Sagittaria latifolia)*

Bulrush.

Found: Tall plant, North America, Africa, Australia, East Indies, Malaya. In U.S. year round, in wet and swampy areas.

Eaten: Roots and white stem base, raw or cooked.

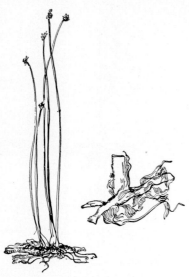

Fig. 86. Bulrush *(Scirpus validus)*

Wild Potato.

Wild potatoes (and other species related to the white or Irish potato, tomato)

Found: Small plants, worldwide, numerous in tropics. Berries of some species reported as poisonous.

Eaten: Raw or cooked.

Fig. 87. Wild Potato *(Solanum Jamesii)*

Fig. 88. Cattail *(Typha latifolia)*

Cattail.

Found: Tall plants, Europe, northern Asia, North America, Africa, Australia and some Pacific islands. Available year round, always near water.

Eaten: Bake or roast roots and chew out starch, discarding fiber, may also be eaten raw. White portions of the new shoots and the flowering spike edible (before blooming.)

Wild Rice.

Found: Tall grasses, North America and Asia along swampy streams, rivers, bays. Base of stems and root shoots in U.S. best in spring or summer, grain in late summer and fall.

Eaten: Lower stem and root shoots are sweet. Remove tough covering and chew central portion. Grain is excellent.

Fig. 89. Wild Rice
(*Zizania aquatica*)

Fruits and Berries

Fig. 90. Juneberry (*Amelanchier canadensis*)

Juneberry.

Found: Small trees, North America, northern Asia, Europe, in forest and mountain areas. In U.S. summer and early fall.

Eaten: Small purplish fruit, fresh or dried.

Papaw.

Found: Tree, North American papaw in fall. Along streams. Related custard apple family found throughout tropics.

Eaten: Banana-like tasting fruit, skinned and eaten raw. Black or yellowish-green when ripe.

Fig. 91. American Papaw
(*Asimina triloba*)

FIG. 92. Wild Grapes in Other Parts of the World Will Look Like Those at Home

Hackberry.

Found: Trees, North America, temperate Asia, northern India, Europe, either in arid or moist habitats. U.S. in fall, winter.

Eaten: Raw or cooked.

Fig. 93. Hackberry *(Celtis occidentalis)*

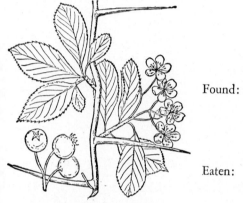

Fig. 94. Hawthorn *(Crataegus)*

Hawthorn.

Found: Bushes, open waste lands of temperate Asia, Africa, Europe, North America, Mexico, East Indies. U.S. in fall and winter. In winter, look on ground beneath the bushes.

Eaten: Tiny red or yellow apples, raw or cooked.

Persimmon.

Found: Trees, North America, South America, Asia, Africa, Australia, Pacific islands.

Eaten: Ripe (soft) fruits only, eaten raw or cooked.

Fig. 95. Persimmon *(Diospyros virginiana)*

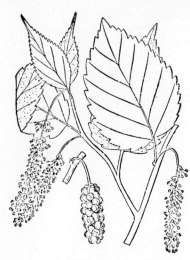

FIG. 96. Mulberry *(Morus)*

Mulberry.

Found: Trees, all north temperate regions and subtropics, U.S. in summer.

Eaten: Raw or cooked.

Cherries, Plums, Apricots.

Found: Trees and bushes, north and south temperate zones, U.S. in summer and fall.

Eaten: Fruit containing single seed, raw or cooked.

FIG. 97. Wild Cherry *(Prunus virginiana)*

FIG. 98. Golden Currant *(Ribes aureum)*

Currants and Gooseberries.

Found: Low sometimes prickly shrubs throughout the Americas and in Europe, Asia, North Africa, Australia and elsewhere.

Eaten: Berries raw or cooked.

Blackberries and Raspberries.

Found: Shrubs, nearly worldwide, U.S. in summer, in open land and forest margins.

Eaten: Raw or cooked.

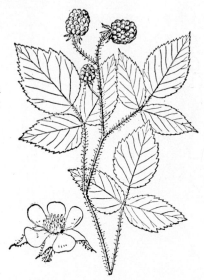

FIG. 99. Wild Raspberry *(Rubus strigosus)*

FIG. 100. Elderberry *(Sambucus canadensis)*

Elderberry.

Found: Bushes, North America, South America, Europe, Asia, Australia.

Eaten: Reddish or purple berries eaten raw or cooked.

Blueberries and cranberries.

Found: Shrubs, the arctic, north temperate and tropical areas. U.S. in summer and fall with some berries remaining through winter. Abundant in burned over areas of north.

Eaten: Raw or cooked.

FIG. 101. Blueberry *(Vaccinium angustifolium)*

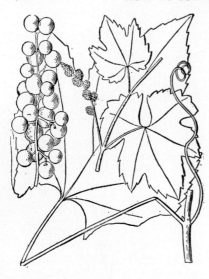

Grapes.

Found: Climbing vines, nearly worldwide, U.S. in fall and winter.

Eaten: Raw or cooked.

Fig. 102. Frost Grape *(Vitis bicolor)*

LEAVES, STEMS AND SHOOTS

Burdock.

Found: Worldwide, particularly in open waste land. Stems available U.S. spring and summer.

Eaten: Tender leafstalks of this weed peeled and eaten raw or cooked as a green. Root is edible.

Fig. 103. Burdock *(Arctium Lappa)*

Fig. 104. Sorrel *(Oxalis violacea)*

Sorrel.

Found: Small plants, nearly worldwide.

Eaten: Leaves raw as a salad. Tubers of some species cooked.

Goosefoot.

Found: Weeds, all temperate and tropic regions, U.S. in spring and summer.

Eaten: Leaves cooked as greens, seeds roasted.

Fig. 105. Goosefoot *(Chenopodium album)*

Fig. 106. Plantain *(Plantago major)*

Plantain.

Found: North and South America, Europe, Asia, New Zealand, some Pacific islands. U.S. spring and summer.

Eaten: Young leaves of this common weed may be boiled or eaten raw.

Purslane.

Found: Fleshy plant, worldwide. U.S. summer and fall.

Eaten: Fleshy leaves and stems boiled.

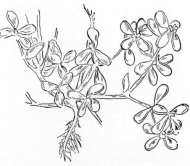

Fig. 107. Purslane *(Portulaca oleracea)*

FIG. 108. Dock *(Rumex crispus)*

Dock.

Found :   Weeds, north and south temperate
            regions. U.S. spring and fall.

Eaten :   Young basal leaves boiled or raw.

Dandelion.

Found: Weeds, most of civilized world.

Eaten: Young leaves, cooked. Roots may
           be eaten raw.

FIG. 109. Dandelion
(Taraxacum officinale)

CHAPTER V
Wild Animal Food

Animal food is any food not derived from plants. It may be in the form of fish, birds, mammals, crayfish, insects, mollusks and so on. It is in general more nourishing than wild plant food and often more available; thus a knowledge of the animals you can eat, where to look for them and how to catch them will increase your chance of surviving.

FISH

Learn to look upon bodies of fresh water as food reservoirs, and when lost or stranded in any type of country, try to strike a river or stream. Generally speaking, animal life is more abundant in the water than on land, it is concentrated in a more limited area, and quite often is easier to get. Your chance of surviving along a body of water is excellent. You can catch fish with crude equipment or with none at all if you know *when, where* and *how* to fish.

Fig. 110. Fishing with a Bark Line

When to Fish

Different species of fish feed at all times of the day and night. In any body of water many factors govern feeding activity; *but in general, early morning and late afternoon are the best times to fish with bait.* Fishing is usually good just before a storm breaks. Jumping minnows and rising fish are feeding signs.

Where to Fish

FIG. 111. Catfish Caught on Makeshift Hook and Bark Line

Pick a good place to fish or your efforts are wasted. It is usually easier to locate fish in small shallow streams, than in large streams, lakes or rivers where they can find suitable habitats over a much wider area. Peer into the water away from the sun, or reflections will make it impossible to see fish.

In streams, fish usually congregate in pools and deep calm water. The heads of riffles, small rapids, the tail of a pool, eddies below rocks or logs, deep undercut banks, in the shade of overhanging bushes, wherever you see submerged logs and rocks—all are likely places to fish.

Fish the mouths of small tributary streams when the main rivers or streams are high or muddy. Fish seek shelter here at such times.

When streams are low and the weather is hot, fish congregate in the deepest pools and at places where cool underground water enters the main stream. At such times fish are much more likely to hide under rocks. (See Fishing with Hands, page 79.)

In the cool spring weather of temperate climates, fish keep to the shallow water that is warmed by the sun.

Bait

Experiment with baits. Look for bait in the water, for this is the source of most fish food. Insects, crayfish, worms, meat of shellfish, wood grubs, immature forms of aquatic insects, small minnows and fish eggs are all good. So are the intestines, eyes, and flesh of other fish. Fruits are seldom good baits. After catching your first fish, open it and examine the stomach and intestines. See what it was feeding on and try to duplicate it. If it is crayfish, turn over rocks in the stream until you get one. Usually the rest of the fish will be feeding on the same food. Meat will attract crayfish.

Make live bait appear to act natural and try to conceal the hook. Don't let

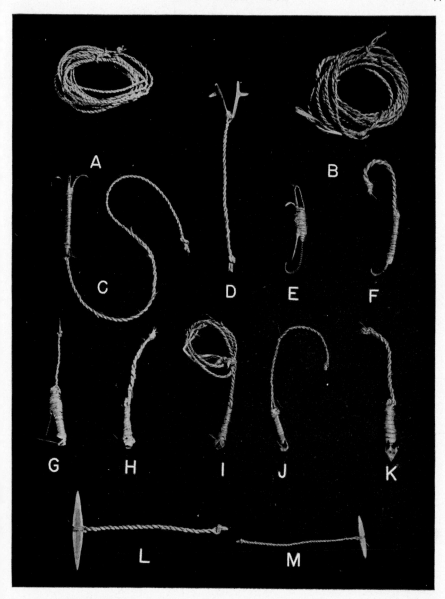

FIG. 112. Makeshift Fish Hooks. a. and b. Bark Lines; c. Triple Thorn Hook; d. Gorge Hook Made from a Thorny Vine; e. Latch Barb Hook; f. Plain Thorn Hook; g. Straight Thorn Hook with Latch; h. i. j. k. Variations of Thorn Hooks Made from Rattans and Trees; l. m. Wooden Gorge Hooks

your bait remain still. Move it slowly from time to time. When fish are scattered or are feeding near the surface, allow the bait to drift with the current. If you see fish breaking water and feeding, work your bait down to them. In all probability they will continue to feed at that spot, unless disturbed.

In clear shallow water, approach fish upstream as they lie heading into the current. Move slowly when the water is clear. If fish are shy, try fishing for them at night.

FIG. 113. Twisting a Fishing Line from Bark

How to Make Hooks and Lines

Hooks can be made from pins, needles, wire or any piece of available metal; out of wood, coconut shell, bone, thorns, flint, sea shells, tortoise shell or a combination of these. (See Figure 112.)

Lines may be made from a great variety of plants (see pp. 104-105). Inner bark of trees is best. Plant fibres and bark may be rolled into a line by twisting the fibres together. This is done by securing the knotted ends of two strands of fibres to a solid object. Holding a strand in each hand, twist them clockwise and then cross one above the other counter-clockwise. Continue adding fibres to lengthen your cord and when necessary to keep it a uniform thickness. Two strands twisted in this manner are four times as strong as one strand, and a twenty or thirty foot line can easily be made in an hour with the more easily worked materials.

METHODS OF CATCHING FISH

There are many technics of catching fish. The method chosen should be suitable to the conditions. Some are much more effective than the use of hook and line.

Set Lines

If you have extra hooks and lines, bait and set them overnight. A skewer or gorge hook is excellent for overnight sets, as the fish have ample time to swallow the baited hook. Fasten your lines to low-hanging branches that will bend when a fish is hooked; otherwise you may lose hook, line and fish.

Fishing with Hands

Catching fish with the hands is most successful in small streams with undercut banks, or in cut-off channels or sloughs where clear shallow ponds are left by receding flood waters. Reach under the bank or rocks and move your hand slowly. When you feel a fish, work your hand gently toward his head, grasping him firmly just behind the gills.

Fig. 114. As One Strip of Bark Runs Out Add Another

Spearing Fish

Where fish are large and numerous, spearing works well. Any straight sapling with a solid core will serve as a spear. Fashion a point and harden by lightly charring it in fire. Bamboo, though hollow, is excellent. Two points should be shaped just beyond a joint. A wooden spear must often be repointed, so if time and facilities are available, spearheads of bone, shell, or stone should be shaped, or heavy thick thorns may be utilized. A knife or bayonet tied to a long straight shaft, or a large fish hook, heated and straightened is good. Try your luck with a fish spear trap. Spearing is most efficient if the fish are the kind that lie on or near the bottom or rise to the surface for air. Many species of fish can best be speared at night with the aid of a torch. A light dazzles the fish, reflects from the scales, and shows the bottom clearly.

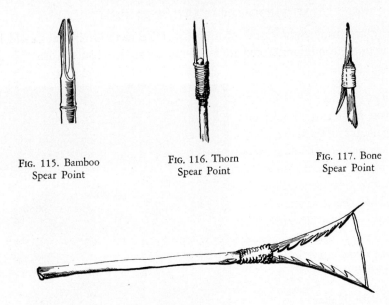

FIG. 115. Bamboo
Spear Point

FIG. 116. Thorn
Spear Point

FIG. 117. Bone
Spear Point

FIG. 118. Fish Spear Trap. When a Fish Is Speared the Trigger Stick Is Released
and the Barbs Clamp Tight

Knife

In shallow water fish can be caught by slashing them with a knife or bayonet. Clubs or machetes can be used to dispatch fish when attracted by torchlight at night in shallow water, or driven from pools over shallow riffles.

A Makeshift Net

A scoop net for catching small fish or bait can be made from a piece of mosquito netting, a perforated parachute, underwear, clothing, the cloth-like material at the base of coconut leaves, or a knotted mesh of hibiscus or coconut fibres. Stitch or tie these along a circular frame made by bending together the ends of a forked sapling. If no fish are visible, hold the net on the downstream side of rocks or submerged vegetation. Muddy the water upstream and as it flows over the net, strike the rock or vegetation with a downstream stroke of your foot. At the same time scoop upstream with the net.

It is often possible to catch fish in small pools by trampling about until the water is muddy. The fish will come to the surface and can be scooped out with a net, speared, or even grabbed with the hands.

Poisoning Fish

Throughout warm regions of the world there are various plants utilized by the natives for poisoning fish. The most common method of using them is to

FIG. 119. Native Crushing Derris Root (University of Kentucky)

macerate or crush the plant parts used (most often roots) and mix this in water. Drop large quantities of the crushed plants into the head of pools or small streams containing fish and within a short time the fish rise helpless to the surface. The poisonous principle is usually rotenone which is harmful to cold blooded animals, but the fish killed by it may be consumed by man without any ill effects whatsoever.

Commercial derris or rotenone can be used essentially like the crushed derris roots prepared by natives. It has no effect if dusted over the surface of a pond. It must be mixed to a chocolate malted milk consistency with a little water, then distributed in the water containing fish. If the concentration is strong, it will work within two minutes at a temperature of 70° F. or it may take an hour at 50° F. Fish sick enough to turn over on their backs will eventually die. An ounce of 12 percent rotenone will kill every fish for a half mile down a stream of the size pictured in the photograph. After putting in the poison, follow slowly down the stream and pick up the fish as they come to the surface, sink to the bottom, or swim crazily to the bank. A stick dam or obstruction will aid you in collecting fish as they float down stream. A few facts to remember about the use of rotenone are:

1. It is very swift acting in warm waters at 70° F. and above.
2. It works more slowly in cold water, and is not practical in water below 50° or 55° F.
3. It can best be applied in small ponds, streams or tidal pools.
4. Don't use too much or it will be wasted; however, too little will not stupefy the fish enough to catch.

A small container of 12 percent rotenone (1 to 2 oz.) would be a valuable addition to any emergency kit. It should not be exposed unnecessarily to air or light. It will retain its toxicity best if kept in a dark-colored vial.

Lime thrown in a small pond or tidal pool will kill all fish in the pool. Burn coral and sea shells to obtain lime.

Poisoning of fish should only be resorted to in times of emergency. A list of fish poisoning plants will prove helpful to those who must secure their own food in remote places of the world. If you have an opportunity, try to get a native of the country to point out these plants and if possible demonstrate their use.

Some Fish Poisoning Plants

Anamirta cocculus (tuba) is a climbing plant found in the South Pacific Islands and southern Asia. The crushed seeds thrown into water will stupify fish.

FIG. 120. Gathering Fish Poisoned with Derris

FIG. 121. Pick up the Fish as They Come to the Surface

Plants of the genus *Derris* (tuba) are climbing shrubs or woody vines used throughout the tropics to kill fish. The powdered or macerated roots are mixed in water and thrown into pools or streams.

Duboisia myoporoides is an Australian shrub with white axillary clusters of flowers and a berry-like fruit. The crushed plants are thrown into water to kill fish.

Croton tiglium (tuba-tuba) is a small shrub or tree with seeds borne in three-angled capsules. It is found in waste places of the islands of the South Pacific region and does not occur in the forests. The pulverized seeds of the fruit will kill fish.

Tephrosia (tuba) contains numerous species of bean-like shrubs widely used in the tropics to poison fish. The leaves and stems are crushed and bruised and whole bundles thrown into the water.

FIG. 122. *Anamirta cocculus*   FIG. 123. *Derris eliptica*

Barringtonia asiatica (tuba-tuba) and related species are large trees, usually found near the sea, in Malaya and parts of Polynesia. The fruits are fleshy, more or less four-angled in cross section, and one-seeded. The crushed seeds are mixed with bait or thrown into a pond.

Lonchocarpus (barbasco, cube, timbo, haiari) is a group of plants, small trees, or woody climbing shrubs with alternate pinnate leaves found in tropical America and the West Indies. The flowers vary in color but are never yellow. The powdered or macerated roots are used for fish poison.

FIG. 124. *Duboisia*

FIG. 125. *Croton tiglium*

FIG. 126. *Tephrosia*

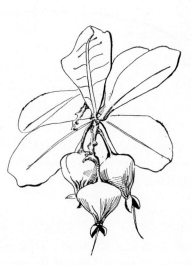

FIG. 127. *Barringtonia*

The stems, seeds, pods, and roots of various species of *Mundulea* in tropical Africa are utilized according to the species.

Swimming to Catch Fish

Fish seek concealment and shade, so if the water is clear and there are large rocks on the bottom, swim down and feel under them just as you might do in catching fish under a bank. Slip into the water quietly and swim slowly beneath the surface until you can get close enough to strike a large fish with a hook or gaff attached to a wooden handle and line. Drop the gaff after striking the fish and haul your prize in upon regaining the bank.

Shooting Fish

Fish can be shot with a sidearm or gun. Aim well under them. A hand grenade thrown into a stream or school of fish will furnish all you can eat.

Ice Fishing

When ice is clear enough for fish to be seen, you can stun them by striking the ice above them with a large rock or the butt end of a log. Chop a hole and

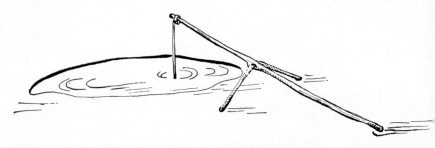

FIG. 128. Ice Fishing

pick up the fish. This method is most effective in shallow water. When water is deep and the ice thick, cut a hole and fish through it. If possible, build a brush shelter and fire nearby. Rig up an automatic signalling device so you can watch several lines at once.

EELS

Eels are fish with a snake-like appearance, found throughout the world in both fresh and salt water. They are smooth skinned and swim under water. Snakes are scaled and usually swim on top. Eels are excellent eating and can be caught in muddy water or at night by using many of the methods described for fish. They are easily speared at night under a torchlight. After catching them, strike them a sharp blow toward the end of the tail to stun them. Eels, like catfish, should be skinned before cooking.

FROGS

Skin frogs before cooking them, as many species secrete irritating and poisonous fluids from their skins. Particularly avoid those marked with yellow and red. Frog legs are a real delicacy, but there is no reason why you shouldn't eat the entire body. Frogs are widely distributed throughout the world in warm and temperate climates and are found along the banks of streams, lakes, ponds, swamps and marshes.

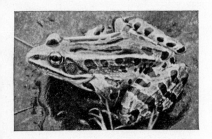

FIG. 129. Frog   FIG. 130. Salamander

At night frogs may be located with a light or by their croaking. Approach slowly. In warm weather when frogs are active, club them with a stick. Snag the larger ones with a hook and line. Frogs are very tenacious of life and frequently escape after they are stunned. Stick your knife through the spinal cord just behind the head.

OTHER AMPHIBIANS

Newts, salamanders and other amphibians are found in some of the places where you find frogs. They can be seen swimming in the water or crawling on the forest floor at night. In the day they can be caught by looking under rocks, in streams, damp woods and under rotting logs. All of them are harmless. They inhabit fresh water only. The best way to catch them is with a dip net.

Skin and gut them, but avoid eating parts that contain glands.

MOLLUSKS

Mollusks such as terrestrial and aquatic snails, and bivalves similar to our fresh water mussel are found the world over under all water conditions. All of them are edible, but they should never be eaten raw. They may carry parasites causing serious diseases, or be contaminated from polluted water. You can usually pick them up in your hands or locate them by feeling around in the mud with your feet. Streams and rivers are the best places to look for them.

FIG. 131. Look for Fresh Water Mussels Along All Streams

Seek out the shallow water with a sand or mud bottom in which mussels can bury themselves, and look for the narrow trails they leave in mud, or for the dark elliptical slit of their open valves.

CRUSTACEANS

Crabs, crayfish, lobsters, shrimps, and prawns are found in fresh water throughout the world. All of them are probably edible, but they spoil rapidly

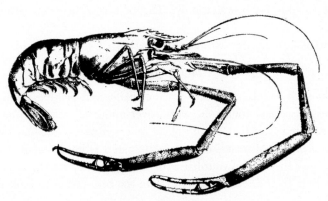

FIG. 132. Fresh Water Shrimp

and some contain parasites harmful to man. They should always be cooked. The salt water forms can be eaten raw with little danger provided they are fresh.

Fresh water crabs and crayfish can be scooped up in a dip net or picked up from moss beds under rocks and brush in streams. Many species of crabs and lobsters are nocturnal and can be most easily caught at night. This is particularly true of the land crabs. All the meat within the skeleton of crabs, crayfish, and lobsters can be eaten, but the gills are usually discarded, since they are the first to spoil.

Fresh water shrimps are abundant in tropical streams. They can be seen swimming or found clinging to branches or vegetation in the water. Look for them along a stream where the water is shallow and sluggish. The shelled tail is the part most commonly eaten.

Prawns will rise to a light at night and can be scooped off the surface of the water.

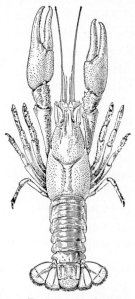

FIG. 133. Crayfish

REPTILES

Lizards, Snakes, Turtles, Alligators

Fresh water snakes frequent sluggish water, rocky, muddy and vegetation covered banks, piles of driftwood and overhanging bushes. In such places they bask in the sun when it is not too hot. All of them are edible, some

FIG. 134. All Lizards Are Good to Eat

delicious, but caution should be used in securing them, as the bites of some are fatal. Land snakes, including the poisonous species, are also edible. (See page 200.)

Lizards are found almost everywhere. They are most abundant in the tropics and subtropics. They can be clubbed, and they are easily snared with a grass or bark noose on the end of a stick. Remove their scaly skins and broil or fry the meat. There are only two poisonous lizards and they are confined to the American Southwest, Mexico and Central America; their flesh however can be eaten. Many of the lizards such as the monitors, inhabiting southern Asia, Africa, and Australia, look exceptionally fierce and dangerous. In spite of their appearance, however, they are good to eat. The flesh of iguanas is much like white meat of chicken. Crocodiles and alligators are also good to eat. Skin them by first heating over a fire to loosen the plates.

Turtles are found over most of the land areas of the temperate and tropical zones and in nearly all the waters of the earth. The marine, fresh water, and land forms are all edible. Small fresh water ones can be grabbed or clubbed on the bank or caught on hook and line. Most of them are slow swimmers. In clear water, you can catch a turtle by swimming under water. Grip well to the rear of the shell, but don't try this technic on the large forms such as the snappers. They can inflict a serious bite.

FIG. 135. Look for Grubs in Rotten Logs

INSECTS

Insects are abundant throughout the world and the larvae or grubs of many are edible and nourishing. Insect forms of one kind or another live in prac tically every conceivable habitat. Grubs are found in rotten logs, in the ground, and under the bark of dead trees. They should be boiled or fried, but they can be eaten raw. Grasshoppers should always be cooked, as some contain harmful parasites. Termites are a native delicacy, cooked or raw, and in jungle country they are generally available. Be cautious of eating caterpillars, as many are irritating and some are poisonous.

FIG. 136. Immature
Termite

FIG. 137 White
Grub

BIRDS AND MAMMALS

Birds and mammals are edible and easily seen, but they are usually the least abundant or available forms of animal life in an area.

First seek the lower animals such as fish, reptiles, insects, crustaceans, and mollusks for food. They are far more abundant and much easier to obtain.

FIG. 138. Keep Your Eyes Open for Nests Containing Eggs

When you have satisfied starvation pangs by eating them, you may consider ways and means of catching the birds and mammals. This is only a very general rule and of course there are many exceptions. In the far north mice and rabbits are often the most numerous and available source of food, and at nesting colonies birds may be caught by the hundreds. As all birds and mammals are edible, it is not necessary to recognize specific ones, but it is necessary to know their general, and, where possible, their specific habits in order to obtain them for food. You must be able to secure them for any prolonged stay in wilderness areas.

General Principles

A few general principles concerning birds and mammals will prove helpful in hunting or trapping them:

1. Land animals make conspicuous signs, such as, tracks, feces, runways, trails, dens, and feeding marks that serve as indicators of their presence and relative abundance. Look for such signs. They will tell you whether it is worth while to stop or to continue to a more favorable place.

2. Many mammals large and small travel on trails and runways. This is especially true of small rodents such as mice, ground squirrels, rabbits and ground hogs. By hunting and trapping along these trails you eliminate large areas of less suitable ground.

3. Birds and mammals are creatures of habit. Their normal daily activities of eating, sleeping, drinking, and traveling are fairly regular, and continuously repeated. If you observe them, you can anticipate their movements. They can be hunted or trapped most successfully during their periods of activity.

4. Birds are less fearful of man during the nesting period than at any other time, and with patience you can catch them. Their nests and young are generally well hidden, but they can be located by watching the parent birds which return often and regularly. Birds nest in every conceivable habitat—rocky cliffs, sandy beaches, marshes, on trees, in the woods and in the fields. Some live in colonies. In the tropics, some birds are nesting all year round. Spring and early summer are the seasons to look for bird eggs in temperate or arctic regions.

5. Birds and mammals tend to congregate in the most favorable habitats. Some of the places to look for them are:

   (1) The edges of woods and jungles.
   (2) Trails, glades, and openings in forest or jungle.
   (3) Streams and river banks.
   (4) Lake and ocean shores.
      A. In some environments such as tropical rain forests and desert regions, more mammals are active at night than during the day. Thus a country seemingly destitute of life during the daytime may "become alive" at night.
      (1) Hoofed animals forage both day and night.
      (2) Many rodents and carnivores are active only at night.

B. Birds and mammals are most active early in the morning and late in the evening and are generally quiet during the middle of the day.

6. Birds detect danger by sight and hearing but rely little, if any, on a sense of smell. Most mammals, in addition to good eyes and ears, have a keen sense of smell.

8. Animals have natural camouflage, but movement makes them visible. Stop often when hunting for food. By doing so you become less visible and the animal life that has "frozen" at your approach begins to move. You may see more animal life in one hour of sitting than in several hours of hiking.

FIG. 139. Fixed Rabbit Snare Across Trail. (Fish and Wildlife Service)

A few examples will be helpful in illustrating how some of these principles can be applied specifically to food getting. When you enter an area of open country where mice, voles, and lemmings are abundant, you will see trails and ground tunnels crisscrossing through the grass and weeds. If the vegetation is matted or snow covers it, you may have to kick under it to observe these signs. In addition, there will be tiny droppings in the trails and in some cases the bases of bushes and trees will be white where the bark has been gnawed completely off. Here is a place to stop and get food. Upon closer observation you will probably see mice scurrying ahead as you walk. Lift up logs and kick into all matted or dead grass. You can club these small mammals or step on them. They don't move about more than a few hundred feet. In the woods, knock open hollow logs and standing hollow dead stubs and investigate all round grass or leaf nests in trees or on the ground.

Wherever rabbits or hare are fairly abundant, you will jump seven or eight in an hour's walk. You will find them "bedded down" in grass on a sunny hillside, in brambles, or among vegetation at the base of trees or logs. If you see one bedded down, approach slowly and shoot or club it. Before retiring for the night, set snares in runways. If snow is on the ground, these runways will be clearly evident by the tracks. In the north, rabbits and hare seek out the swamps during the winter and are concentrated in these habitats. If you jump a rabbit, don't shoot at him on the run. Whistle shrilly and the chances are that he will stop just before disappearing into the brush. That's your chance for a still shot. These are only a few of the countless ways in which you can utilize animal habits in your search for food.

FIG. 140. Set Snares in Runways

TRAPPING

Any trap to be effective must be constructed and set with a knowledge of animal habits. There is no "catch all" among traps. A trap set at random to catch whatever chances to come along is worthless. Decide upon the kind of animal you wish to trap, bait your snares with the kind of food it eats, and keep the surroundings as natural as possible.

The fundamental principle of successful trapping is to determine what the animal you wish to trap is going to do and then catch him doing it. It is easier to determine this for some animals than others.

Small mammals such as mice, rats, rabbits, or squirrels are most easily trapped, because their activities are confined and regular and thus more easily anticipated.

Remember that wherever birds and mammals are naturally abundant, or for one reason or another are congregated or follow very definite and observable habits, trapping will prove effective.

FIG. 141. Rabbit in a Hanging Snare

Hanging Snares

A snare is a noose that will slip and strangle or hold any animal caught in it. It is fastened to the end of a bent pole or sapling, and spread open in a well worn runway or in front of an animal den or bird nest. The size of the loop will vary with the kind of animal to be trapped. Make it large enough to admit the animal's head, but not its entire body. *On a rabbit trail the loop should be about 4" in diameter and hang 1 1/2" to 3" above the ground.*

FIG. 142. Running Bowline

The trigger or cross piece holds the sapling down until an animal puts its head in the noose and with a jerk frees the trigger. The bent sapling lifts the animal off the ground where it soon strangles.

Fixed Snares

Fixed snares are fastened to stationary objects such as logs, trees or a forked stake. (See Figure 139.) To be most effective the snare should be set near a bush or limb where the animal will get tangled and strangle itself while struggling. This is particularly useful for catching rabbits and hare.

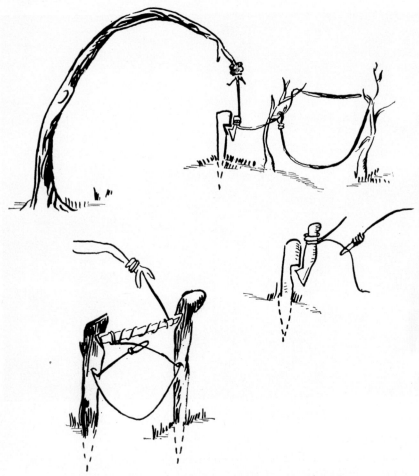

FIG. 143. Hanging Snares Set on Trail. Closeup of Triggers

In the jungle, small mammals and especially birds such as pheasants and jungle fowl are more readily snared by building a low fence of sticks on either side of the runway to lead them to the trap. The treadle spring snare is very effective for such a set. A spear trap should be used for large mammals. (See Figures 145 and 146.)

Deadfalls

Deadfalls will trap both birds and mammals and the basic principles can be infinitely varied to meet specific conditions. The trigger should be long and the weight tilted at a steep angle. Place a small flat stone under the upright so that it will not sink into the ground. Bait the trigger and the trap will fall when the bait is disturbed. The bait should always be tied on before the trap is set. (See Figure 147.)

These traps can also be sprung with a long string or strip of bark. If they are placed in front of a den or over a regularly used trail, no bait is necessary.

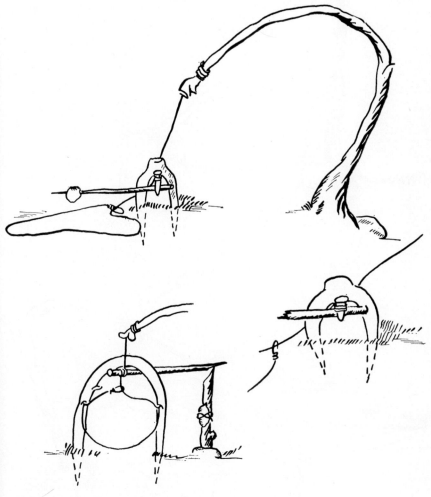

FIG. 144. Baited Hanging Snares and Triggers

Trapping with Bird Lime

Bird lime is any strong adhesive (generally made from the sap of plants), used to catch birds just as flies are caught with fly paper. This method of

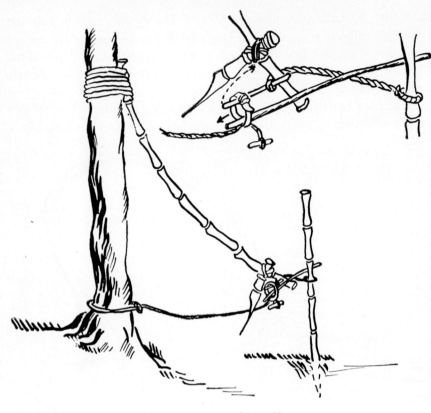

FIG. 145. Spring and Spear Trap

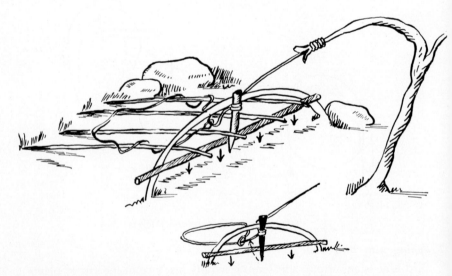

FIG. 146. Treadle Spring Snare. Treadle Should Be Covered with Leaves or Grass

FIG. 147. Deadfall with Figure Four Trigger

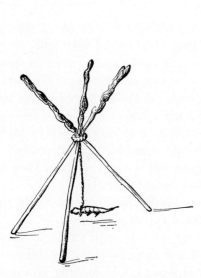

FIG. 148. Tripod Smeared with Bird Lime
and Baited with a Mole Cricket

FIG. 149. Noosing Wand

trapping is common in many parts of the world. The adhesive is usually smeared on slender sticks that adhere to the wing of birds and prevent flight.

When using bird lime, study the habits of the bird you wish to trap so you can set the sticks where they will come in contact with its wings. A tripod of sticks baited with an insect is often effective. (See Figure 148.)

The sticky qualities of bird lime are neutralized by dust. Try to place your sets in dust-free areas, but if this is not possible, lose no time in grabbing the entangled bird.

Bird lime can be used in either jungle or desert, but it is not effective in cold weather. It can be made by boiling the sap of various Euphorbias. In many places bird lime is made by boiling sap of fig trees. The sap of the bread-fruit tree swells when exposed to air and forms a glutinous substance utilized as bird lime. In parts of South America it is made from the milky sap of the Sapodilla tree which furnishes chicle for chewing gum. Heated chewing gum makes a good substitute and is supplied in emergency rations.

Trapping Tricks

Squirrels, coons, opossums, and other mammals that live in hollow trees can be extracted by inserting and twisting a short forked stick. Pin the animal against the side or bottom of the hollow and then twist the stick. The fur and loose skin will twist around the fork and the animal can be pulled out. Keep tension on the stick when withdrawing. A short fork takes a secure hold, a long fork does not. These same mammals can be smoked or drowned out of dens and clubbed as they emerge.

There is no better way to attract mammals to a trap or within shooting distance of a hide than by placing salt along a trail or at a water hole.

A noose fastened to the end of a long pole can be used to snare an animal as it comes out of its burrow. If there is more than one entrance to the burrow, block all but one. Roosting and nesting birds can also be noosed in this manner. Some birds can actually be touched while incubating eggs or brooding young; others are more wary. All will return to their nests or roosts provided the surroundings have not been too greatly disturbed. Conceal yourself by building a blind of vegetation and remain still and quiet within. Drop the noose over the head and pull up and back against the bill.

Birds that nest in hollow trees such as woodpeckers, owls, hornbills, etc., can be blocked in the hollow tree or noosed as they go in or out.

A tethered live bird acts as a decoy for other birds of the same species. Imitation distress sounds and calls will lure some birds within striking or noosing distance. A very effective distress sound can be made by kissing the back of your hand.

A fish-baited hook placed along the beach or in the water will catch shore birds, herons, and fish-eating ducks. Gulls, terns, albatross and other ocean birds can sometimes be caught by trolling slowly with a minnow or piece of fish.

When all else fails, resort to fire. Game, nesting birds, and lower animal forms can be burned or driven out by setting fire to open grasslands. This cruel and wasteful method is not to be considered unless your life hangs in the balance.

If you learn a few trapping technics, if you are resourceful, and, above all, if you observe the habits of the wildlife, you should be able to obtain enough wild meat to sustain you. In the wilderness, resourcefulness and observation are your greatest tools.

HUNTING PRINCIPLES

Game animals rely upon their senses of sight, hearing and smell to detect danger. Some have only one or two of these senses highly developed, while others have all three. An experienced hunter takes advantage of the shortcomings of his quarry; the novice, however, when hunting unfamiliar game should proceed on the assumption that they are naturally wary and that they possess keen senses of sight, sound and smell. Be over-cautious until experience indicates the best hunting technics for the quarry at hand.

To be consistently successful in hunting, you must know how to *find* game, how to *approach* game and how to *shoot* it. In a tough spot you may have only one chance; a failure may mean your life. Learn a few do's and don'ts of hunting.

Some of the hunting principles that follow can be applied to almost any type of mammal shooting, but are especially applicable to large game such as deer, antelopes, caribou, sheep, goats, buffaloes, and wild boar.

Finding Game

1. The greatest advantage you can have in hunting is to see your quarry before it sees you.
2. Look for fresh signs such as tracks, beds and warm or moist droppings; they indicate the recent presence of game.
3. Whether in the woods or in the open, peep cautiously over ridges, examining first the distant and then the closer ground.
4. *In the woods move slowly and stop often. A motionless man has an immense advantage over a moving animal.*
5. One of the surest ways to get a shot is to locate a water hole, feeding ground, or well traveled trail and wait quietly for the game to come to you.
6. In dense forested country where the range of vision is limited and the

FIG. 150. Elk—Stalk Game by Utilizing Their Habits and You'll Get a Shot

FIG. 151. Mountain Sheep—With Patience You Can Get Close Enough for a Shot

game must be closely approached to be seen, *silence* is essential. Avoid treading on dry sticks and leaves or brushing against bushes.

7. In open or mountainous country game is generally seen and shot at a distance. Silence is not such an important factor as in the woods, but you must keep under cover.

8. Whether looking for game or stalking it, move up or across wind, never down wind. This applies equally in open or forested country. Go out of your way to utilize cover and contours even if it requires a wide circuit.

9. In open country keep the sun behind you, as it is difficult to shoot into the sun. You will be less visible to the game and it will be more visible to you.

10. If your quarry has sighted you but has not fled, do not approach it directly; tack back and forth across your line of approach. Move when the animal is feeding and freeze when it looks up or ceases the activity that is absorbing its attention.

11. Get above mountain game; it seldom suspects danger from above.

12. Never silhouette yourself on a skyline, as you become immediately visible and suspicious to game.

13. Camouflage your clothing so it blends with the landscape.

Shooting Game

14. Never make a shot unless it is the very best you can do. Take your time, for a miss will scare the game and increase your difficulties many fold.

15. Many animals are curious of strange noises and objects and can be made to stand for a good shot, or to approach within range by attracting their attention with a whistle or moving cloth.

16. The head, neck, or just back of the shoulder are vulnerable spots on many animals. Aim for one of these.

17. Don't follow a wounded animal too closely; give it time to bleed and weaken, otherwise it may run for miles.

The principles of hunting set down here will prove invaluable to the novice, but remember that a knowledge of the habits of the game and the locality are equally important factors in successful hunting. Your chances of success increase with each day spent in hunting an area or a particular animal, so don't be discouraged if at first you are unsuccessful.

TABLE 1

SOME PLANTS FROM WHICH CORD, LINES AND ROPES MAY BE MADE

Throughout the world there are numerous plants whose roots, outer and inner barks, and leaf and stem fibers can be twisted and used as cord or rope for fishing, lashing and climbing. Fiber from palms, rattans, bamboo and various vines are common in the tropics. The tough inner or outer bark of trees is the easiest and simplest material to use. Soaking often helps to separate the fibers.

NAME	PART USED	WHERE FOUND
1. Leather wood (*Dirca*)	Strands of split bark.	Eastern North America.
2. Basswood or Linden (*Tilia*)	Shredded layers of inner sapling bark.	Temperate countries of northern hemisphere. Rich humus soil.
3. Mulberry (*Morus*)	Inner bark of trunk and roots.	Temperate regions of northern hemisphere.
4. Spruce (*Picea*)	Barked rootlets.	Cold climates of northern hemisphere. Southern mountainous country.
5. Hemlock (*Tsuga*)	Fibers of roots and the roots themselves.	Northern North America and Southern mountains.
6. Tamarack (*Larix*)	Fibers of roots.	Cold climates of northern hemisphere. Swampy wet region.
7. Elm (*Ulmus*)	Shredded bark of trunk and roots.	Temperate climate of northern hemisphere.
8. Indian Hemp (*Apocynum*)	Bark fibers.	Temperate regions of northern hemisphere. Open land.
9. Yucca (*Yucca*)	Fibers in leaves.	Southern United States, Mexico, tropical America. Many are semi-desert plants.
10. Breadfruit (*Artocarpus*)	Strands of inner bark.	South Pacific Islands, Malaya, Southern Asia.

NAME	PART USED	WHERE FOUND
11. Plantains & Bananas (*Musa*)	Fibrous tissues in mature leaf stalks. Musa produces manila hemp.	Throughout tropical and sub-tropical countries.
12. Coconut palm (*Cocos*)	Fibers of coconut husks and midrib of the leaves.	Throughout tropical countries.
13. Liana (*Entada scandens*)	Whole smaller stems and fibers of large stems.	Native of tropics of both hemispheres. South Pacific Islands. Also furnishes drinkable sap.
14. High climbing fern (*Stenochlaena palustris*)	Wiry stems, very durable under water.	India and South Pacific Islands. Another species in Africa and Madagascar. Found in swamps or near the sea.
15. Climbing Cane (*Flagellaria*)	Stems.	India, Australia and South Pacific Islands.
16. Climbing or scrambling aerial plants. (*Freycinetia*)	Flexible stems.	Indian Archipelago, New Zealand, Pacific Islands, etc.
17. A climber of open country. (*Pachyrhizus erosis*)	Stem fibers.	Tropical America, East and West Indies, South Pacific Islands. Found in thickets in open country.
18. Common tropical weeds (*Urena sinuata and lobata*)	Fiber from inner bark.	Common in tropics.
19. Shaw trees (*Stercula*)	Fibrous inner bark. Rope not affected by wetness.	Tropics of both hemispheres.
20. Wild Hibiscus (*Hibiscus cannabinus*)	Stem fibers.	South Pacific Islands.
21. Screw pine (*Pandanus*)	Leaf fibers.	South Pacific Islands.

CHAPTER VI

Firemaking and Cooking

Fire will lengthen your survival time by enabling you to keep warm, cook your food, and destroy the harmful germs commonly found in food and water. You should be able, with matches, to build a fire under all weather conditions. No one who may have to shift for himself in a remote area should ever be without matches carried in a waterproof case. If you remember and practice a few basic principles of fire building, you can always make a fire.

(1) Select a dry sheltered spot.

(2) Use only the driest of tinder to start the fire.

(3) Have a good supply of kindling on hand before you strike the match.

(4) Start with a tiny fire and add fuel as the flame grows.

(5) Fire needs air. Add fuel sparingly.

(6) Blow lightly on the burning wood. This helps the flame along.

(7) Fire climbs. Place fresh kindling above the flame.

(8) Use dry dead wood.

FIG. 152. Fire with a Camera Lens

Fire Site

Use judgment in the selection of a fire site. Don't select a windy spot. Don't build on damp ground if dry is available. Pick a spot where your fire won't spread. In rainy weather, build under a leaning tree or rock shelf. If snow is on the ground, build your fire on a platform of logs, or metal salvaged from your plane; however, you can build or keep a fire going on bare snow or ice.

Tinder

Tinder may consist of dry grasses or plant stems, dry inflammable bark, such as birch, or dry leaves. The most available tinder in dry weather is the tiny,

FIG. 153. Use Small Dry Tinder

brittle branchlets from dry, dead limbs. Twigs not much thicker than a straw should be broken in lengths of several inches and arranged in a wigwam pile three to four inches high, the shortest and thinnest twigs being underneath. Touch a match to these and add kindling as the flames grow. A fuzz stick or shaving clusters may be used in place of small twigs. Select some dry branches the diameter of your finger and shave them halfway through for most of their length to form a cluster of shavings. Stand these in a wigwam with curls down, and light them.

Kindling

Have plenty of kindling at hand to keep your fire burning. Soft woods make the best kindling as they light easily and burn rapidly. Split wood burns faster than round branches. Branches lying flat on the ground are generally damp. Select dead branches off the ground. Most dead branches snap when broken. Live ones bend and are usually not brittle.

Fuel

All woods do not burn alike. Some scarcely burn at all, others burn quickly and make a hot flame. Some burn slowly and make good coals; some smoke, others don't. Use whatever is at hand, but where there is a choice, select the best fuels for the purpose. In general, hardwoods make a slow-burning fire with lasting coals, and soft woods make a quick, hot fire with coals that are soon spent.

In the Arctic fire is essential. Dried lichens, moss, heather, scrub willow, and driftwood all make good fuel. The resinous white heather is the most valuable arctic prairie fuel. Willows and alders grow along practically all arctic rivers, and their stems and roots alike serve as fuel. Even in mid-winter, willows can be found in wind-swept spots.

Seal blubber is the best natural fuel. It can be burned in a shallow stone lamp or tin can with a wick of thoroughly dry powdered moss, grass or decayed wood. Another method is to soak a small piece of cloth in seal grease. Then place a small pile of dried bones or other non-combustible material on top of the rag. Lay several strips of blubber on top of the bones and light the rag, which will burn like a wick and start the blubber frying. The blubber oil will trickle down on the bones and flare up as soon as they become hot. Fat and hides of land animals are also usable fuel.

Lubricating oil will not light with a match unless first vaporized by dripping on a piece of hot rock or metal. It can, however, be burned in a container with a wick of rope, cloth, dried bark or moss. If you come down with your plane in the Arctic, drain your oil before it congeals, mix it with gasoline, pour it into a container and burn it with an improvised wick.

Banking a Fire

It is essential to bank a fire properly if you expect to have it burning the next morning or the next week. Use green logs or the butt of a decayed punky log for a slow-burning fire. Eliminate as much draft as possible. The coals or the charred backlogs can be blown into a flame when needed. Dry coconut husks, punk and fungus are excellent for keeping a fire going and for carrying it from place to place. It requires less work to keep a fire going than to start a new one.

Fire in Wet Weather

The trick of making a fire in wet weather is to find enough dry tinder and wood to get it started. Even wet wood will burn on a good fire. Look for dry wood under overhanging rocks, in caves, on the under side of leaning trees and logs, and in hollow trees. Rain does not soak far into a standing dead tree; split it open and use the interior. Cut away the wet exterior of small dead limbs to get dry wood. If your matches become wet, you can dry them by rotating them rapidly between the palms of the hands.

In wet weather, a fire can be started with certain inflammable tinders that will ignite even when damp. The resinous pitch in pine knots or dried stumps burns like an oil torch. Slivers of dry pitchy pine make excellent tinder and kindling. The loose bark from living birch trees contains a resinous oil which is easily ignited and burns fiercely.

Fire Without Matches

Sun and glass.—Sunlight focused on a pile of tinder through the lens from a flashlight, binoculars, telescopic sight or camera, will produce coals that can be fanned into a flame. It may be necessary to take the lenses apart and use a single element.

Flint and steel.—Sparks struck from a piece of flint, quartz or pyrite into a pile of tinder can be used to start a fire. Use the back of your knife blade

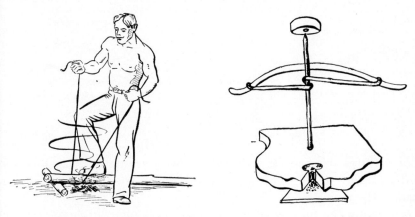

FIG. 154. Fire Thong   FIG. 155. Bow and Drill

or any piece of hard steel to strike the sparks. Let the sparks fall on a spark-catcher of shredded cloth, dry moss, bird and seed down, dead fungi, punk or pulverized bark. Once the spark catches, blow it gently until it flames. Experiment with the driest tinders you can find. Charred rags catch better than anything else; so if your matches are running short, char some of your clothing by burning it without air in a closed container such as a tin first-aid kit or a ball of clay.

Wood friction.—Choose dry, well-seasoned wood to make a fire by friction. Dead branches slightly punky are the best, and in general, soft-grained woods are better than hardwoods. Resinous, gummy woods are worthless. The best woods include balsa, yucca, elm and the root of willow and cotton-wood. The right kind of wood makes a fine carbon dust with the formation of an ember. If you get a coarse, gritty powder, discard the wood and try another.

Fire with bow and drill.—The bow and drill is the easiest method of making fire by friction. When a dry, soft shaft of wood is spun into a block of the same material, a black powdered dust will form and eventually catch a spark. Figure 155 shows the necessary materials. To make a fire with these materials, draw the bow back and forth causing the drill to spin in the block. Start slowly with long full strokes and work faster. When a volume of smoke begins to rise through the fire pit, you have a spark sufficient to start a fire. Lift the block, add tinder and blow gently until you get a flame. Fire has been made with a bow and drill in less than seven seconds.

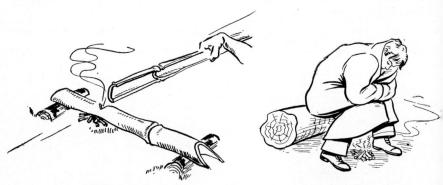

FIG. 156. Bamboo Fire Saw   FIG. 157. Keeping Warm

Fire thong.—Fire can be made by drawing a dry rattan thong back and forth on a soft, dry piece of wood. Wedge tinder into a split in the hearth log to catch the embers.

Fire saw.—The fire-saw, commonly used in the jungle, consists of two pieces of wood and plenty of "elbow grease." Split bamboo or a soft wood will serve as a rub stick, and the dry sheath of the coconut flower makes an effective base wood. Good tinder is the brown, fluffy covering on the trunk of the Apiang palm, the dry, fabric-like material found at the base of coconut leaves, and the fine, skin-like membrane lining the bamboo cavity.

These methods, however, are always a last resort, and should be tried only as such. Fire with matches is infinitely easier; always carry them in a waterproof case.

Fires for Warmth

A small fire is better than a large one for nearly all purposes. A very small fire will warm you thoroughly if you sit or kneel over it, draping your coat, blanket or parachute so as to direct all of the heat upward.

A reflector fire will keep you warm while you are sleeping. The base of a tree, a large rock or a log are ready-made reflectors. Lie or sit between the fire and reflector, as this will prevent you from "baking" on one side and "freezing" on the other. A reflector can be constructed of logs, snow, boughs or sod.

Cooking Fires

When fuel is scarce, make a hobo stove from an empty tin. Such a stove will conserve heat and fuel and is particularly serviceable in the Arctic.

The criss-cross fire is the best all-around cooking fire, as it burns down to a uniform bed of coals in a short time. (See Fuels.) The simplest fireplace consists of two rocks, two logs, or a narrow trench on which a vessel can

FIG. 158. Broiling Fish—Simple Crane   FIG. 159. Reflector Fire

rest with the fire below. Arrange the fireplace so that it will have a draft. If the fire does not draw well, elevate one edge of the log or stone. Replenish a fire by stacking the wood on criss-cross. It will burn to coals much sooner.

COOKING METHODS AND TECHNICS

Cooking renders most foods more palatable and digestible, destroys bacteria, toxins, and harmful plant and animal products; cook your food whenever possible. *The best cooking is done over a bed of glowing coals, not flames.* Where containers are used, construct a crane over the fire to support the cooking vessels.

Boiling requires a container. When meat is tough or food requires long cooking, it is often a wise procedure to boil it first and then roast, fry or bake it. Boiling is the easiest method for the Arctic. It should be used in any case where you want to save the juices. At high altitudes, food has to be boiled longer than at low altitudes. Do not try to boil food above 12,000 feet; it requires too much time and fuel.

Water in a scooped-out log or clay pit can be boiled by dropping heated stones into it. In the tropics, half a green coconut or a bamboo stem cut well above and just below the joint can be used for containers. They will not burn completely until well after the water boils. After placing food and water in a freshly-cut bamboo joint, tie green leaves over the open end and support the vessel against a stone. (See Figures 162 and 163.)

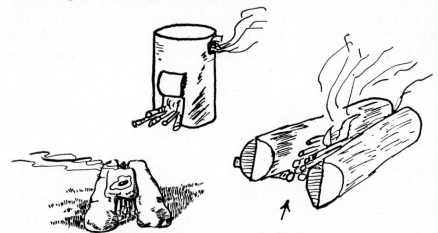

FIG. 160. Stone, Tin Can and Log Fireplace

FIG. 161. Crane

You can boil water in vessels made of bark or leaves. The container will not burn below the water line, but it may catch fire above unless moistened. If you use a small fire and keep the flames low, you will experience little difficulty.

Birchbark and banana leaves make excellent containers. Cut out about a

FIG. 162. Cook or Boil Drinking Water in a Bamboo Joint

FIG. 163. Cover Container and Stand Upright in Fire

twelve inch square of bark, make two diagonal folds between all four corners
open them up, turn the bark over, and fold it in thirds. Open again and fol
in thirds the other way. Then pinch up each corner so that the triangle i
pointing out. Fold this along the side and pin in place with a thorn, or slive
of wood. Make sure your bark contains no holes.

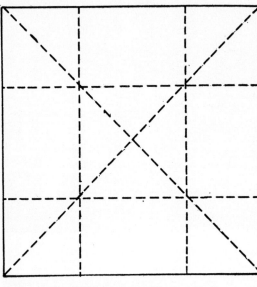

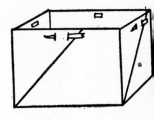

Roasting or broiling is
quick way to prepare wil
plant foods and tende
meats. Simply run a sticl
through the piece to b
cooked and hold it over th
coals. Keep the piece as clos
to the coals as possible. Thi
hardens the outside quickl
and holds the juices in.

FIG. 164. Diagram for Making a Bark
Container

Baking is cooking witl
moderate, steady heat in an oven. The oven may be a pit, closed vessel or
wrapping of clay or leaves. Without cooking equipment, most of your fish an
meat must be either broiled or baked. To bake in a pit, get a good bed of coals

then drop in a covered shell vessel con
taining water and meat, tubers wrappe
in leaves, or fish or bird wrapped in we
leaves and mud. Cover whatever you ar
baking with coals, and then fill the pi
with a few inches of earth. A stone-line
pit will hold more heat and cook mor
quickly than an earthen pit.

Steaming is slower than boiling, bu
it can be done without a container. Di;
a hole and fill it with stones. Build a fir

FIG. 165. Steam or Baking Pit

to heat the stones. Cover the stones and coals with leaves, then put in your food
Cover this with more leaves and then a layer of dirt. Punch a hole down to th
food and pour in some water. Close the hole and the food will steam. Thi
method is suitable for foods such as shellfish that require little cooking.

Utensils

Large leaves, a slab of bark, turtle, coconut, or sea shells will serve as plates. Some kind of container is necessary for carrying water. An excellent one can be made by punching out all but the last node from a convenient length of bamboo. Fit with a wooden plug for a stopper and sling it over your shoulder on a piece of vine. A water belt can be made of short bamboo nodes strung together.

Cooking Wild Food

Fruits.—Succulent fruits are best boiled. Large, tough or heavy-skinned fruits are best baked or roasted.

Potherbs (Leaves, stems and buds).—Boil until tender; several changes of water with subsequent rinsing will help eliminate bitter juices or undesirable tastes.

Roots and tubers.—These can be boiled, but are more easily baked or roasted.

Nuts.—Most nuts can be eaten raw, but some such as acorns are better cooked. Acorns should be broken up, boiled with ashes from the fire to eliminate tannin, moulded into cakes and then baked. Chestnuts are good roasted, steamed, or baked.

Grains and seeds.—Parch grains and seeds. They are more digestible and tasty that way.

Sap.—The sap of plants containing sugar can be dehydrated to a syrup or sugar by boiling to remove the water.

Large game.—May be cleaned and cooked for its food value. Remove the entrails and the glands in the anal and reproductive regions, as they will impart an objectionable taste to the meat. Animals the size of a domestic cat or larger should be boiled first, then roasted or broiled. If meat is very tough, stew it with vegetables. Broil meat as quickly as possible over hot coals. Slow roasting makes tough meat tougher. Cook small pieces at a time.

Small game.—Small mammals and birds may be cooked whole or in part. If tough, or if the flavor is strong, boil first and then broil. If fruit is available, stuff the animal and bake or roast.

Fish.—Fish can be roasted on a grill of green sticks or baked in leaves and clay. Fish wrapped in leaves should be placed on green logs on the fire to keep the flesh free of ashes.

Reptiles and amphibians.—Frogs, small snakes, and salamanders can be roasted on a stick. Large snakes and eels are better if boiled first then roasted. Turtles should be boiled until the shell comes off. Then cut up the meat and cook with tubers and greens to form a soup.

FIG. 166. Cooking Breadfruit ("Yank")

Crustaceans.—Crabs, crayfish, shrimps, prawns, and the like can be steamed, boiled, roasted or baked. They require very little cooking. However, they spoil quickly and the safest way to cook them is to drop them alive in boiling water.

Mollusks.—Shellfish should be steamed, boiled or baked in the shell. They make excellent stews in combination with greens and tubers.

Insects.—Insects such as large grubs, locusts, grasshoppers, ants, termites, etc., can be fried, boiled or roasted, but they are generally more palatable if disguised in a stew containing other foods.

Eggs.—Eggs can be hard boiled with the shell on and carried for days. They can be poached in a bark container or fried on a hot rock. Turtle eggs don't get hard with boiling. Fresh eggs are among the safest of foods, and they are edible at any stage of embryo development.

Salt.—Salt is necessary for proper functioning of the human body. It can be obtained by boiling sea water. The ashes of burned nipa palm boughs, hickory, and some other plants, contain salt that can be dissolved out in water. Evaporate the water and a black looking salt remains.

Preparing Food Without Fire

Fresh papaya leaves contain papain that renders meat soft and tender in a short time. It is especially useful when freshly killed meat must be eaten raw or cooked.

The citric acid in limes, lemons and other citric fruits can be used to pickle fish and other flesh. Dilute two parts lime juice with one part sea water, add raw fish, and allow the mixture to stand for half a day or more. The citric acid will "cook" the fish.

PRESERVATION OF FOOD

Wild food is scarce in some local areas and abundant in others. Whenever you can get more than you need immediately, preserve it, especially if there are indications that you may have difficulty in getting more.

Freezing

In cold climates, meat will be the principal food you will get in excessive quantities. It will keep indefinitely when frozen.

Drying

Drying food not only preserves it, but decreases its weight without losing any of its calories. Dry foods can be eaten uncooked when necessary. Food can be dried by wind, air, sun, or fire with or without smoke. A combination of these can be used. The main object is to get rid of the water. In hot, dry

FIG. 167. Before—Wild Food Collected in Two Hours' Time Along a River

FIG. 168. After—Same Food Cooked and Ready to Be Eaten

climates the sun and air will be sufficient, but in humid climates fire must be used and the dehydrated product kept dry. Cut the food to be dried in small strips so that a maximum area will be exposed to the drying influence.

Smoke-Drying Meat

To smoke-dry meat, build a stick grate three to four feet above a slow-burning fire, and lay strips of lean meat one-fourth inch thick on this lattice. Do not let the fire get hot enough to cook the meat or draw out the juices. The smoke which rises naturally from the burning wood is sufficient. Continue the smoking until the meat is brittle. It will then keep for long periods, and can be chewed while traveling or cooked in a stew if time permits. Avoid using resinous or oily woods to smoke meat; they will blacken it and give it a disagreeable flavor.

Fish and Birds

To dry fish, cut them in strips or split them down the back. Leave the heads on small ones and hang them over the fire by threading a stick through their gills. Small birds may be gutted and dried whole.

Fruit

Plantains, bananas, breadfruit, apricots, cherries, grapes, potatoes, tubers, leaves, figs, dates, apples, berries, in fact most wild fruits, can be dried. Cut them into fine slices and place in the sun. A fire may be used if necessary.

CONCENTRATED RATIONS

Two of the best concentrated foods are pemmican and pinole. These keep indefinitely, contain a maximum of calories for their weight, are easy to prepare, and do not require cooking when used. A man can live entirely on either one for long periods. Pemmican can be made by pouring hot suet (fat) over shredded dried meat. Keep in a waterproof container and cook or eat raw.

Pinole is prepared by parching corn grains in hot ashes, on heated rocks or in an oven. The browned kernels are then ready to eat or can be pounded to a fine meal. A small handful of this in a cup of cold water has a pleasant flavor, and will keep a man going all day. Most grass seeds can be prepared in this way, though few of them will have the same nutritional properties of corn.

POISONOUS ANIMAL FOODS

No birds or mammals are poisonous to eat, though the liver of polar bears may cause serious sickness. In South America, some mammals may have flukes. Snake flesh is generally safe if cooked.

Some sea foods are poisonous at certain times and places. Only along tropical shores, especially in the vicinity of coral reefs, is there any real danger. The alkaloids in the flesh of poisonous fish are not destroyed by cooking. (See pages 151-153.)

Spoiled meats and fish are far more dangerous to eat than animals that are themselves poisonous. Poisoning from such food is common in the tropics and constitutes a real hazard. Sea food is especially likely to spoil and should be eaten when fresh. Fish should be gutted at once to prevent spoiling. Good fish will be firm, spoiled fish soft and flabby.

Meat and the flesh of all fresh water fish should be cooked whenever possible for they may contain flukes and other parasitic worms harmful to man. Salt water fish are generally free of harmful parasites.

In populated parts of the tropics, cholera, typhoid fever, and dysenteries can be contracted from eating raw foods handled by the natives. Flies carry the above diseases, too, and are more dangerous in native villages than in the open country. Protect your food from flies. Sterilize it by cooking.

VITAMIN DEFICIENCIES

When living off the land or sea, there is often little choice of food. If the diet is restricted to a few foods over a period of at least a month, vitamin deficiency diseases are likely to develop. Under extreme conditions, especially at sea, there is nothing you can do but grin and bear it.

Although these diseases are painful and appear serious, they disappear almost miraculously when you reach land and get fresh fruits and vegetables.

Vitamin deficiencies often occur through ignorance where proper food is available. You cannot live on lean meat alone, but you can remain active and healthy for long periods on fat and lean meat. Stefansson lived entirely on meat and fat for a year.

Vitamin A—Vitamin A deficiency causes night blindness, followed by extreme muscular weakness, and in late stages, blindness. Carotene, which supplies vitamin A, is found in yellow fruits and vegetables. Vitamin A in pure form is found in fat, egg yolk, liver, and in oily fresh and salt water fish.

Vitamin B_1 or Thiamine—Absence of vitamin B_1 causes fatigue, headache, and finally beriberi. Vitamin B_1 occurs naturally in egg yolks, grains, and lean meat.

Vitamin B_2 (Riboflavin)—A deficiency of this vitamin causes irritations of the digestive tract. It is found in a wide variety of foods, such as lean meat, liver, eggs, grains.

Vitamin C—Scurvy is the result of a deficiency of this vitamin and is characterized by irritability, lethargy, soreness and stiffness of the joints, loosening of the teeth, nosebleed, and hemorrhages under the skin. Vitamin C is abundant in liver, citrous fruits, green vegetables, and wild herbs such as sorrel, purslane and dock.

Vitamin D—Vitamin D deficiency causes rickets. This vitamin is produced in the skin by sunlight and is found in liver oils.

Pellagra is a vitamin deficiency disease caused by a lack of vitamin B_1 and complicated by other dietary deficiencies. It is characterized by skin lesions, digestive disturbances, nervousness and paralysis.

If the symptoms of any vitamin deficiency diseases should appear, make a special effort to vary your diet. An adequate supply of vitamins can generally be obtained by eating a variety of foods. If you manage to survive for a month on land, the chances are you have eaten enough different kinds of foods to keep yourself supplied with all the necessary vitamins. If any of the above symptoms are showing, get busy and experiment with some new foods. Green grass contains vitamins A, B, and C. Try it.

CHAPTER VII
Shelter

The ability to provide yourself with adequate shelter will increase your chances of surviving and greatly reduce your physical hardships.

Shelter and sleep are as necessary to a stranded man as food and water. You will tire as quickly from loss of sleep as you will from lack of food.

When lost or stranded, decide what you need to make you safe and comfortable for the night, and then look for these things. Avoid the things that are most likely to prevent a good night's sleep. In a strange country begin to look for a site at least two hours before sunset; don't wait until dark. Consider these factors in selecting your camp:

FIG. 169. A Natural Rock Shelter and a Leaf Bed—A Little Ingenuity Will Give You Additional Protection from Wind and Rain

1. Available food.
2. Good drinking water.
3. Enough level ground for your bed.
4. Protection from wind and storm.
5. Bedding and shelter material.
6. Protection from floods, wild animals, rock falls, high tides, wind and cold.
7. Concealment from enemies.
8. Absence of insect pests.
9. Firewood.

Natural Shelters and Windbreaks

Make camp with the least possible expenditure of time and energy. A ravine or narrow valley between steep hills collects cold, heavy air at night

FIG. 170. Windbreak Shelter

FIG. 171. Tarpaulin Shelter

and will be several degrees colder than the surrounding heights. A natural terrace, a clump of bushes, a small depression, or a large rock on the leeward side of a hill will break the wind and make a comparatively warm site.

When you find your site, examine it well. Rocky crevices and caves may harbor poisonous snakes; hollow trees and logs may contain ticks, mites,

FIG. 172. Parachute Tent Pitched High to Give Room. Use Rest of Chute for a Blanket

FIG. 173. Parachute Tent Pitched Low to Make Floor. Pile Leaves Under Floor for Bed.
Waterproof and Camouflage by Covering with Overlapping Leaves, Branches, or Bark

scorpions and stinging ants. The time you spend making yourself comfortable for the night will pay good dividends the next day.

Brush Shelters

With a little time and effort a brush shelter can be made of two poles leaned against a log and covered with boughs or palm fronds. A more elaborate lean-to can be built. (Figure 175.) Tie cross pieces to the uprights with

FIG. 174. Log Shelter

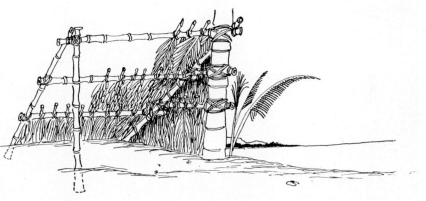

FIG. 175. Lean-to

vines or bark. Cover the frame with evergreen boughs, elephant grass, palm, or banana leaves, or strips of bark depending upon the available foliage. Start the boughs at the bottom row and work up shingle-fashion. A section of your parachute makes a good tent when pitched as shown in Figures 172 and 173. (See diagram, Figure 180.)

Snow Shelters

In a cold climate the primary purpose of a shelter is to break the air movement and retain the heat from your fire or body. The shelter should be small, windproof, and as nearly closed as possible. The smaller the air space around

your body and the less the air circulation, the warmer your shelter will be
A snow cave meets the above requirements and is easy to construct. Select
a spot where the crust is firm or where the snow covers low-hanging evergreen
boughs. Scoop or kick a hollow beneath the crust or limbs. (Figure 181.)

If you build a fire, there will be danger of carbon monoxide poisoning

FIG. 176. Plaiting a Palm Leaf ("Yank")

so a more open shelter is necessary. Dig a trench in a low drift or bank. Line
the floor and roof the trench with boughs. Build a fire at the entrance and
reflect heat inward with a reflector of logs, boughs or snow blocks.

Make the roof strong to support a layer of snow. This will help hold the
warm air in. If you do not have a fire, cover the entrance and don't worry
about air. You will get plenty. If you insulate your body from direct contact
with the snow and prevent circulation of air, you will keep warm.

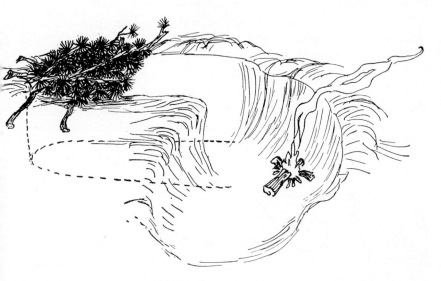

FIG. 177. Snow Bank Shelter

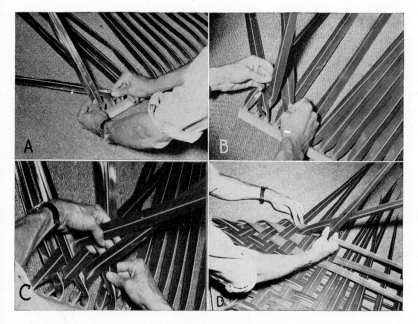

FIG. 178. Thatched Palm Leaves Make Excellent Water-repellent Shelters and Comfortable Beds

Desert Shelters

In desert country you are concerned with protection from sun and heat although wind is an important factor and cold often becomes disagreeable a night.

In the early evening, desert sand may be so hot you can't sleep on it, ye after dark the desert becomes chilled. To insure a maximum of warmth throughout the night, spread a coat, parachute, or blanket of vegetation ove the ground while it is still hot. This prevents the rapid radiation of heat and will help keep you warm through the night.

Natural shelters such as vegetation, overhanging rocks, and depression will offer shade, provided you shift with the sun. A cave or covered trench is practical where the sand or soil is loose.

Beds

A good bed serves two functions; it allows the body to relax completely and it insulates against ground chill. To do this it must be dry, smooth, soft and free of insects.

Warmth.—A cold man can't relax. He will wake up more fatigued than when he went to bed. The ground is cold at night and conducts body heat away. To sleep warm you need more insulation below than above you as the ground is a better heat conductor than the air.

If it is cold and there is no snow, the ground chill can be removed by building a large fire over the spot you intend to sleep on. Spread the coals and stamp them into the ground; then make your bed over the heated area.

In the open, several fires with reflectors may be necessary to keep you warm

Smoothness.—Hard, level ground is more comfortable than soft, uneven ground. Avoid hummocks, small depressions, sticks and small stones.

Sand feels soft but is really hard, and if you are restless it soon becomes very uncomfortable. To make a good bed, scoop out hollows to fit your body contours, especially the hips.

Level surface.—Don't sleep with the head downhill. A level surface is best, but a slight slope will do. Too steep a slope will cause sliding and rolling

Dampness.—Dampness is a problem in tropical forests during the wet season. It can be overcome by sleeping off the ground.

A dry jungle bed can be constructed as in Figures 183 and 184. Two logs five to twelve inches in diameter can be substituted for the uprights.

A hammock or platform can be made from vines and leaves or a parachute. The same section used as a tent can be doubled and hung as a hammock.

Insect pests.—A smudge produced by burning wet or green wood, leaves, or grass will help keep mosquitoes and flies away.

FIG. 179. Parachute Hammock—Swing Hammock with Shroud Lines

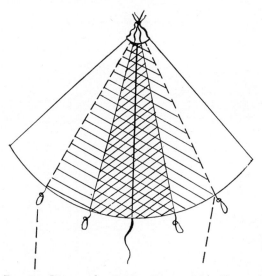

FIG. 180. Diagram for Cutting Chute to Make Tent and
Hammock. Cut Out Four Sections as Shown by Dotted
Lines. Fold Double to Make Hammock.

FIG. 181. Snow Tunnel Shelter

FIG. 182. Bough Bed (Laid)

FIG. 183. Jungle Bed

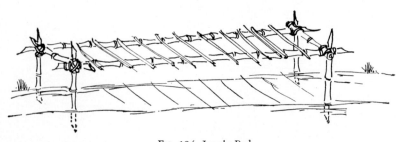

FIG. 184. Jungle Bed

Any place free of flies and mosquitoes, no matter how uncomfortable otherwise, will be acceptable. The only real protection against mosquitoes is a net. (See pages 189-193.)

Bed Construction

Grass, sedge, dry leaves or boughs are all good bedding material. Balsam, spruce, or hemlock make the best bedding in cold climates. Such beds must be properly constructed to give a maximum of insulation and comfort.

Insert the branches in the ground with the tips leaning all in the same direction and with the under or curved surface downward. Plant rows the length of your bed about six to eight inches apart. Cover with fine feathery tips.

FIG. 185. Bough Bed (Inserted)

Water Proofing

Keeping yourself and equipment dry is a major problem in the tropics. A very good waterproof fabric can be made from the broad leaves of young banana trees. Build a hot fire on a flat stone or a platform of small stones. When they are well heated, rake the coals off and place banana leaves one at a time on the hot stones. Let the leaf remain for a minute or two until it turns darker and becomes glossy. The heat "rubberizes" the leaf, making it more pliable and water repellent. The leaves will last for some time and can be used to shingle a lean-to, make a ground cloth, crude poncho, or a wrapper for matches, food, and other small articles.

CHAPTER VIII
Survival in Special Areas

Wherever or whenever conditions are exceptionally adverse, survival will be dependent upon specific information. The more you know concerning a particular area or set of conditions, the longer your survival time will be.

OCEAN SURVIVAL

Survival on the ocean depends to a large extent on the rations and equipment you have with you, the use you make of them, and the degree of skill, ingenuity, and resourcefulness you employ. The Navy, Coast Guard and Merchant Marine have equipped all life boats, rafts and planes with survival

Fig. 186. Eighty-Three Days on a Raft

FIG. 187. Rescue After Existing Nearly Three Months on the South Atlantic

equipment adequate for emergencies at sea. Know where this is stored in your raft or plane before the need for it arises. Check your equipment before starting out on a mission, and know how to use it. Take care to see that fishing tackle is included. Fish may be your only source of food and water. Under severe conditions of cold or heat, clothing becomes as necessary as water or food. Be dressed for the emergency and take extra clothing with you when you abandon ship. Before leaving, drink all the extra water you can. Your body is a good storage tank. Many useful articles can be made from a canvas tarpaulin if you take it along. As soon as you are adrift, make inventory of such articles as safety pins, campaign bars, knives, and military insignia, and save them for future use. The most useless appearing articles may be put to practical use when the going gets tough.

Survival without equipment depends more on fresh water than on food. Without water, a man in good health will become delirious in about four days, death will occur in from eight to twelve. If you have water and are in good health you may live weeks without food. Survivors have been known to live for 10 days or more on as little as two or three ounces of water per day

FIG. 188. Downed Fliers Release a Smoke Signal (*British Combine*)

without causing any apparent bodily damage. *The amount of water and food you need depends upon weather conditions, physical exertion, and individual resistance.*

The record for survival at sea was set by a Chinese seaman who drifted 133 days in the Atlantic. He subsisted on fish and rain water, and was able to walk ashore when rescued.

Living Without Food or Water

If you lack water, don't eat. Your body uses up water in digesting and assimilating food, and the elimination of the waste products also draws water from the tissues. Abstain from both food and water for the first twenty-four hours. After that, ration what you have; and when that is gone, live off your body fat and protein. When these are converted to energy, water is released by the tissues and will help to maintain kidney activity. Keep your body protected as much as possible from sun and wind, since heat and air movement increase evaporation. Heavy clothing in warm weather, strenuous exercise and worry induce sweating with a subsequent loss of water.

One pound of body fat will provide your system with an equivalent of two good meals. The rate at which body fat and protein is converted to heat and energy will depend on the air temperatures and your activity and mental state. *You can live longer on your stored energy by relaxing mind and body and guarding against exposure to extreme temperatures.*

When taking little or no food you can't expect a bowel movement. It is nothing to worry about and you don't need any treatment for this condition.

Water

Rain, ice, and dew are the only sources of water. Do not mix salt water, animal fluid, or urine hoping to stretch your water supply. *Don't drink sea water;* it will only aggravate your thirst and increases water loss by drawing body fluids from the kidneys and intestines, eventually resulting in serious convulsions and delirium. You will have some difficulty in passing urine which will be dark and thick. Such a reaction to dehydration is natural. Urine contains waste products from the body and may be almost as concentrated as sea water. Drinking it will only increase thirst and draw water from the body tissues.

Water evaporates through the skin. Some survivors have reported that by remaining in the sea for hours at a time they prevented the evaporation of water from their bodies and even absorbed enough to increase kidney activity. *The blood of birds and the blood and body fluids of fish are drinkable and nourishing if chewed out.* Break the back bone and drink the spinal fluid.

Collect rain water in any available receptacle, using clothing, parachute, or sails. Devise methods before there is an actual need. If the shower promises to be light, take measures to get every drop of water. Wet your cloth or canvas catchment in the sea so that fresh water will not be absorbed by the fabric.

The amount of salt water contaminating the rain water will be negligible, but the amount of fresh water lost through absorption if you fail to first wet your canvas will be considerable. In a driving rain, a piece of canvas or any large flat surface held at an angle to the wind will catch the water. Your body can store water, therefore drink all you can hold when water is plentiful. Little of the water taken in large quantities when you are dehydrated is lost through perspiration or excessive urination.

Food Getting

The condition of your body will determine whether or not you can or will eat starvation foods. *The sea is far richer in different forms of life than the land or fresh water, and if fresh water is available there is little danger of starving to death.* The problem is to tap this wealth of food. *No one at sea*

should be caught without fishing tackle on his person at all times, but ever
if this happens the situation is far from hopeless.

Fish

*Fish caught at sea are good to eat, cooked or raw. Not any of them are likely
to be poisonous.* Flying fish are widely distributed, palatable, and probably are
the most available source of food if you have no equipment. Many survivors
have lived on them alone. In time some may glide into your boat or against it.

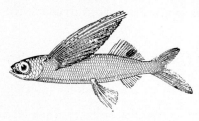

At night they are attracted by a light, become helpless within its radiance, and
can be scooped in a net. Shine your light
on the side of your boat or on any surface
that will reflect it and the flying fish will
often glide toward the light and in or
against the boat.

FIG. 189. Flying Fish

The heart, liver and blood of fish are
good to eat, though in some fish they
are less palatable than the flesh. Intestinal walls are edible, but the contents
may be dangerous unless cooked. The stomachs of large fish may contain
small fish partly digested; they are excellent. Fish eyes contain a high percentage of water.

Small fish can be caught with a skewer or gorge hook made of wood or
metal and a short line improvised from shoe laces, canvas or clothing. If you
have hook and line, but no bait, a strip of leather cut from the tongue of your
shoe, a button, or a piece of canvas fastened to the hook and trolled behind
your boat may prove effective. It must be kept moving so as to resemble a small
fish.

If you have a knife you may be able to stab large fish near the surface, or
spear them by tying your knife to the end of an oar. Slash with your knife in
schools of small fish. Natives get bait in this manner.

Fish spoil quickly in warm weather; therefore clean and eat them without
delay and immediately dry what is left. If the sun is hot, fish can be partially
cooked by cutting them into thin slices and placing them on a dry metal surface.

Fishing Line

To make a fishing line cut a piece of canvas about a yard square, being
careful to follow the weave of the fabric so the threads or ravelings may be
drawn. Be sure the canvas is dry; wet canvas is difficult to unravel. Place 8
or 10 strands between the thumb and forefingers of each hand and roll or
twist the thread clockwise, at the same time passing the right hand over the
left counter-clockwise. This will form a small rope with a breaking point well

over 100 lbs. When about 18 inches of line is completed, cut off the strands at intervals of about two inches so that each thread will be progressively longer. As the end of each strand is reached, feed in a new strand, until 50 or more feet of line have been made.

A two-strand line when made as described will have a breaking point well over 20 pounds.

Fabric from clothing can be utilized in the same way.

Fishhooks

Fishhooks can be made from wood split from seat benches or gunwales. Shape the shaft and cut a notch near the end in which to seat the point.

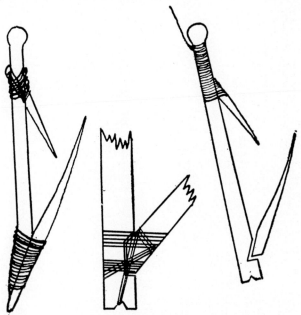

FIG. 190. Construction of Wooden Fish Hooks

Sharpen the point so the hardest part of the grain will form the extreme tip as well as the barb. This section should form an angle of about 30° with the longitudinal axis of the shaft and be lashed firmly in position, using single strands from the canvas. Make the line fast by binding it tightly to the shaft. (See Figures 190 and 191.)

Bait Grapple

A grapple for collecting and pulling in seaweed can be made from four heavy slivers of wood cut from a raft or boat. Cut three notches near the end of the heaviest sliver of wood in which to seat three pieces and lash them in position. Make the line fast to the shaft by cutting three or four notches near the end and lashing it tightly with canvas threads. (See Figure 192.)

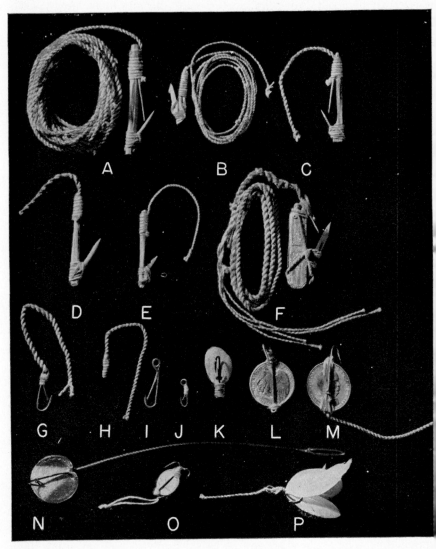

FIG. 191. An Improvised Hook and Line May Well Save Your Life at Sea. a. Wooden Latch Hook and Canvas Line; b. Wooden Snell Hook; c. Hook from Splinter of Wood and Shoe Nail; d., e. Wood and Fish-spine Hooks; f. Pocket Knife Hook for Large Fish; g., h. Latched Hooks from Military Insignia; i., j. Safety Pin Hooks; k. Wooden Spoon Hook; l., m., n. Artificial Lure from Coin and Snelled Hook; o. Dime Fastened to Double Hook; p. Safety-Pin Hook and Feather Lure. A knife makes a useful tool for bending hooks.

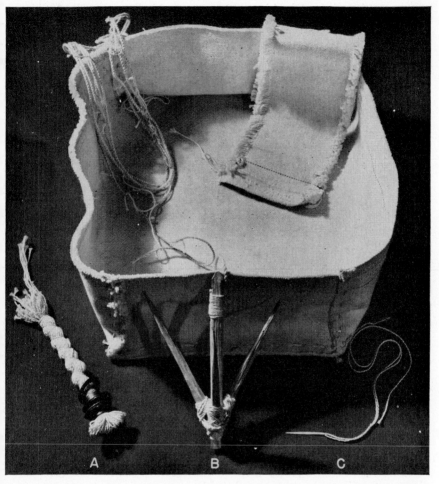

FIG. 192. Bait Grapple and Container. A—Wick; B—Grapple; C—Fish Spine Needle

Bait

Small forms of life drifting about in the sea furnish food directly or indirectly for all the larger forms of aquatic life. This drifting life is most abundant in northern seas, and in some areas is so dense that it colors the water. It can be gathered with a tow net or improvised dip net. Use the small creatures as bait for fish, but don't eat them as they are salty and contain sharp spines that will injure the stomach and intestines. Likewise, don't eat jellyfish; they possess stinging cells that are poisonous. (For poisonous fish see pages 150-152.)

Containers

Containers that will serve as water or fire buckets can be made with an improvised needle and some canvas. If the bucket is to be watertight the seams must be reinforced with a narrow canvas binding and calked with fish slime that is then allowed to dry into the seams. A seamless watertight container can be made from canvas as described on page 114, Figure 164.

The tail-half of a fish carefully skinned back, then scraped, stuffed with seaweed or rags and dried in the sun will make an oil or water container. Leave the tails and fins attached to the skin. The air bladder of large fish can be dried and used in the same way.

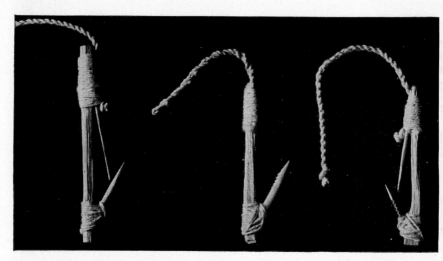

FIG. 193. Wooden Shafted Hooks with Wood, Fish Spine, and Shoe Nail Barbs.

Fire Pots

The bottom of a canvas fire pot should be kept wet; the sides will act as wicks and prevent the pot from burning. Rags, a few seat shavings, and the oil from fish livers should be saved and lighted as a signal to attract rescuers. Extract the oil by placing the fish livers in the sun. A wick can be made from the canvas threads. (See Figure 192.)

Fishing at Sea

Your success with fishing equipment will depend on how you use it. Remember the following.

1. Never fasten your line to something solid; it may snap when a large fish strikes.
2. Try to catch small fish; large ones may destroy your tackle.
3. Fish are more apt to see and strike a moving bait than a still one.
4. Use part of any bird or fish you catch for bait. It need not be fresh. Bird intestines threaded on a hook are excellent.

5. Many species of fish are confined to certain depth zones by light, pressure, and food. Some range through a wide variety of depth zones while still others migrate from zone to zone at different times of the day. Try fishing at different times of the day and night at all depths. Don't give up; sea life is not evenly distributed; sooner or later you will have luck.

6. When you hook a large fish, keep a taut line and play him. Don't force him, you may break your line or tear the hook loose.

7. Watch for schools of fish breaking water. Schools of small fish are good indications of the presence of large fish and vice versa. Birds often follow schools of small fish.

8. Many species of fish and drifting sea life come to the surface of the sea at night. Fish shallow and use a drag net.

9. Many small fish are attracted by shade. Lower the sail or tarpaulin into the water; fish may gather under it.

Seaweed

Raw seaweeds are tough and salty, absorb water from the intestines, and are difficult to digest. Eat them only if you have plenty of water. Small edible crabs, shrimp and fish inhabit the seaweed along the coast and patches of sargasso weed far at sea. A grappler dragged behind the boat will collect seaweed. Shake it vigorously and examine carefully as the crabs, shrimp and fish will be well camouflaged in it.

Birds

All sea birds are edible and nourishing, though they may have a fishy flavor and musty odor. Birds are relatively scarce on the open sea, but along coral islands and mid-ocean rocks thousands may be found. Three members of a torpedoed merchantman survived 83 days on a raft catching 25 or 26 birds during that time.

The number of birds you can expect to see on the open North Atlantic is comparatively small. In the North Pacific Ocean most of the seabirds are found near the coasts. Many tropical sea birds breed throughout the year and eggs and young can be found at all times. In the southern oceans many species of birds may be seen and caught hundreds of miles from shore. Land birds migrate miles over water; they often alight on boats to rest and at such times exhibit little fear of man.

Gulls, albatross, terns, gannets (boobies) can be caught by dragging a baited fishhook behind a boat, or lured within shooting distance in the same manner. A flat sharp-edged, triangular-shaped piece of metal or shell, dragged behind the boat will attract gulls and albatrosses. A shiny or colored object is most effective and a bait of fish or intestines adds to its attractiveness. The bird dives, seizes the lure, and the sharp points catch in its bill and hold fast.

Gannets once settled on a boat or raft will often allow themselves to be captured without atempting to fly away. If they are shy they may be caught in the following manner: Tie a knot with two pieces of line as illustrated in Figure 194, fastening two of the free ends of the knot to the boat. Place some fish entrails or similar bait within the loop. When a bird is attracted to the food, pull the knot together about its legs. A simple overhand knot can be used for the same purpose. Whatever bird you catch, use all of it. The smaller feathers can be used to make a fly or lure. A spinner can be fashioned

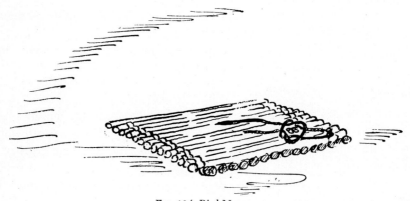

FIG. 194. Bird Noose

from the long plates of the bill. The bones can be utilized for skewer or barbed hooks and the quills stripped to make string. The skin is highly nutritive, but if warm clothing is the pressing problem, skin the bird down the back, dry in the sun and use the thick downy breast feathers for a cap, ear muffs, scarf, or shoe lining.

Indicators of Land

Large numbers of birds indicate some kind of land nearby. Most of the tropical sea birds do not range far from their breeding grounds. This is particularly true of the "boobies" or gannets which are found throughout tropical seas within fairly close proximity to land. Their habit of diving into the sea for food is in itself a characteristic almost sufficient to distinguish the bird as a gannet. The only other sea birds which dive from the air are the brown pelicans, also seen close to land, and the much smaller terns and the long tail-feathered tropic birds which may or may not be far from land. Note the direction of flight of sea birds, for in some species it will be a reliable indication of the distance and direction of land. Frigate birds are easily distinguished from any other sea bird. When you see them in the evening, you can

Casualty Removal Adaptation (Land)

Casualty Rig Adaptation (Sea)

be reasonably sure that land is not too far away on their line of flight. Gulls are primarily birds of the shore lines and are not found in the open ocean. In northern seas, especially in the Bering Sea, adjacent parts of the North Pacific Ocean, and in parts of the North Atlantic and Arctic Seas, various species of auks are a good indication that land is near. The very distinctive tufted and horned puffins and the common murre are generally not seen very far out to sea, and their flight at dawn and dusk shows the direction of land.

Fixed cumulus clouds in an otherwise clear sky are likely to have been formed over high or mountainous land. Take note of any stationary cloud especially where moving clouds are passing by, for it is an indication that land lies beneath it beyond the horizon. Lagoon glare, a greenish tint in the sky or on the under side of a cloud, is caused by the reflection of sunlight from the shallow water of coral reefs. The reflection of light from any surface such as sand, shoal water, ice or snow may be reflected in the sky or on clouds and is an indication of land. Drifting wood or vegetation is an indication that you are approaching land.

Morale

High morale will bring you through. Without it you may fail. Living without equipment in an open boat on the high seas is the severest test of morale. Don't let your thoughts and imagination become your greatest enemy. Keep fishing and experimenting to the limit, for activity is the best cure for depression.

Remember:

> "Life's battles do not always go
> To the stronger or faster man,
> But sooner or later the man who wins
> Is the man who thinks he can."

THE SEASHORE

Where and What to Hunt

The sea beaches and shores of the world contain more easily-available wild food than any other division of the earth. If you are stranded on the seashore in a warm climate you should have little difficulty sustaining yourself indefinitely.

Types of oysters, mussels, scallops, crabs, lobsters, shrimps and prawns are found along all seashores. At low tide, start hunting on the beach by turning over the stones nearest the low tide level and examine crevices and sheltered nooks of rocks. Examine the sand and the line of sea detritus that marks the level of the high tide. *The best hunting will be in the shallow water below*

FIG. 200. Three Pacific Fleet Airmen Who Survived 34 Days on a Tiny Rubber Lifeboat

the tidal zone and in the tidal pools. Some of the animals which inhabit rocky shores, stony beaches, or sand and mud in one area may be looked for anywhere in the world under similar physical surroundings. They may differ in genera and species, but a picture of typical forms is a sufficient guide to their recognition.

The outer margins of rocky or coral reefs usually contain channels, and on the surface of the reefs are pools that contain edible sea life. On sandy beaches you can expect to find bivalve mollusks and sand crabs. The loose, soggy soil of salt marshes and mud flats is the home of fiddler crabs, the mud snail, and various other types of mollusks and crabs.

FIG. 201. Blue Crab

FIG. 202. Hermit Crab

Crabs also inhabit mangrove swamps throughout the tropics. Some live in holes in the mud, others burrow under the mangrove roots. Still others live among the trunks and branches. In all these swamps, oysters, barnacles and mussels are found fastened to the mangrove roots near the water line and in the mud.

Oysters and fish are numerous at the mouth of mangrove rivers and streams. Catfish are often plentiful, but the most abundant fish in such areas is the mud skipper. It is small but edible, and will be seen out of water on rocks, limbs, roots and mud banks. On the mud flats at the seaward edge of mangrove swamps, small rays and sharks may be speared as they come in with the tide. The wings or flaps of the ray may be cut off and eaten. Mullet and larger fish can be speared or netted. Birds such as ibis, egrets, herons, flamingoes and ducks are generally present in great numbers.

Be careful in traversing a mangrove swamp. Wait for low tide. (See page 28)

Some fish can be obtained best at night. They swim near the surface close to shore reefs. By remaining still you can hit them with clubs or spear them In shallow lagoons, mullet and other bottom feeders can be spotted with a torch and speared or slashed with a machete.

In daytime at ebb tide the larger fish can be shot as they swim over the

FIG. 203. Gathering Shellfish
(*Life*)

FIG. 204. Spearing Lobster
(*Life*)

FIG. 205. Common Lobster

FIG. 206. Spiny Lobster

FIG. 207. Some Common Edible Marine Mollusks of the Southwest Pacific

FIG. 208. Some Edible Fresh Water Mollusks of the Southwest Pacific
(Smithsonian Institution)

Fig. 209. Some Edible Marine Mollusks of Alaska and the Northwest Pacific

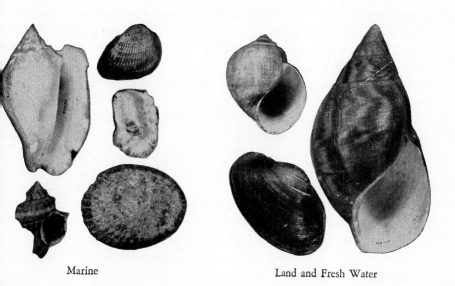

Marine   Land and Fresh Water

Fig. 210. Some Edible Mollusks of Africa (Smithsonian Institution)

reefs with their backs out of water. They frequently swim into the pools on top of the reefs at high tide and can be trapped there by building a net across a channel through which they must leave when the tide falls. A seine of coconut leaves is useful for driving fish into a trap. Stingrays and flounders lie in shallow water where they are difficult to see but easy to spear. (See page 209.)

Crabs and lobsters may be speared, can be caught with the hands, bait-trapped, or caught with a scoop net. They are most active at night and should be hunted in shallow water along the beach. As far as is known, all crabs and lobsters, whether fresh water, marine or land forms, are edible. Salt water crabs can be eaten raw, but all fresh water and land crabs should be cooked.

Marine shrimps and prawns may be found anywhere in shallow water, but they prefer rocky coasts and reefs. They can best be captured with a dip net.

Salt Water Shrimp

Marine mollusks, such as oysters, clams, scallops, welks, periwinkles, barnacles and conches, form a large part of the food supply of natives all over the world. Along many shore lines the supply is practically inexhaustible. They can be gathered by simply walking along the beach and picking them up. They can be eaten cooked or raw. Shifting bottoms, sedimentation, rough water and swift currents generally constitute unfavorable environments for oysters, clams and scallops. Hunt them in sheltered coves, lagoons, tidal pools and crevices. Snail types are found chiefly on rocky shores or under coral blocks and slabs of stones, while most of the bivalve mollusks will be found buried beneath the surface of sand or mud. Many mussel-type (bivalve) mollusks live in burroughs or holes in muddy or sandy bottoms and must be found by digging. Some will be deep, others shallow. Some types, such as the razor clam, can burrow faster than a man can dig. If you can't locate burrows, watch for squirts of water or bubbles from beneath the sand or mud and dig there. Oysters are found largely in shallow water.

The sea cucumbers found on almost all rocky shores and reefs are edible, raw or cooked. Strip out the long muscles on the inside of the body.

Spiny, globular sea urchins of temperate and arctic shores are harmless to handle and the eggs within their bodies are edible, but the needle urchin of tropical shores have long spines that will penetrate the flesh. One specie contains poisonous glands.

Dangerous Mollusks

There are only two groups of mollusks that should be avoided. These are the cones and the terebras. They have poisonous teeth and their bite can be fatal. They are distributed principally throughout the tropical and subtropica

FIG. 211. Dangerous Cones and Terebras
Left—Cones   Right—Terebras

FIG. 212. Parrot Fish

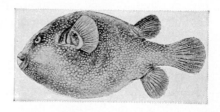

FIG. 213. Trigger Fish   FIG. 214. Pufferfish

FIG. 215. Porcupine or Spiny Pufferfish

shores of the world, but are nowhere common, and they are easily recognized.

In the north pacific area the black mussels living on exposed reefs at low tide are occasionally poisonous, though normally edible. The poison is derived from a tiny one-celled protozoan on which the mussel feeds.

Poisonous Fish

Some fish are poisonous to eat because of:
   (1) Poisonous alkaloids within their bodies.
   (2) Poisonous foods they have eaten.
   (3) Bacterial decomposition.

Most of the information concerning fish poisoning is not based on scientific study and there are no steadfast rules to go by. It may safely be stated that the danger is greatly exaggerated but you should nevertheless take precautions by following local native customs concerning nonedible fish.

The principle symptoms of fish poisoning are nausea, vomiting, diarrhea, itching, cramps, paralysis and a metallic taste. The symptoms appear suddenly, from one to six hours after eating. No antidote is known and the poison is not destroyed by cooking. Such sickness is not to be confused with the far more common fish poisoning caused by bacterial decomposition which may be destroyed by cooking. In either of the above cases, as soon as the symptoms appear, drink sea water and force yourself to vomit.

Poisonous fish are seldom if ever found in the open sea, but shore forms such as pufferfish, porcupine fish, trigger and parrot fish possess toxic substances in their flesh. All these occur around rocky or coral reefs and muddy or sandy shores. *Do not eat any of the puffer or porcupine fish, as practically all are poisonous.* These fish do not have true scales. Their bodies are covered with smooth skin or by a rough shagrin, or bristles or spines. The gill openings are short oblique or vertical slits. By inflating themselves with air they become balloon-like, hence their name of puffer or balloon fish. (Figures 214 and 215.)

Many of the trigger fishes are brilliantly colored. All have a sharp dorsal spine, scales that do not overlap and the eyes set very far back. (Figure 213) They can be caught easily but none are desirable as food. The striped trigger fish is common in the Southwest Pacific.

In certain seasons of the year in localized areas the red snapper and parrot fish around tropical islands are said to be poisonous, and these should be eaten sparingly until proven to be nontoxic. It is thought that these fish become poisonous by eating poisonous marine organisms or plant-like growths around these islands. Parrot fish have true scales and their mouth is formed of long plates resembling the beak of a parrot. (Figure 212)

In certain regions large barracuda have been reported as poisonous, but this was probably ptomaine poisoning.

All the fish along the shores of the North Pacific and in the Arctic Ocean are good to eat. No poisonous varieties are known. The eggs of some sculpins are deadly poisonous. Therefore don't eat any fish eggs found in clusters or clumps on rocks, logs or reefs.

In addition to the abundant sea food, the seashore provides birds, mammals, drinking water and many edible plants. It should be quite evident that the seacoasts of the world offer a wide variety of foods and that this is particularly true of the tropics. No equipment is essential, but the task of surviving becomes a hundred-fold easier if you have matches, a head net and machete. Don't get caught without them.

TROPICAL PLANT FOODS

There are numerous edible plant foods found only in the tropics that may sustain you in emergencies. Because these plants must in most cases be specifically identified before you can make full use of them, only a few of the more common and widely distributed ones are discussed. Try to learn and use these plants before an emergency arises.

FIG. 216. Picking a Pandanus Fruit

FIG. 217. Tropical Jungle (U. S. Marine Corps)

FIG. 218. Celery-like "Millionaire's Salad" from Base of Coconut Palm Crown ("Yank")

FIG. 219. Cutting Bamboo Shoots

Palms are found throughout the tropical world, and are most numerous near the equator. They grow in all types of habitats and vary in form from tall trees to shrubs and vines. The leaves are generally pinnate or palmate, and many, but not all, palms have the well-known leafy crown. Palms are one of the best sources of plant food for inexperienced individuals. They are widespread, conspicuous, and a great many of them contain drinkable sap, edible fruits, buds or starchy cores within the trunks. Palms also furnish alcohol, sugar, oils, fibers, shelter, and clothing material.

The terminal bud or growing point of most palms is edible either cooked or raw. It is located on the tip of the trunk, enclosed by the crown of leaves or sheathing bases of the leaf stem. Eat any that are not too bitter.

The sap of many of the palms is drinkable and nourishing.

The fruits of palm trees are generally produced in clusters below the leafy crown. The fruits of the coconut, nipa and date palm are excellent food, but the fruits of many other old-world species are not edible. Some contain minute crystals that cause intense pain. *Eat old-world palm fruits with caution. Most of the new-world palm fruits are edible or at least not poisonous or irritating.*

FIG. 218a. Palm Buds

Enormous quantities of starch are stored in the trunks of some of the palms. It is edible in all species in which it is found, but is not worth trying to get unless you have an axe or machete.

From this general information it should be evident that in an emergency, or if you lack specific knowledge concerning edible palm species, you can obtain and eat the fruit, sap, starch or buds with reasonable safety and success. A little specific knowledge, however, will greatly facilitate your use of palms for food.

The Nipa Palm

The nipa palm looks like a stemless coconut palm with long leaves rising in tufts from the rootstock to a height of about 15 feet. The short, erect flower stem produces a cluster

FIG. 220. Nipa Palm *(Nipa fruticans)*

of seeds that are edible when young and resemble coconuts in taste. This palm is found growing only in brackish tidal marshes and mangrove swamps of the islands and coasts of the Indian Ocean. The flower stems give off large quantities of an edible sugary sap commonly collected in jointed bamboo funnels. The cabbage is edible and the leaves are one of the best thatching materials.

FIG. 221. Coconut Palm *(Cocos nucifera)*

Coconut Palm

The coconut palm is widely cultivated throughout the tropical world, being common in Africa, tropical America, Asia and the South Pacific Islands. It is usually found growing near the seashore, but sometimes occurs some distance inland. The large terminal bud or cabbage is an excellent vegetable cooked or raw. The nuts furnish meat and water, and a sugary sap can be obtained by cutting the flower spikes. The nuts are available the year round. The jelly-like flesh of half-grown coconuts is more nourishing and can be eaten in greater quantities than the hard oily meat of the mature nuts. A sprouted nut is excellent food. (See palms page 47.)

The Sago Palm

The sago palm occurs on the islands of the Indian Archipelago and the Malay Peninsula in damp lowlands, fresh water swamps and along streams, lakes and rivers. The hard trunk contains an accumulation of starch which is at a maximum when the tree is between the ages of 10 and 15 years, just before the flowers are produced. Lesser amounts exist in immature or flowering

FIG. 222. Sago Palm *(Metroxylon)*

trees. To obtain the edible starch, cut down the tree, split and remove the hard outer shell, and slice the core into small fragments. Boil these or wrap them in leaves and bake. Chew the starch out of the pith. A flour can be obtained by crushing the pith, washing and straining it through a cloth or netting to remove the fiber. The terminal bud may be cooked and eaten.

Sugar Palm

The sugar palm is common throughout the open lands of the Indian Archipelago. It is more abundant in the hilly districts of the interior than on the seacoast. The mature tree is 30 to 40 feet tall with a dense crown of leaves. The terminal bud is considered edible but should be eaten with caution. Starch can be obtained from the trunk. A sugary sap can be collected by cutting the flower spikes. The black fibrous material at the base of the leaf stalk makes excellent cord.

FIG. 223. Sugar Palm *(Arenga)*

FIG. 224. Buri Palm *(Corypha)*

The Buri Palm

The buri palm is a very large fan-leaved palm found only in tropical Asia. The leaves may be as large as nine feet in diameter. The pithy portion of the trunk contains starch, difficult to obtain because of the thick, hard, outer shell. The sap is sugary and the buds are edible. The leaf and leaf stem fibers are used for making cord and rope.

FIG. 225. Piva or Peach Palm *(Guilielma utilis)*

Piva or Peach Palm

The piva palm is confined to regions of tropical America. Its slender trunk, 20 to 40 feet tall, is easily recognized by its alternating light and dark bands of spines. The mature fruits are red or yellow and grow in large clusters. They may be eaten boiled or roasted and they taste like sweet potatoes or chestnuts.

Fig. 226. Bacaba and Patawa Palms *(Jessenia, Oenocarpus)*

Bacaba and Patawa Palms

These palms are found in the moist forested regions of the Guianas and Brazil. The pulp of the fruit can be chewed and eaten. The oily kernel within the pulp is also edible. The fruit is smooth, dark purplish in color and about three-quarters of an inch long.

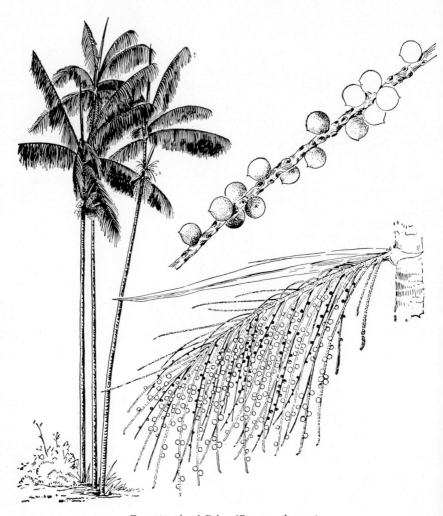

FIG. 227. Assai Palm *(Euterpe oleracea)*

Assai Palm

The Assai palm and related species are native to the forests of tropical South America where they generally grow together in large masses. The Assai palm grows in swampy places particularly along the banks of rivers within the tidal limits. It attains a height of 30 or 40 feet with a stem about as thick as a man's arm. When the fruit is mature, the soft purple pulp is edible.

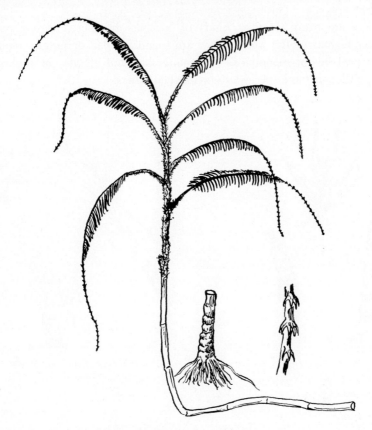

FIG. 228. Rattan Palm *(Calamus)*

Rattan Palms

There are many species of rattan or climbing palms with smooth reed-like stems seldom more than an inch or two in diameter and usually growing to a great length. Nearly all are native to Asia, being particularly abundant in Malaya and the Southwest Pacific Islands. The leaf stalks are spiny and in many species prolonged through the divided blade into whip-like tails at the end. They are common in the virgin forest. It is safe to try eating the terminal bud of all species. The swollen base of the vine in some species contains edible starch that can be obtained and utilized as described for sago. Drinking water can be drained from lengths of the stem and the stems themselves serve as cord or rope. (See top of page 47.)

Bamboo

There are many different kinds of bamboo distributed throughout the warmer regions of the world. They are found in open or jungle country in either lowlands or mountains. The young shoots of all may be cooked and eaten, although some species are better than others.

FIG. 229. Bamboo

FIG. 230. Sugar Cane *(Saccharum officinalis)*

Sugar Cane

The cultivated sugar cane and similar appearing wild species grow throughout the tropical regions of the world, usually in open country along the banks of rivers and streams. Cultivated varieties are commonly found around abandoned plantations and similar dwellings. The sugar content is high and can be obtained by removing the hard outer stem layer with a knife or the teeth and chewing the soft inner pith.

Bananas and Plantains

Bananas and plantains are found in the tropical and subtropical regions of both hemispheres. They are herbaceous plants in which the leaf sheaths encase the stem. Bananas and plantains look much alike and it is not necessary to distinguish between them. The fruit of both is eaten raw or cooked, although most plantains must be cooked to be edible. The fruits of the different species vary in shape and size. The slender terminal flower bud of some species is excellent when cooked, and the rootstock and leafsheaths of many of them can be cooked and eaten in emergencies.

FIG. 231. Bananas and Plantains *(Musa)*

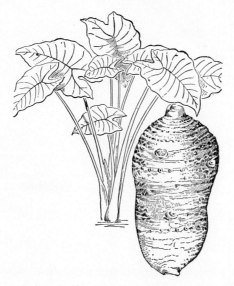

FIG. 232. Taro *(Colocasia antiquorum)*

Taro

Taro is related to our jack-in-the-pulpit, calla lily, and skunk cabbage. There are numerous species in the Pacific regions, many of which are used by the natives as food. Taro is especially abundant in the Pacific Islands and also occurs in India, Ceylon, the West Indies and Eastern Asia. It thrives best in damp or wet areas. The roots are rich in starch, though they are pungent and irritating unless thoroughly baked or boiled. The tubers may weigh from one to twelve pounds, and have a mottled bluish-gray appearance. The young leaves are edible if boiled thoroughly in several changes of water.

FIG. 233. Buck Yam *(Dioscorea pentaphylla)*

Yams

Yams are sweet potato-like vines found throughout most tropical and sub-tropical regions. The large tuberous roots of cultivated and wild species are dug up by the natives and either boiled or roasted. They grow in jungle thickets and in forests. Some species are poisonous unless properly prepared. The buck yam is common in the jungles and thickets of tropical Asia, including the South Pacific Islands.

Manioc, Cassava, Tapioca

The fleshy and starchy root of bitter and sweet manioc yields the greatest portion of the daily food of the natives of tropical America. There are about 50 species and they are most abundant in the wet areas of Peru, the Guianas, Brazil, the Antilles and Southern Mexico. Bitter and sweet manioc, a shrubby

FIG. 234. Manioc *(Manihot)*

plant about six to eight feet high, is the species commonly eaten in South America. It is also cultivated widely in the old-world tropics. The two varieties cannot be distinguished except by taste. Sweet manioc can be eaten cooked or raw, but bitter manioc must be cooked (as directed on page 61) to rid it of poisonous hydrocyanic acid. If in doubt as to whether you have bitter or sweet manioc, play safe: cook it.

Arrowroot

The six or seven species of Tacca are distributed over tropical America, Africa, Asia and the South Pacific Islands. The various species grow in open country or on sandy or rocky soil near the sea. The carrot-like and potato-like tubers of all species are rich in starch and are edible when cooked. They should not be eaten raw. (See Figure 236.)

Seaside Purslane

One or the other of the seaside purslanes are found on the shores of most tropical countries within the influence of brackish or salt water. They are smooth, succulent plants with fleshy stems and leaves, and salty taste. The entire plant can be boiled and eaten.

FIG. 235. Seaside Purslane *(Sesuvium portulacastrum)*

FIG. 236. Arrowroot *(Tacca leontopetaloides)*

FIG. 237. Wild and Hog Plums *(Spondias dulcis)*

FIG. 238. Figs. *(Ficus pretoria)*

Wild and Hog Plums

These are native to the tropics of both hemispheres and the fruits of some of them are edible. The Polynesian wild plum yields a yellowish fruit which tastes something like a pineapple.

Figs

Numerous species of edible figs are widely distributed throughout the tropics of both hemispheres. Wild figs resemble cultivated figs and are easily recognizable. The wild figs are usually small and all have a milky juice. Insects are often found in them, but the fruit may still be eaten unless definitely decayed. (See Figure 238.)

Fig. 239. Sour Sop *(Annona muricata)*

Fig. 240. Sweet Sop *(Annona squamosa)*

Custard Apple, Sour Sop and Sweet Sop

This genus of small fruit trees is largely represented in tropical America, but various species are widely cultivated throughout the tropics. A wild custard apple is found in tropical Africa and is large, well-flavored and juicy. A similar cultivated species with pale green fruit is found in settled areas of the Pacific Islands. The sour sop is cultivated throughout tropical America and is found both wild and planted in the South Pacific Islands. The leaves are strongly scented when crushed. The spiny green colored fruit is sometimes as large as a man's head. It can be used to prepare a thirst-quenching beverage.

Stamvrugte and Star Apple

Members of this genus are found in the tropics of both hemispheres. The star apple is found in the West Indies and Central America, while the stamvrugte is found in tropical Africa on rocky outcrops and mountains. The fruit is red when ripe, about an inch in length, and has a tart flavor. (See Figure 242.)

Sour Plum

The sour plum is a large, often thorny, shrub or small tree bearing yellow fruits resembling plums. It is found throughout the tropics of America, Asia, Africa and the Pacific Islands, often near the seashore. The genus contains numerous edible species. The pulp of the fruit, but not the seed, is edible.

Fig. 241. Sour Plum *(Ximenia caffra)*

Fig. 242. Stamvrugte *(Chrysophyllum magalies-monlonum)*

Fig. 243. Breadfruit *(Artocarpus)*

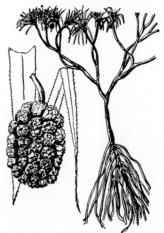

Fig. 244. Screwpines *(Pandanus tectorius)*

Breadfruit

There are many species of breadfruit native to the Southwest Pacific Islands. They are closely allied to our mulberry and osage orange and all have a milky sap. The fruits of some species are excellent boiled or baked, and the seeds of all are edible when cooked. Some species are seedless. The pulp of some can be eaten raw. The fruiting season of the different species varies, supplying a year-round supply of the fruit. The common breadfruit tree is moderate in size with dark, green-lobed leaves, and bears a roundish, rough-surfaced green or brownish fruit. It forms one of the most important food staples in the South Pacific Islands. The milky juice of the tree can be used as glue for caulking canoes or prepared as bird lime.

Screw Pines

The screw pines are confined to the eastern hemisphere, and a large number of them are limited to the islands of the Indian Archipelago. They are found principally in close proximity to the sea, sometimes covering large areas with an almost impenetrable mass of vegetation. Most of them are large bushes with long, narrow, leathery leaves, thick and often twisted stems, and many prop roots. The red fruits and the seeds are available the year round, and are edible either cooked or raw. The fruit itself consists of rounded grains or sections enclosed in a hard rind. The terminal leaf bud may also be eaten cooked or raw. (See Figures 216 and 244)

FIG. 245. Sapodilla *(Achras sapota)*   FIG. 246. Mango *(Mangifera)*

Mango

Mangos are tropical asiatic trees, cultivated or wild. The common mango is one of the most delicious of tropical fruits, and is commonly found cultivated in nearly all tropical countries. The fruits of the wild species are edible, but some have a strong turpentine flavor. The ripe fruits are generally yellow in color.

Sapodilla

The sapodilla is a medium sized evergreen tree bearing brown fruits within which are large smooth black seeds. It grows wild in central and tropical South America, and is found wild and cultivated in other parts of the tropics. The fruit should be eaten raw, not cooked. (See Figure 245.)

FIG. 247. Baobab Tree and Fruit *(Adansonia)*

FIG. 248. Cashew *(Ana cardium occidentale)*

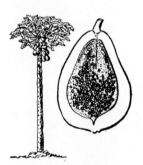

FIG. 249. Papaya *(Carica papaya)*

Baobab

The baobab tree occurs in Africa, Madagascar and Australia. It is easily recognized by its stout, bottle-shaped trunk which is sometimes 30 feet in diameter. The fruit is large, oblong or globular, four to eight inches long, with a woody shell enclosing numerous seeds embedded in a soft bready substance. The seeds are nutritious, the flesh tart, and the white gum which exudes from the tree makes an agreeable drink when diluted with hot water. Fibers of the wood can be used to make rope or twine.

Papaya

The papaya is native to tropical America, but it is found cultivated and wild in all tropical countries. It is a straight, green or brown stemmed plant six to twenty feet high with large, melon-like fruits. The tree has a milky sap. The fruits of the wild plants are small. They can be eaten raw, and unripened fruits may be boiled as a vegetable. The milky sap contains the enzyme papain which will tenderize meat if put on it before cooking. (See Figure 249.)

Cashew

The cashew is a spreading, moderate-sized evergreen tree found semiwild in fields and on the sides of dry bushy hills in tropical regions of Central and South America and is cultivated throughout the tropics. A grayish, kidney-shaped nut hangs from the red and yellow fruit. The fruit can be eaten raw, but the nut is poisonous unless roasted until all the oil is removed. (Figure 248.)

SUBSISTENCE IN THE FAR NORTH

As you travel north or south from the equator, disease-transmitting insects, parasites, diseases, poisonous snakes, plants and animals decrease; physical hazards such as snow and cold increase. Trees become scattered and stunted, finally giving way to tundra, grasses and seas of ice. Food in the form of plant and animal life grows less abundant while the body requires more nourishment. Living off the land becomes increasingly difficult, but is possible with a gun, fire, equipment and suitable clothing. The arctic explorer, Stefansson, lived on the meat of land animals killed during every month of the year as far north as 80° latitude.

In general the plants and animals of the arctic zone and of the subarctic forests are circumpolar in distribution, so living off the land will be basically the same throughout these global areas. In other words the plant and animal food you can expect to find will be much the same in Alaska, Northern Canada, Labrador, Greenland, Northern Europe, Iceland, and Siberia. (See Map.)

FIG. 250. Lemming

Although plant and animal food is present in the arctic, it is not always easily available. Vegetation is scattered, but is most plentiful along the banks of lakes and rivers. Game may be abundant over a large area yet scarce in local areas at specific times.

ANIMAL FOOD

You can live on meat alone if you eat both lean and fat. You cannot remain healthy on a diet of lean meat only.

Within the arctic circle are such animals as musk ox, wolves, polar bears, foxes, muskrats, lemmings and seals; and such birds as ptarmigan, gulls, owls,

FIG. 251. Crash Landing in the Far North (U. S. Air Force)

FIG. 252. Improvised Shelter Beneath Plane Wing (U. S. Air Force)

hawks, geese, brant, swans, dovekies, crane, loon, ducks, snow bunting and pipits.

Many of these animals migrate south during the long arctic winter, others do not such as caribou and musk ox. Some ptarmigan remain north of the circle

FIG. 253. Ptarmigan—Look Sharply for Them, as They Change Plumage to Blend with the Summer Grass and Winter Snow

and can be approached and shot, clubbed, or snared. Hare are found in the same local regions the year round and can be snared along their runs. Lemming can also be trapped or clubbed along their runways. You may have to dig down in the snow for them.

Farther south where trees occur, a greater diversity of birds, mammals and plants are found. Many of the deer family are in this area. The porcupine is often encountered, and can be easily clubbed on the ground or shaken from a tree. Porcupines feed on bark. Limbs stripped bare are good signs of their presence. To avoid their sharp needles, pick them up by the loose skin under the chin.

In summer, birds and bird eggs will abound in certain areas. Gulls, terns, murres and dovekies nest in colonies along the coast, while ducks and geese can be found in the vegetation along the streams and lakes.

FIG. 254. Ruffed Grouse—Grouse Can Be Shot, Snared or Clubbed in Timbered Areas.

Seals are the staff of life in the Arctic, but it requires exceptional skill and knowledge to spear them. Even with a gun they are not easily obtained. Other large aquatic mammals such as whales and walrus are even more difficult to get.

Areas devoid of life occur in the Arctic as elsewhere, seals especially being concentrated in favorable areas and absent in many parts of the polar ocean. Even in those places where they are found in numbers they cannot always be hunted successfully. In winter they are hunted where there is an even layer of ice over water of fair depth. They can be expected in numbers where the ice is broken by current holes and tidewater cracks. Where the ice is thick and unbroken they will be scarce. Seals snort at their water holes and remain for some time taking air. Sneak up to the hole while the seal is taking a breath or dozing. Flatten out on the ice and remain still when it looks around. Move slowly and silently. They can hear slight sounds, even through the ice. Construct a white shield of parachute silk (as illustrated in Figure 255) and using this as a blind, slip up on the seal. When you get ready to shoot, try for a brain shot; otherwise, he may escape into his hole.

The walrus comes up to breathe, but does not scratch breathing holes and is thus harder to locate. It is probably the most dangerous animal of the arctic region.

The polar bear is found in practically all arctic coastal regions, seldom far from sea ice.

The caribou and reindeer are the most abundant of arctic land mammals. Their presence can be located by tracks, but careful stalking is necessary for a shot.

All of the large animals may supply food, implements, fuel and clothing. When hunting these animals with a gun, remember they are wary, and stalking them will take all your skill and patience. (See page 101.)

FIG. 255. Stalking Seal

Fish are plentiful in small northern streams. Salmon can be found from early spring to fall in coastal streams and rivers from Oregon through Alaska and from the New England states northward. When they are traveling upstream to spawn, they can be picked up by hand or clubbed. Salmon die after spawning in the headwaters. Their flesh deteriorates the farther they get from salt water. The flesh of these live but dying salmon may be poisonous. Watch for white salmon and let the pink ones pass. Trout can be caught in the larger lakes by fishing through the ice.

PLANT FOOD

When animal life fails and even such food as mice, fish and grubs are not available, you can still find plant food that will stave off starvation. In summer there is no great problem finding plant food and even in winter berries and roots are available beneath the snow, if you know where to look for them.

In arctic and subarctic regions you may safely seek and try plant foods with the assumption that none of them are likely to be poisonous. The water hemlock is in most cases the only seriously poisonous plant but buttercups should also be avoided. The Amanitas (mushrooms) are present, but in many cases not even these are poisonous or at least deadly poisonous in far northern regions. It is important that you be able to recognize the relatively few nutritious plants from the far greater number that have no food value.

Berries

The salmon-berry is the most important of the northern berries. It is circumpolar in distribution and always grows in a peaty soil. Its fruit is yellow and looks like a raspberry. The plant grows close to the ground, often covering many acres. These berries are available in summer and may be found frozen on the stalks in the winter and early spring. They can be eaten raw but are better cooked.

The crowberry is a small evergreen heathlike plant. The berries are brownish black, single seeded, juicy and sweet. They often can be found on the bushes in winter. They are circumpolar in distribution.

Currants, cranberries, strawberries, raspberries and blueberries are found where conditions are favorable for vegetative growth such as timbered regions, bogs, hillsides, and along streams. Remember the spots where you have found them, and look in the same types of places again.

Roots and Greens

Snakeweed is a low plant with white or pink flowers in dense solitary spikes and is common on dry tundra. The rootstock is edible raw although slightly astringent, but is starchy and potato-like when roasted. It is circumpolar in distribution. (Figure 262.)

Wild rhubarb or alpine knotweed is a plant three to six feet high with small flowers. It grows on moist open or alluvial soil along river banks. The leaves and red stems are edible when cooked. After it becomes frosted it may be poisonous. It is circumpolar in distribution. (Figure 261.)

Wooly lousewort is a low plant with wooly spikes of rose-colored flowers. It is found on dry tundra regions of North America. The yellow root is sweet like carrots and may be eaten raw or cooked. (Figure 263.)

Licorice-root is a legume with pink flowers. It is found throughout the north as far as the Arctic Ocean. Its long tap roots taste like licorice when raw and carrots when cooked. In summer the root becomes tough and woody. (Figure 260.)

Bark and Buds

The bark and buds of certain northern trees that are eaten by animals can also be eaten by man. The bark and buds of aspen can be eaten raw or cooked

FIG. 256. Crowberry *(Empetrum nigrum)*

FIG. 257. Salmon-berry *(Rubus chamaemorus)*

FIG. 258. Cranberry *(Vaccinium macrocarpon)*

FIG. 259. Mountain cranberry *(Vaccinium Vitis-Idaea)*

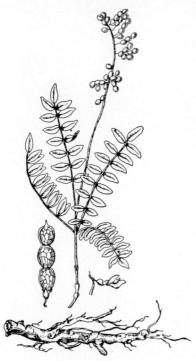

FIG. 260. Licorice-Root *(Hedysarum boreale)*

FIG. 261. Alpine Knotweed *(Polygonum alpinum)*

FIG. 262. Snakeweed *(Polygonum bistorta)*

FIG. 263. Wooly Lousewort *(Pedicularis lanata)*

but should preferably be boiled to a gelatinous mass. The buds of basswood, poplar, maple, the shoots of spruce, tamarack and the inner bark of willow, alder, hemlock, basswood and birch are all edible. The leaves of mountain sorrel, young willows and fireweed can be eaten when boiled.

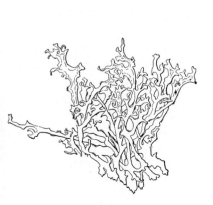

Fig. 264. Iceland Moss *(Cetaria islandica)*

Fig. 265. Reindeer Moss *(Cladonia rangiferina)*

Fig. 265a. Rock Tripe *(Umbilicaria)*

Lichens

The most widespread and surest source of emergency food in the far north are the lichens, some of which are mosslike in appearance. Often these small plants cover large areas, growing on rocks, trees, logs and in sand and gravel. They sometimes grow where there appears to be no soil. The lichens are gray, brown, or black in color and are rich in carbohydrates, furnishing food for many northern mammals. Some are eaten by Eskimos and European peasants during famine periods. None are poisonous, but some contain a bitter acid that causes internal irritation unless they are cooked in water, dried until brittle, and then powdered and boiled.

Among the most useful edible species are the following:

Iceland moss grows best on sandy soil and resembles a brown seaweed. It should be boiled for an hour or longer. (See Figure 264.)

Reindeer moss is gray-green in color and has a small globular "fruit" in a cup-like receptacle. It should be washed to remove grit and then boiled or roasted. It grows on the ground over extensive areas and is the most abundant of the food lichens. (See Figure 265.)

Rock tripe or famine food are flat leathery crinkle-edged lichens that grow on acid rocks throughout the north. They are smoky colored and brittle when dry, but dark-green on the upper surface when wet. The taste is bitter but not unpleasant. Rock tripe should be dried before being boiled, or it will cause diarrhea. When properly prepared it is nutritious and easily assimilated.

Plant life above tree line in the high mountains of the temperate and even tropic zones is similar in many respects to that in the far north and the Arctic. If it is necessary to live off the land in such regions, proceed as if you were in the far north.

CHAPTER IX

Environmental Hazards

Physical and biological hazards take a heavy toll of stranded men even when food and water are available. The ability to evaluate these and a knowledge of how to surmount them will give you confidence, diminish your hardships, and lengthen your survival time.

PHYSICAL HAZARDS

In this chapter a number of these environmental hazards are discussed, together with ways of avoiding injury or illness from them.

Effects of Sunlight and Heat

Sunburn prevention is much easier than treatment. Many people are severely burned because they fail to realize that the effects of sunburn are not felt until

Fig. 266.—Be Prepared in Dress and Equipment for the Type of Country Over Which You Must Fly.

183

several hours after the exposure. If you wait until your skin turns pink or feels hot before you cover it, it will already be too late. Hazy and overcast days are sometimes the worst because there is much reflected light and little warning of sunburn. Danger of severe sunburn is greatest on a mountain snowfield, on open water, desert sands and beaches.

A "sunburn powder" of lime can be made by burning sea shells or coral in an open fire, and then crushing them. Mix the powder with water or oil and apply it as a paste over your face and body—for protection, not as a cure. Coconut oil (made by exposing coconut meat to the sun) is a good sunburn preventive. The best preventive is to keep covered as much as possible, with clothing or a makeshift covering.

For sunburn treatment, use the burn ointment and dressing in your first-aid kit. Tannic acid is effective in treatment of severe sunburn. Gather the *dark brown* bark from a tree, boil it, and then apply the solution to the burn. Inner bark of oak, hemlock, or chestnut wood and all parts of the mangrove tree are particularly rich in tannic acid. Boil betel nuts. They contain a high percentage of tannin.

Heat Stroke (Sunstroke) and Heat Exhaustion

Loss of salt is a main cause of heat stroke, heat exhaustion and other less acute effects of heat. Muscle stiffness after exercise will be reduced if you get plenty of salt. You sweat freely in the tropics and can easily lose salt beyond the danger point unless you replace it by taking extra salt on your food, and in or with your drinking water. If salt is not available, several swallows of ocean water a day will help replace the salt lost by sweating, will not be harmful if you are getting plenty of other water, and will relieve a sluggish, tired feeling.

In cold climates loss of salt is reduced, but you may be fooled in a hot, dry climate, at high altitudes, or in warm, windy areas where salt is lost through sweating but the sweating is not apparent because of rapid evaporation. When your body requires salt, even a strong solution will not taste salty.

Ascorbic acid also is lost through sweating. Replace it by eating citrus fruits.

In the tropics don't travel in direct sunlight without head protection. A head covering of leaves or cloth will be better than nothing. Don't overexert during the hottest hours of the day, especially if you are in poor condition. If the humidity is not too high, you can cool off when exerting in the heat by soaking your clothes. The resulting evaporation will keep you comfortable.

Sunstroke is the result of direct exposure to the sun. It may affect you suddenly, but is usually preceded by dizziness, nausea and headache. Your face will be flushed, your skin hot and dry, and your body temperature high. If the air is dry, you may not even feel unusually hot or uncomfortable preceding a sunstroke. The best preventive is to keep your head covered or wet, drink plenty of water with salt, and cool your body by wetting it and your clothing. For treatment, lie in the shade with your head higher than the rest of your body; drink water with salt in it (a tablet to a glass of water), and bathe your head and body. *Heat exhaustion* is the result of long exposure to heat when the temperature and humidity are high. It may occur without exposure to the sun. The symptoms are different from a stroke. The skin is clammy and the temperature normal or below. Drink salt water, lie in the shade with head low, and cover up to keep warm.

Snow Blindness

Snow blindness is a painful inflammation of the inner side of the eyelids caused by constant exposure to the reflection of the sun's rays from snow. Its effect may range from slight inflammation to temporary blindness of several days' duration. The first sign of inflammation is a feeling of sand in the eyes. Preventive measures include travelling at night, use of a shade to protect the eyes from *below,* blackening of the eyelids, cheeks, and bridge of the nose, wearing a dark mask with small eye slits, or best of all, *dark glasses.* Cold water will relieve the pain. If temporary blindness has resulted, wear a dark bandage over the eyes.

Severe headaches are often indirectly due to excessive glare and exposure to sun. Eye inflammation often occurs among survivors at sea. It may be caused by exposure to wind, cold, water glare, salt water or a combination of these. Protect the eyes at the first sign of soreness.

Acclimatization to the Tropics

Men unaccustomed to tropical climates have less resistance to infection, and are also exposed to intestinal and gastric infections to an unusual degree. While you are adjusting to tropical conditions, "go easy" until you determine the kind and quantity of food, water intake, and amount of exercise you need for keeping physically fit.

When air temperatures are higher than body temperatures, the pulse rate, rate of breathing, and body temperature all tend to rise, for the heat loss does not keep up with heat production. A healthy man, well-acclimated to working under tropical conditions, may for hours run a body temperature of 103° or even 104° F., while exercising in the heat without marked ill effects. The individual acclimatizes to heat by sweating more freely. This must be accompanied by a greater water intake and an adequate amount of salt.

While diarrhea from infected food and water is always a danger in the tropics, constipation also should be guarded against. It may come from over-eating, over-exertion, lack of an adequate water supply, worry and interruption of regular habits. If safe liquids are available, drink them freely and eat fruits. Coconut milk or several swallows of ocean water will act as a mild laxative. Don't use a laxative when nausea or abdominal pains are experienced since a ruptured appendix may be the result.

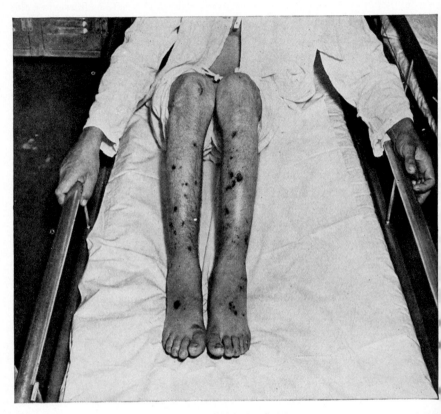

FIG. 267. Salt Water Sores

Exposure to Water

Long exposure to salt water (as when adrift in a boat or a raft) may result in sores and swelling. Fats or greases will help prevent salt water sores.

Immersion foot is caused by continued immersion of the feet in cold or ice water (60° F. down) or by continued hiking in wet cold footgear. Pain is followed by swelling and numbness, and blisters and sores may result. The best preventive is to keep your feet as dry as possible (dry out socks and shoes) and to exercise your feet regularly. Don't wear tight boots or socks that bind the legs. In treatment, *don't rub or apply direct heat* and avoid breaking the skin. Keep the legs above body level and apply cold compresses or packs, keeping a layer of dry material between the compress and the feet to avoid wetting them.

Strenuous Exertion

In any climate, severe headaches are common after strenuous, unaccustomed exertion. An aspirin will ease the condition, but the best relief is sleep or rest. If you are hungry, moderate eating of hot broth or sweets will help. Nibble at food more or less continually. If you are not hungry, don't force yourself to eat but wait until you are rested and your appetite returns. This may be as long as twelve hours. Try not to exert over a long period of time without eating.

Effects of Cold

Regulating Heat Loss. Survival in extremely low temperatures is a matter of balancing heat loss and bodily heat production. You can balance heat loss to some extent by food intake and exercise, but since there is a definite limit to the amount of food you can utilize and to your muscular activity, *your main reliance for keeping warm must be in the reduction and regulation of heat loss by wearing proper clothing.*

Clothing should consist of a number of light garments that can be taken off or put on as the need arises to regulate heating and chilling. None should be tight enough to reduce blood circulation.

Outer garments should be windproof, but not so airtight as to cause excessive heat production and sweating. Inner garments should act as insulators. They should be form-fitting, light, soft, and loose enough to permit escape of perspiration. Your shoes should be big enough to allow you to wear at least two pairs of heavy socks.

Clothing is the "switchboard" by which you can balance heat production with heat loss. If you are overdressed and the day calm and sunny, it may be necessary to strip to the waist to prevent overheating. When walking or exercising lightly, removal of the windproof outer garment is often sufficient to prevent sweating. *Control of sweating is essential, for wet clothing conducts heat from the body and increases your chance of freezing.*

When keeping warm is a problem, never expose any more of the body than is absolutely necessary, since enough heat can be lost from uncovered hands, face, head and poorly insulated feet to chill the entire body.

Frostbite.—Local freezing of face, feet and hands is an ever-present danger at low temperatures. *Don't rub frozen parts, or expose them to heat rapidly.* Rubbing will break the skin and lead to infection. Thaw frozen parts slowly. Frozen flesh is white and stiff, while milder frostbite is dark red. Wrinkle the face continually to determine whether any part is frozen. The ears are especially susceptible to frostbite. Press your warm hands against them. When fingers become cold or frost-bitten, warm them against the bare skin of the body. Place frozen toes against the warm flesh of a companion or cup your hands around them. Dry grass, moss or feathers placed inside shoes or between socks provides insulation against frostbite. A cloth tied over the face below the eyes and allowed to hang loosely at the bottom will protect your face and allow your moist breath to escape. Frostbite is especially apt to occur when you are traveling into a wind. A 60-mile wind at 0° F. feels colder and does more damage than a 15-mile wind at –30° or a calm at –50° F. Body heat is blown away by wind. Wild animals seek shelter in a cold wind, and you should do the same.

Remember that:

(1) Temperatures are often warmer below the snow than above it and any windbreak will help conserve body heat.

(2) Generally, hollows and valleys will be colder than protected slopes and ridges.

(3) Lowest temperatures occur during clear, still weather. Temperatures usually rise during a blizzard or snowstorm.

(4) Plenty of rest and food are most important in the Arctic. Never travel until you are exhausted. Take frequent rests, and sleep when you feel like it. Unless you are exhausted, the cold will waken you before you freeze.

(5) For temporary rest and protection, dig into the snow with your back to the wind and your arms pulled out of your sleeves and held against the body for warmth. Don't sit directly on the snow if you can place something under you.

(6) If you get wet in extremely cold weather, make a fire immediately in the most sheltered spot available, and dry out. Without fire, keep moving until your body heat has warmed and dried your inner garments.

(7) Breathe only through the nose. This will warm the air before it reaches your lungs and reduce the danger of frosting them.

(8) When your whole body has been exposed to severe cold, exercise and rub your limbs to increase circulation, and get something warm inside you.

BIOLOGICAL HAZARDS

The sources of the greatest dangers are not always the most apparent. Many of the small forms of life, particularly the arthropods, can cause more real discomfort and danger than even a scarcity of food or water.

They may be irritating in themselves, but *their greatest danger lies in the fact that through their bites they transmit various weakening and frequently fatal diseases.*

The general information which follows is designed to tell you what to expect from them, how to evaluate the danger and discomfort, and how to take precautionary measures against them.

Supplement this general knowledge at every opportunity by getting specific information from medical authorities about the presence, transmission and prevention of diseases apt to occur in your particular area of operations.

It is not necessary for you to know a great deal about the diseases themselves. They are caused by minute parasitic plants and animals that enter the body, multiply, and set up a series of disturbances. What you're primarily concerned with are the parasite carriers which are responsible for getting the disease-causing organisms into your body. If you can keep the carriers away, or avoid them, you escape the diseases.

HAZARDS FROM THE SMALLER FORMS OF LIFE

Arthropods are small animals with jointed appendages or legs, and include the centipedes, spiders, insects, ticks and crustaceans.

These smaller forms of animal life which act as carriers are like all other forms of life in that they require certain conditions of environment for their existence. Some forms are widely distributed and others are localized, while the habits of many make it easy to avoid them. They may not be able to live in bright sunlight, or they may come out only during the day or only at night. They may not range far from their breeding areas, or may be limited in altitude or latitude by their inability to survive low temperatures. Lack of proper breeding places will limit their numbers.

Because of all these factors, you will have only a very limited number of these disease carriers to take precautions against at any one time or place.

A carrier which may be dangerous under certain circumstances or in a particular area may be perfectly harmless at another time, or in another area. Frequently the particular disease organisms which they carry and transmit to man by their bite must at some time in the course of their life pass through one or more other animals or hosts. When these hosts are specific, *nothing else will do.* In such cases, if the hosts or man are absent, the disease organism will not exist in that area and cannot be transmitted, no matter how many potential carriers are present.

Malaria is a good example of a disease requiring a specific carrier and a specific host—in this case, man.

Malaria is transmitted to man by some (not all) species of infected Anopheles mosquitoes, and not by any other kind of mosquito.

The disease itself is caused by a microscopic protozoan (Plasmodium) which is injected into the blood stream through the bite of an infected mosquito.

These protozoa enter red blood cells, absorb their contents, and grow and divide into numerous individuals which are discharged into the blood stream by rupturing of the cell wall, and in turn each attack a new red blood cell. (The patient has chills and fever during the period when the discharge is taking place.) After a number of days, some of these parasites develop into male and female forms and remain in the blood cells. If at this time the infected man is bitten by the right variety of Anopheline mosquito, the male and female protozoa are taken into the stomach of the mosquito. They unite to produce offspring which escape into the body cavity of the mosquito, and in turn are injected into a man when the mosquito bites him. *This life cycle can't take place unless the protozoa can spend part of their time in the blood of man and part in the stomach of the right kind of mosquito.*

Therefore an area which is free of Anopheles mosquitoes, or one which may have such mosquitoes but which has not been inhabited by man for some time, will be free of malaria. A great many other disease organisms require specific hosts to complete their development. *It is important for you to know the areas in which all the requirements for a specific disease exist, and how to recognize and avoid the transmitting organisms in those areas.*

Mosquito bites are at the best unpleasant, and at the worst can lead to delirium and even death, if you are exposed to them in large numbers over a long period.

Mosquitoes are much more numerous in some areas of the arctic and temperate regions during late spring and early summer than they are at any time in the tropics, but tropical mosquitoes are much more dangerous because they transmit diseases, among them malaria, yellow fever, dengue fever and filariasis.

All mosquitoes require water for breeding purposes. While only a small amount is necessary, they naturally will be most numerous near large areas of surface water and will not be found in desert areas unless they are blown there by the wind.

In temperate regions, various methods of getting away from heavy swarms of mosquitoes may be used.

Any breezy spot will be relatively free of mosquitoes and other small flying insects, but take care not to sleep *downwind* from a swamp or other wet area. A raft anchored off a lake shore, or a platform built in a tree so situated as to catch the breeze, may enable you to get a night's rest. When the breeze is from the sea, the shore will be mosquito-free. For temporary relief in an emergency, get into water and rest with only your nose and eyes above the surface. If you can climb 25 to 30 feet up a tree, you usually will "lose" mosquitoes, which normally do not fly that high; but first sprint to get rid of a swarm which may otherwise follow you.

Since mosquitoes can readily bite through light cloth it may be necessary to pad the inside of your clothing with leaves and thin strips of bark. Keep your clothing loose, except at wrists and ankles. A mosquito head net is a most important piece of emergency equipment, since your face and neck are the most difficult portions of your body to protect, and the net will also do duty against blackflies and other pests. Coconut palm cloth, handkerchief, leaves and other makeshifts will help if you don't have a head net. Dangle these at the side and back of your neck.

Effective mosquito repellents are very useful and may be effective for several hours. At your base or station they are available from the dispensary.

Mosquitoes and Malaria

You have already learned how certain mosquitoes transmit malaria to man. Malaria may exist in any tropical climate where men live and where it is

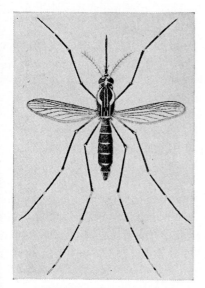

FIG. 268. Aedes Mosquito

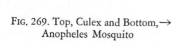

FIG. 269. Top, Culex and Bottom, →
Anopheles Mosquito

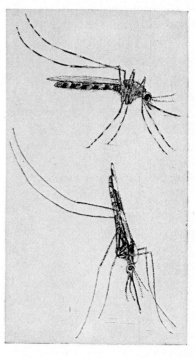

wet enough for mosquitoes to breed. It can also be contracted during the summer in many temperate regions, but is not found in the cool climates of the northern and southern hemispheres.

Take every possible precaution against malaria, particularly when you are alone and on your own. The greatest danger is in regions with a large native population which may be infected. In such an area, almost any Anopheles mosquito may be a carrier (in most regions a great majority even of the Anopheles mosquitoes are not infected).

The Anopheles mosquito is identifiable by the fact that it rests with its tail end pointing upward at an angle. Its wings tend to be spotted. It is only active in the early evening and at night, though it may be well to take precautions in dark or shaded areas, particularly on cloudy days. Because of its night-feeding characteristics, it is highly advisable in malaria regions to get a camp made and mosquito netting arranged well before dark. Since most malaria victims contract the disease while sleeping, a head or tent net should always be used for protection. Use atabrine or quinine as directed by your medical advisers.

Mosquitoes Transmit Yellow Fever and Dengue Fever

The Aedes mosquito transmits yellow fever and is largely responsible for transmission of dengue fever. Unlike the malaria-carrying Anopheles, the Aedes will bite at any time of day or night. (See Figure 268.)

"Shots" will protect you against yellow fever, which is most common in the Caribbean, West Africa, and in parts of Central and South America.

Dengue fever is transmitted like yellow fever. It is weakening but seldom fatal. It is widespread in the tropics and subtropics.

The mosquitoes which transmit it seldom range more than a quarter-mile from the little pools of water where they breed (can, tree-holes and the like) but they are especially abundant near human habitations.

Mosquitoes Transmit Filariasis

Filariasis is a round-worm infection transmitted by mosquitoes in the tropics and subtropics. The mosquito deposits minute larvae worms which bore through the skin and reach the lymphatics. There the worms mature and deposit the eggs which pass into the blood stream. Occasionally, affected portions of the body develop abnormal swelling which may reach huge proportions. There is no effective treatment of the infection at present.

Flies

Flies vary greatly in size, breeding habits, and in the discomfort or danger they can cause men. Some are vicious biters and the larvae of others infest wounds or even unbroken skin. Many contaminate food.

Like mosquitoes, some flies are active only at night, others only by day, and still others roam both day and night. In general, protective measures used against mosquitoes will be effective against flies, though some fly pests, such as the sand fly and the no-see-ums or punkies, are so small that they will go through ordinary mosquito netting. Many such pests are limited in range to comparatively short distances from their breeding areas, and can be escaped by moving out of the vicinity.

Black flies or buffalo gnats may cause you discomfort or danger, may transmit filarid worms and are found throughout the world in wet forested areas, particularly in the vicinity of running water. Various biting deer flies and horse flies are abroad only in the day and may be numerous in regions where there are hoofed animals. They are stout-bodied and usually brightly colored. No-see-ums or punkies are tiny mottle-winged flies. They are found in fresh and salt wet areas throughout the world. They have an itching bite. Some species may carry filarid worms. If these gnats are abundant, move on; they are often local in distribution and are seldom encountered more than a half mile from their breeding areas. (See Figure 271.)

Sand flies are tiny moth-like flies which bite at night. They breed in humid places out of the sun and wind, such as crevices in trees and rocks. They can pass through ordinary netting, and are disease transmitters in such widely separated areas as Colombia and the Peruvian Andes, the Mediterranean, India, Ceylon, and China. They transmit verruga, pappataci and kala-azar fever. These flies seldom fly more than ten feet above the ground and dislike air currents. Sleep off the ground or in a breeze. (See Figure 270.)

Tsetse flies are found only in central and south tropical Africa. While some species transmit a sleeping sickness which may be fatal, the proportion of those infected is very small and so is the chance of contracting the disease. All require shade, usually bite only during the daytime, and prefer dark-skinned natives to whites. Avoid the forested and brushy borders of bodies of water in areas of possible tsetse fly infection. (See Figure 272.)

Screwworm flies are found in the Americas and southern Asia, especially the tropics, and are most likely to be abundant in the vicinity of unburied corpses and animal carcasses. They are active during the day and often deposit their eggs in wounds where the larvae feed on the living tissue. Danger is greatest when sleeping in the open as the flies deposit their eggs in the nostrils, particularly if these passages are irritated by colds or wounds. The larvae burrow into the nasal tissues causing severe pain and swelling. Stupefy the maggots with chloroform, then remove them with forceps. Where these flies are numerous, don't sleep during the day in the open without covering your face or using a net. (See Figure 273.)

Blowflies with somewhat similar habits may be encountered in parts of Africa, India, Australia and the East Indies.

Bot fly larvae bore into the skin producing painful swellings and boil-like lesions. Apply tobacco to the open boil to kill the larvae and squeeze them out without breaking them. (See Figure 274.)

Fleas

Fleas are small wingless insects that move about by jumping and live on warm-blooded animals. (See Figure 276.)

In some areas their bites may transmit extremely dangerous diseases such as plague and endemic typhus. Fleas that live on rodents, particularly rats, can

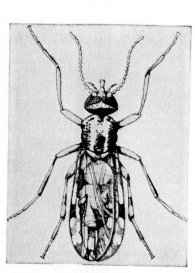

FIG. 270. Sand Fly

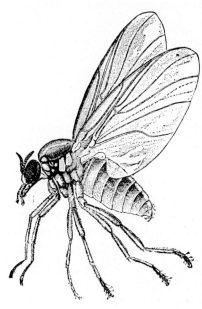

FIG. 271. Black Fly

FIG. 272. Tsetse Fly

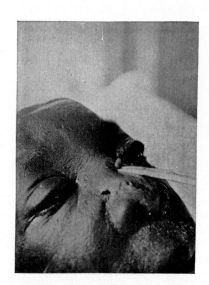

FIG. 273. Screwworm Infection

Bureau of Entomology
and Plant Quarantine

FIG. 274. Human Bot Fly

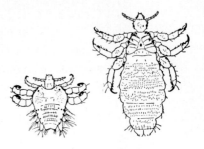

FIG. 275. Lice

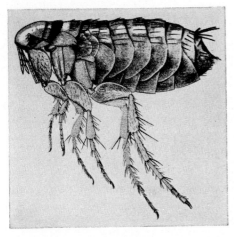

FIG. 276. Flea

FIG. 277. Human
Bot Larva

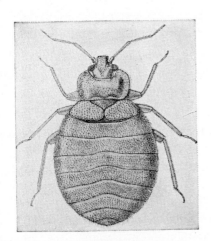

FIG. 278. Bedbug

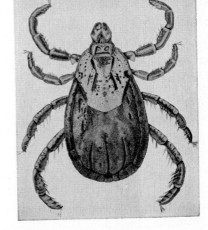

FIG. 279. Hard Tick

Bureau of Entomology
and Plant Quarantine

transmit plague to man after feeding on plague-ridden rodents. Plague, a fatal bacterial disease, is apt to be contracted only in regions where epidemics are flourishing. It persists among wild rodent populations in various parts of the world, and occasionally breaks out in epidemic proportions.

If you must make use of rodents as food in plague-suspect areas, hang up the animals as soon as they are killed and do not handle them until they get cold. Fleas will soon leave dead animals.

The *tiny chigoe, jigger* or *sand flea* occurs in immense numbers in tropical and subtropical countries, particularly in dust near human habitations. The females burrow into the skin usually on the legs, feet and under the toe nails where they produce painful sores. The flea appears as a black speck under the skin and may be dug out with a sterilized needle or knife.

Precautions against fleas include use of derris or louse powder, and (in areas of sand flea infestation) wearing tight-fitting leggings or boots.

Lice

Lice or cooties are wingless insects that live and feed on birds and mammals. Head, body and pubic lice infest men living under unsanitary, crowded conditions. You need not worry about becoming infested with them in the wilds. Their greatest danger lies in transmission of such diseases as typhus, trench-fever, and relapsing fever.

Both the lice and their eggs, which may be deposited on hair or clothing, must be killed. Control measures include use of general-issue louse powder, exposure of clothing to direct sunlight for a few hours, washing frequently in hot, soapy water, or leaving clothing near an ant hill, since certain types of ants feed freely on lice and their eggs. (See Figure 275.)

Bedbugs

Bedbugs are brown wingless bugs with flattened bodies, which are found throughout the world but are most abundant in temperate regions. They feed at night, on human blood when available, and have a characteristic, disagreeable odor. They will leave bedding spread in bright sunlight. (Figure 278.)

Ticks

Ticks are distributed over much of the world and are especially numerous in the tropics and subtropics.

The hard or wood ticks are found chiefly in wooded or brushy areas; the soft or leathery ticks in caves, around rocky ledges, and in the nests and burrows of animals. Both types may transmit disease, but fortunately *the percentage of ticks which are infected is in most areas extremely small.*

Hard ticks, which may cause secondary infection or transmit Rocky Mountain spotted fever or tularemia, are reasonably easy to guard against. In temperate regions they are numerous only in late spring and summer, and are found in the woods away from direct sunlight. They are most common along a path or trail. *Since it takes several hours for most hard ticks to bite, a thorough check of your body and clothing two or three times a day will eliminate danger of disease infection.* (See Figure 279.)

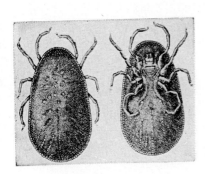

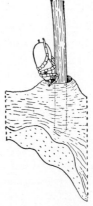

FIG. 281. Chigger (Nearly Invisible to Naked Eye)

FIG. 280. Soft Ticks

Soft ticks bite quickly and fill with blood in 10 to 60 minutes. They may transmit relapsing fever, a weakening but usually not fatal disease.

In examining your body for ticks, look particularly at the base of the head, or hairy portions of the body under the arms, in the groin and where clothing is tight. Don't crush them on the body and be sure to get the head out or it may cause infection. A lighted cigarette or match held close to the tick's body will cause it to loosen its grip and it can then be removed entire. Kerosene or oil will have the same effect. In tick-infested areas avoid sitting on fallen logs and wear trousers tucked into boots.

Rocky Mountain spotted fever is found in many areas of the United States but particularly in the Rocky Mountain regions. It has a high mortality rate, but is comparatively rare. Closely related tick-borne diseases occur in the Mediterranean area, Brazil and elsewhere. Tularemia, a bacterial disease of rodents which can be contracted either from insect bites or through contact with infected animals, is present in the United States, Europe, Japan, and Russia, but is nowhere very common. Don't handle, prepare or eat rodents that were noticeably sick or very sluggish when killed.

Mites and Chiggers

Mites and chiggers are tiny arthropods, some almost invisible to the human eye, which cause annoyance and irritation through their bites or through diseases transmitted by them. They include the human itch mite which causes various skin diseases such as scabies, Norwegian itch, and barber's itch; and the harvest mites or chiggers, which cause irritating sores and may transmit Japanese river or Kedani fever in certain areas of the Far East, including South Pacific Islands. Human itch mites infest the skin and live beneath the scabby crusts made by their burrowing and feeding.

Washing in strong soap followed by application of sulphur ointments will help eliminate mites and chiggers after exposure to them. To protect against chiggers before exposure, dust fine sulphur or louse powder on your skin and inside your clothing, particularly around the ankles. Tucking trousers into boots also will help.

Human itch mites are particularly prevalent in areas where people live in crowded or unsanitary conditions.

Spiders

Spiders in general are not particularly dangerous. Even the much-advertised tarantula is not known to bite with fatal or even serious effect. The black-widow or hour-glass spider of the southern half of the United States, together with tropical members of the same genus, should be avoided as their bites cause severe pain and swelling. All are of a dark color and marked with white, yellow, or red spots.

FIG. 282. Scorpion

FIG. 283. Black Widow Spider

Scorpions

They are usually small (1½ inches in length) but some are as long as eight inches. They sting with their tail spine but usually only when molested. Their stings are extremely painful, but seldom fatal. Since they hide in the daytime and are active at night, they may take refuge from light in shoes or clothing. In areas where they are found, shake out your clothing well and knock your shoes, bottom up, before putting them on.

Centipedes and Caterpillars

Many-legged centipedes, found under logs, stones, or leaves, are numerous in the tropics. Their bites are poisonous but rarely serious.

Numerous hairy or spiny caterpillars will cause severe itching and inflammation if brushed against the skin.

Bees, Wasps, and Hornets

They usually sting only in defense of themselves or their nests. The stings of an aroused swarm may be dangerous and even fatal. Varieties in the tropics range from small, stingless bees to large, militant varieties whose hives should be avoided even when in desperate need of food. In most cases, use of a smoke smudge to stupefy the bees, together with a head and hand covering, will permit you to take honey safely.

Some tropical ants sting severely and attack in numbers, but they can be easily avoided by moving.

Some people are much more susceptible than others to poisoning from stings. To susceptible individuals even a single sting may be serious. Applications of wet mud, ammonia, or soda will relieve the irritation. Juice from the leaves of climbing hemp weed, found near streams, swamps, and seashores, in parts of the Americas, Africa, and the South Pacific, is a good antidote for stings.

FIG. 284. Wasp

FIG. 285. Leech

Leeches

Blood-sucking land leeches are common in very wet areas particularly during the rainy season in Borneo, Sumatra, India, Ceylon, the Philippines, the South Pacific Islands, Malay States, Australia, and in various parts of South America. They cling to blades of grass, leaves, and twigs and fasten themselves on any passing individual. Bites may cause intense discomfort, loss of blood, and may be followed by infection. Remove by touching with a lighted match, cigarette, or moist tobacco, and protect yourself by wearing trousers inside tightly laced boots. Leeches found in mud and shallow water in other areas of the world are not apt to be numerous, and their bites are more irritating than painful, though they can cause severe trouble if swallowed in drinking water. (See Figure 285.)

Flukes or Flatworms

Blood flukes or flatworms, human parasites, are found in sluggish fresh water in Africa, parts of tropical America, Asia, Japan, Formosa, the Philippines and other Pacific Islands. There is little danger in areas remote from human habitation, or in salt water. The flukes pass through part of their life cycle in mollusks, usually snails, and the forms which emerge from the snails penetrate the skins of people who come in contact with them by drinking or bathing in infested water. They live in the blood vessels, feed on blood cells, and escape painfully through the bladder or the feces.

Hookworm

Hookworm is common in the tropics and subtropics. The larvae are usually acquired by going barefooted in areas where human excrement is found. There is no danger from hookworm in wilderness areas, away from human habitation.

Fungus Infections

Parasitic skin diseases (athlete's foot is one) are common in the tropics. They occur most frequently in the armpits, groin, and on the feet. The best protection against them is frequent washing and changing of clothing, particularly shoes and socks, and frequent bathing with plenty of soap. To treat an infection, wash with strong soap, soak the affected part in salt water, and use approved disinfectants as available. Such infections are incapacitating and are always difficult to cure.

POISONOUS SNAKES

Snake Sense

Fear of snakes is out of all proportion to the facts. Common sense dictates a healthy respect for the poisonous varieties, but no more than to cause you to take normal precautions. Cases of bites by poisonous snakes are relatively rare.

Nowhere are poisonous snakes common or numerous over wide areas. Most of them are seclusive and timid, disappearing at the slightest disturbance. The majority of bites are by snakes which are suddenly surprised, stepped on, or grasped.

While the number of varieties of snakes is especially high in the tropics and decreases north and south of the equator, the danger in tropical jungles is actually less than in rattlesnake- and moccasin-infested areas of the United States. If you know a few facts about their habits, and the general and specific areas in which they may be found, you can take normal precautions, give warning of your coming, and forget about fear of snakes.

General precautionary rules are:

1. Keep alert, particularly when climbing steep, rocky slopes.
2. Never tease or pick up a strange snake in a strange country.

This warning may seem unnecessary, but violation of it is the cause of many of the cases of snake-bite which do occur.

3. Knowing exactly what to do if you are bitten will give you confidence.
4. Protect vulnerable portions of your body, particularly the feet and legs. Even light clothing is an excellent protection against many varieties of poisonous snakes.
5. Many snakes roam at night. Therefore, cut down on night travel in snake country.
6. Learn the distribution and habits of poisonous snakes in general, and specifically of those in any area to which you may be assigned.

Snakes are cold-blooded meat eaters and live only in the temperate and tropic regions. Only 200 of the 2400 different kinds which exist are dangerous to man, and most of these will avoid you if given a chance. Only in Australia do the poisonous species outnumber the harmless ones.

Some areas of the world are entirely free of poisonous land snakes, including Madagascar, New Zealand, the Polynesian Islands, Cuba, Jamaica, Haiti, Puerto Rico, the Azores, the Canary and Cape Verde Islands, and Hawaii. While most sea snakes (distinguishable by their paddle-like tails) are poisonous, they do not attack man unless forcibly restrained, and they do not exist in the Atlantic area. Most poisonous snakes are confined to particular types of country and sets of conditions and are encountered only in such places. Certain of these local areas or habitats will harbor more poisonous species and greater numbers of them than others. In such places take every precaution and move out of the area if possible. Snakes feed on mice, lizards, birds, insects, frogs and other small animals and are generally found where such food is abundant.

Snakes cannot stand extremes of either heat or cold. In temperate regions they are active day and night during the warmer months, but hibernate or become inactive in cold weather. In desert and semi-desert regions snakes are most active during early morning and evening. During the heat of the day, they lie in the shade. Give warning of your presence when you seek shade, scan the ground before you stop to rest, and travel in the open as much as possible. Many poisonous snakes are active only at night. When travelling in the dark, use a light, move slowly and avoid brushy areas.

Snakes with few exceptions travel slowly, though many can strike very rapidly. They cannot outrun a man, and only a few can leap entirely off the ground or strike as far as their own length. A sharp blow with a stick will break the vertebral column of average-sized snakes.

By now it should be clear that the danger of being bitten by a poisonous snake is extremely small, almost non-existent except in certain types of country and under certain sets of conditions.

There are no characteristics common to all poisonous snakes, and considerable training is necessary to be able to distinguish poisonous from harmless species. It is, however, comparatively easy to learn the common ones of a particular region.

Colubridae

This family, represented by such familiar snakes as our blacksnake and gartersnake, contains nearly two-thirds of the known species of snakes. None are poisonous except some of the rear-fanged snakes of Africa and southern Asia.

Poisonous Long-Fanged Snakes

The true vipers and the pit vipers are long-fanged venomous snakes. Most of them are thick-bodied with a distinctly flattened head. Many have keeled scales that give them a dull appearance as compared with the polished or satiny appearance of smooth-scaled snakes. (See Figures 286 and 287.)

The pit vipers include all the dangerous poisonous snakes of North America except the coral snake. They inhabit both the eastern and western hemispheres but the most numerous and the largest species are in the New World. All have a deep pit between the eyes and nostril which is *not* easily seen, even at close range.

This family includes the various species of rattlesnakes, *all dangerous* and all confined to the New World, with the majority of species found in the United States and Mexico. The water moccasin is semi-aquatic, inhabiting sluggish waters of southern United States. The copperhead is common in eastern United States. Other pit vipers include the bushmaster of central and tropical South America; the fer-de-lance, a night prowler of southern Mexico and tropical South America; the arboreal palm vipers of Mexico, Central and South America (which frequently inhabit low trees or bushes and palm or banana trees) and the bamboo snakes of Asia.

True vipers are thick-bodied poisonous snakes found only in the Old World: in Europe, India, and particularly in Africa. Well known species

FIG. 286. Gaboon Viper (New York Zool. Society)

FIG. 287. Rattlesnake (Chicago Academy of Science)

include the Russell's viper of India, the cape viper of southern Africa, the puff adder of dry areas of Africa and Arabia, and the gaboon viper of tropical Africa. (See Figure 286.)

Poisonous Short-Fanged Snakes

The elapine snakes (including the cobras, kraits and American coral snakes) are among the most deadly of poisonous snakes, but even light clothing is a

FIG. 288. Cobra (New York Zool. Society)

fairly good protection against them because of their short fangs. They comprise the majority of snakes in Australia, and many species are found in India, Malaya, Africa and New Guinea.

There are ten or more species of cobras, all confined to the Old World and all more or less able to spread the neck to form a "hood." The king cobra is the largest of all poisonous snakes. The Australian blacksnake, the tiger snake and death adder are among the most deadly and abundant Australian elapin snakes.

Coral snakes are small, brilliantly colored snakes confined to the New World. Many have a pattern of rich red, yellow and black bands and few are more than a yard long.

Sea Snakes

Although sea snakes are poisonous, they do not disturb swimmers and are said not to bite unless forcibly restrained. Oriental fishermen are reputed to throw them from their nets with bare hands. Sea snakes usually are found close to shore or in tidal rivers, but they may be seen a hundred miles from the coast. They can be distinguished from river snakes by their flat vertically-compressed, paddle-like tails. Venomous sea snakes are not found in the Atlantic, but may

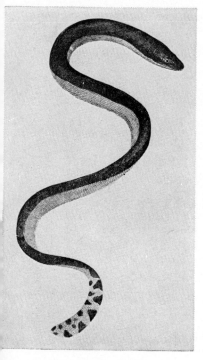 

FIG. 289. Sea Snake   FIG. 290. Sea Snake

occur in large numbers off the shores of the Indian Ocean and the southern and western Pacific.

River Snakes

These snakes frequent the rivers and bays of the East Indies, and are found from Bengal through Malaya to northern Australia. They are poisonous, but they must bite and hold in order to inject poison, and thus are not especially dangerous.

Boas and Pythons

Boas and pythons are not poisonous, are slow moving and rarely attack man unless molested. They are vicious and dangerous if disturbed because of their sharp teeth and power of constriction. The large species live only in dense jungle country, and are found in areas of Burma, Indo-China, the Malay Archipelago, the Philippines, southern India, China, South America, and central and southern Africa. Species such as the regal python and anaconda average between 17 and 22 feet in length.

FIG. 291. Mexican Beaded Lizard (Smithsonian Institution)

Lizards

Poisonous lizards are not found outside the western hemisphere. The only poisonous ones are the gila monster of the American Southwest and the beaded lizard of Mexico and Central America, both *found only in desert areas.* The poisonous lizards are so sluggish, and their mechanism for injection of poison so poor, that cases of their causing injury to human beings are extremely rare. *No lizards, large or small, anywhere in the world, are poisonous except the two mentioned above.* Some lizards are excellent sources of food. (See page 90.)

Summary on Poisonous Reptiles

From the previous discussion, you can see readily that because of their distribution, variations in habits and habitat, small numbers, and the nature of their venom-transfer mechanisms, only a few dangerous snakes are apt to be encountered at any given time or place, and that most of these are seclusive and timid, preferring to get away or remain undisturbed.

Snake Bites

Danger from snake bite is in proportion to the size of the snake, the type nd quantity of venom injected, and the part of the body bitten. While venom may contain several toxins, the most important (the hemorrhagins and the eurotoxins) affect the blood and nervous systems, respectively.

Nausea and desire to void and defecate, thirst, severe headache, and bleeding from the wound, gums, and nose are frequent symptoms of snake bite.

Pain symptoms from the bite of the elapine snakes (cobra, krait, coral nakes) are comparatively mild, but the poison is absorbed rapidly and irectly by the blood, spreads to all parts of the body, and acts quickly by aralyzing the nervous system and respiratory centers. Within the period of n hour a numb feeling grows progressively worse, resulting in partial paralysis f the affected area.

Venom of the viperine snakes will cause severe local pain followed by welling that may continue for hours. It does most of its damage in the blood y liberating hemoglobin or producing internal hemorrhage or clotting. This enom is absorbed slowly through the lymphatic system.

Death dealing bacteria such as the gas-gangrene bacillus (*Bacillus welchii*) nd Streptococcus hemolyticus occur normally in the mouths and venom sacs f snakes and cause secondary infections which greatly increase the seriousness f snake bite.

irst Aid in Snake Bite

Quick and intelligent treatment is the most important factor in reducing ne danger from snake bite.

1. Make a lengthwise cut through each fang puncture, as deep as the uncture, and make additional shallow cuts near the wound to drain the mphatics. Cut parallel to blood vessels and tendons and *don't slash indis- iminately.* Prompt incision will reduce a lethal to a non-lethal dose.

2. Squeeze out the blood and venom, and suck it out if your mouth and ps are free from cuts. It won't hurt you unless it gets into the blood stream. If medical attention can be had in an hour, don't cut.)

3. If a limb has been bitten, place a tourniquet *between the wound and e heart,* making it tight enough to cut off the return of the blood to the heart rough the veins, but not to cut off flow to the wound, as bleeding will help move the poison. You can do this by tightening up the tourniquet so that e pulse stops, then easing it so the pulse can barely be felt. If the wound is the lower part of the arm or leg, put a tourniquet above the elbow or knee d another just above the wound and massage the limb toward the wound encourage the blood flow. Loosen the tourniquet briefly every 20 minutes.

4. Keep quiet. Exercise increases the speed of spreading and absorption of e venom. Avoid all stimulants, including alcohol.

5. Cooling with a wet cloth or ice will retard the flow of lymph thus delaying the absorption of venom.

6. Kill the snake for identification. This is important if there is a chance of getting serum.

7. Don't cauterize (burn out) the wound or use potassium permanganate, as this destroys the tissues and does more harm than good.

8. Act rapidly but keep calm.

POISONOUS AND DANGEROUS AQUATIC ANIMALS

Sharks

The danger of being attacked by a shark or barracuda is greatly exaggerated in the minds of most people. Whether there is any hazard at all depends

FIG. 292. White Shark

FIG. 293. Barracuda

both on the locality and on the condition of the man in question. In general sharks are timid and wary creatures.

Sharks are curious, and will investigate any object in the water but are likely to attack only the dead, or the wounded and bleeding. Blood in the water attracts and excites them through their sense of smell. Any flow of blood should be stanched as quickly as possible. Stay with your companions, as groups are less subject to attack than lone individuals.

Clothing, especially if it is dark colored, is a good protection, as light colored bodies appear to attract sharks. Be careful when cleaning fish at the edge of a raft and don't trail hands or feet in the water when sharks are present.

Barracudas

Barracudas are found in most tropical and subtropical seas, usually along coral reefs and near shoal waters. Danger from them is greater in murky water in reefs than in clear water. Under such conditions they apparently have difficulty recognizing their prey and thus are likely to attack objects in the water indiscriminately. They are seldom encountered in the open seas.

Electric Ray

The electric ray, or torpedo, is found both in open water and along sandy and muddy bottoms, both in tropical and temperate seas. It can give a paralyzing shock, but fortunately it is rarely encountered.

Jelly Fish and Portuguese Men-of-War

These marine animals have long stinging tentacles that produce painful stings and severe swelling which will last several hours. The greatest danger is not from the stings themselves, but from the fact that they may cause a swimmer to develop cramps, panic, and loss of energy which may result in drowning. Clothing should be worn as a protection while swimming in areas where these animals are present, and objects on the water surface resembling large bubbles should be avoided. If stung, make every effort to relax. When near a source of medical supplies, prompt application of ammonia will relieve the pain. (See Figure 295.)

Whales, Dolphins and Porpoises are large sea mammals, not dangerous to man.

Cuttlefish, Squid and Octopus have long, powerful tentacles, but those large enough to be dangerous live in the depths of the ocean and are rarely encountered.

Stingrays

Stingrays (stingarees) are flat fish with a powerful, venomous, tail stinger that can be driven through a man's foot leaving a wound likely to become infected. They frequent sand or mud bottoms, and in warm seas they may grow to several hundred pounds. You can avoid stepping on them by shoving your feet through the sand, or by poking ahead of you with a stick to frighten them out of your path. The sting of a large ray may be fatal. A small one can hospitalize a man. (See Figure 294.)

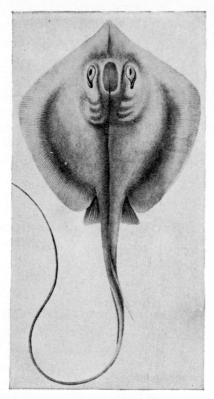

FIG. 294. Stingray   FIG. 295. Portuguese Man-of-War

FIG. 296. Scorpion Fish

corpion, Stone, and Toad Fishes

The stone and scorpion fishes of the Pacific Ocean and some of the toad shes of tropical America are the most dangerous poisonous fishes. Their enomous spines may produce a sting which causes severe pain and swelling, ollowed by prostration. Treat a sting as you would snake bite. These fish are nost apt to be encountered among coral head, where the unwary may accidentally step on them, or touch them with the hands while turning over coral ocks in search of food. The flesh of these fish is edible, but don't pick up nese fish or take them off a hook with bare hands.

ea Anemones and Sea Urchins

Some of the sea anemones may produce an annoying sting. They are small, dant-like creatures which cling to rocks on reefs and in tidal pools. Some pecies of sea urchins found in the southwest Pacific have long, poisonous, eedlelike spines.

FIG. 297. Sea Anemone   FIG. 298. Moray Eel

he Morays and Conger Eel

These are snake-like fish inhabiting coral reefs. Normally they bite only hen touched.

hells

The sharp shells of oysters and other mollusks, coral and starfish, cause ounds which heal slowly. You are almost sure to be cut if you try to wade r swim without shoes through a surf on coral shores.

Crocodilians

The crocodilians are confined to marshy lowlands, sloughs, rivers, and along the coast in the tropics and semitropics. All species are potentially dangerous, some more than others. A blow from the powerful tail of one which is surprised constitutes more of a real danger than the possibility of being bitten. The group includes the crocodiles, alligators, gavials and caimans.

All crocodilians prefer sluggish water and will rarely be encountered in swift water. Most of them are timid; if out on the banks, they will rush for water at the sight of a man. They will seldom attack unless you come on them suddenly or get between them and the water, blocking their natural path of escape. Either on land or in the water, keep a sharp lookout as they are difficult to see.

Crocodiles

The salt water and African crocodiles are the most dangerous of the species. The former is found in coastal swamps, inlets and tidal rivers of the South Pacific ocean. The latter, abundant in some areas of Africa and Madagascar has a reputation as a man-eater. The American crocodile, found along coastal regions of Mexico, the West Indies, Central America, Colombia, and Venezuela, usually will avoid man.

Gavials

Largest of all the crocodiles is the Indian gavial, a timid creature confined to northern India, and living largely on fish. Natives swim in water where gavials are numerous.

Alligators

Alligators are found only in the southeastern portion of the United States and along the Yangtze River in China. They are more active in the water and more vicious and treacherous than crocodiles.

Caimans

Caimans, resembling alligators, are found in the rivers of Central America and in tropical South America, east of the Andes.

Fish

Only four fresh water fish are at all dangerous to man and all four are found in South America. They are the caribe, the electric eel, the candiru, and the stingray.

The caribes (also known as piranhas or pirayas) are far the most feared of this group. They inhabit the Paraguay, Amazon and Orinoco river systems are generally found in schools, and "go wild" if they encounter blood in the water. They are about the size of a large sunfish, and have deep, blunt heads and powerful jaws armed with cutting teeth. They may attack any animal entering the water. People wading or swimming have been severely bitten and even killed by schools of these little fish. They live in smooth water, never in rapids. Clothing (including shoes) will protect against them.

FIG. 299. Caribe

The electric eel of the Orinoco and Amazon river systems delivers the most powerful shock of any fish. It is seldom encountered.

Fresh water stingrays are abundant in the muddy and sandy areas of South American streams, ranging thousands of miles up the river systems. Take the same precautions as against marine stingrays.

The candiru is a tiny fish found in the Amazon and Orinoco river systems, and apparently is attracted by water currents. Cases have been reported of this small fish swimming into the urethra of an individual urinating in the water. Small, hook-like, head spines prevent it from getting out again.

Harmful Mammals

Generally, mammals large or small, flesh-eating or herbivorous are not of great danger to man. You may travel in jungles, grassland, desert or arctic regions without worry from this source. All wild mammals avoid man, and most of them are timid and wary. You will have more difficulty in locating lions, bears, and wolves than you will in avoiding them. You may consider yourself lucky if you get an opportunity even to see some of the supposedly dangerous carnivores. There are conditions under which mammals may be dangerous, but these are usually situations in which they are threatened or attacked by man.

Circumstances under Which Mammals May Become Dangerous

When Wounded.—Large animals such as elephants, bears, tigers, moose, wild boar and water buffalo will attack or charge when wounded, especially f cornered. If you find it necessary to shoot an animal which may be dangerous when wounded, use a large caliber gun if available; try to kill at the first shot.

Protection of Young.—Many mammals, which prefer to run away if given the opportunity, will fight when cornered, or if their young are harmed.

Exiles and Man-eaters.—Old exiles or hermits (such as elephants, boar, or buffalo) that have been cast off by a herd, are often cantankerous, and may charge you if disturbed or irritated. They will be alone or straggling in the vicinity of a herd. Almost all man-eating lions, tigers or leopards are old beasts that no longer can successfully hunt wild animals and have resorted to killing man. Such animals are rare. Take reasonable precautions when sleeping if such an animal is known to be in the area. A hammock or platform in the trees will eliminate danger from tigers or lions, although leopards are excellent climbers. Tigers are found primarily in jungles of southeastern Asia, including India, Burma, and Malaya, Sumatra, Borneo, and Bali. Lions are confined to Africa and a very small region of western India and Persia. They are found in open regions of grass and scrubby trees. Both lions and tigers are shy and seldom seen, but may prove dangerous when suddenly disturbed or in a region where game is scarce.

Stampeding.—Mammals that live in herds can be dangerous if suddenly frightened into stampeding. Wild hogs or boars have been known to attack man.

Bites

Bites from all canines (dogs, jackals, foxes) as well as some other meat-eaters may cause rabies. There is no need to worry unless this disease is known to be prevalent or the animal was particularly vicious or noticeably sick or paralyzed.

The Pasteur (vaccine) treatment for prevention of rabies is highly effective. The treatment may safely be delayed for several days after you have been bitten unless the bite is in the region of the head or neck. In any doubtful case consult a doctor as soon as possible.

Blood-sucking vampire bats, found only in South America, are not dangerous unless their bite becomes infected. Mosquito netting will keep them away, and should be used at night in areas where these bats are found.

Poisonous Plants

As a general rule, poisonous plants are not a serious hazard, but under certain conditions they are dangerous. Plants may be poisonous to eat, poisonous merely to touch, due to toxic juices or oils, and poisonous due to stinging hairs that come in contact with the skin.

The dangers from poisonous plants in other parts of the world is no greater than in any part of the United States where poison ivy, poison oak, and poison sumach occur.

Plants Poisonous to Eat

There are numerous plants which are poisonous to eat in whole or in part. To attempt to learn these would only be confusing. Learn the plants that are edible, and if it is necessary to try strange plants, eat only minute quantities and wait a while before trying more.

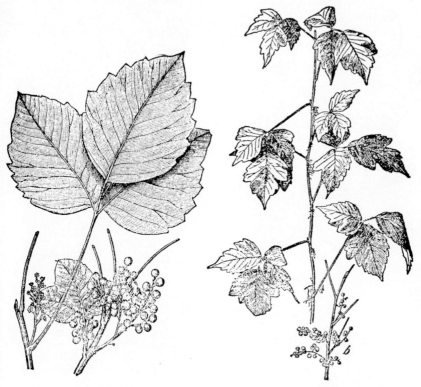

FIG. 300. Poison Ivy *(Rhus toxicodendron)* Grows as a Shrub or Creeping or Climbing Vine

Plants Poisonous to Touch

This group will cause you most trouble. Contact with them may cause severe eruptions, swelling and inflammation. They are particularly dangerous in the vicinity of the eyes. *Some people are immune or only slightly affected by contact poisons, while others are extremely susceptible. This is something you should learn about yourself.* There is a greater danger of being affected when you are overheated and sweating. The plants themselves may vary in toxicity at different times of the year. Don't use the wood of any contact poisoning plants for firewood. Avoid contact with the milky juices of all unfamiliar trees and take particular precautions against getting such juices in your eyes. *It will be helpful for you to learn the appearance and effects of the contact-poisoning plants found in the United States, and to use this background of experience to help you in other parts of the world.* The method of

FIG. 301. Poison Oak *(Rhus diversiloba)*

FIG. 302. Poison Sumach *(Rhus vernix)* Grows Only in Wet Swampy Areas

FIG. 303. Liga *(Semecarpus)*

FIG. 304. Black Poison Wood *(Metopium)*

poisoning, the symptoms and to some extent the appearance of the plants, will be similar.

Most of these plants, both tropical and temperate, belong to two families—the sumach and the spurge.

Poisonous Contact Plants of the United States

The three most important contact poisonous plants in the United States are poison ivy, poison oak, and poison sumach. Their toxic principle is a resinous alkaloid that occurs in all parts of the plant.

Symptoms may take from a few hours to several days to appear. They consists of reddening, itching and swelling of the affected parts, followed by the formation of blisters. The infection may be localized or spread over the body.

All of these plants have compound leaves and a small round grayish green or white fruit. They can easily be avoided by learning where they grow and what they look like. The best treatment after contact with these plants is to wash thoroughly with a strong soap. (See Figures 300-302.)

Poisonous Contact Plants in Other Parts of the World

Most plants in other parts of the world that produce skin eruptions similar to poison ivy and poison sumach belong to the same family.

Some of these plants are:

1. The Rengas trees of India, Malaya and the South Pacific Islands. Their sap causes severe skin eruptions. Liga, a small shrub of this group found in the Philippine Islands can be identified by the black sap along the trunk. (Figure 303.) Many of these plants are large forest trees and there is little likelihood of trouble unless you climb or cut them.

2. Several species of Mangifera to which the edible mango belongs. They are found in tropical Asia.

3. Black poison wood of Central America and the West Indies. (Figure 304.)

4. Carrasco, common shrubs in the West Indies.

5. The Chinese lacquer tree of China and Japan.

Among the spurges the following should be avoided:

1. The beach apple or manzanillo of Central America and tropical South America, the West Indies and Mexico causes skin inflammation and may also cause blindness if the sap gets in the eyes. It is a small tree with smooth, pale-brown bark and "crabapple-like" fruits. It is found in thickets along the coast. Immediate bathing in sea water will counteract the effects of the sap. The fruits are poisonous to eat. (See Figure 305.)

2. The "blind eye," white mangrove found in Australia, the South Pacific Islands and India grows in mangrove swamps, salt marshes and along the

seashore. It is a shrub or small tree whose white sap causes severe skin irritation and may cause blindness.

3. The monkey pistol or sandbox tree of tropical America, Panama, and the West Indies is a large tree with spiny trunk whose sap is irritating and

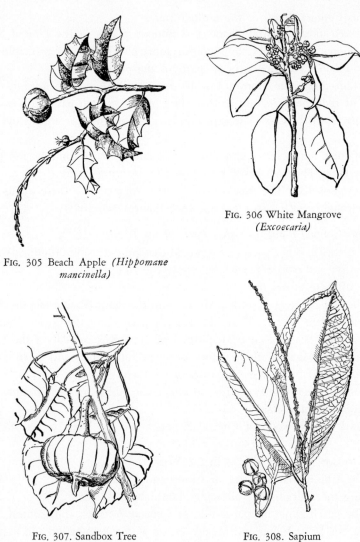

FIG. 305 Beach Apple *(Hippomane mancinella)*

FIG. 306 White Mangrove *(Excoecaria)*

FIG. 307. Sandbox Tree *(Hura crepitans)*

FIG. 308. Sapium Jamaicense

may cause temporary blindness. The small pumpkin-like fruit is also poisonous.

4. The milky juice of a number of species of the genus Sapium found in the tropics of both hemispheres causes serious skin inflammations.

5. The castor oil plant belongs to this family and contains poisonous and purgative qualities. A remedy that many natives use for milky juices in the eyes is to wash the eyes immediately with warm milk.

The Upas or Ipoh tree is notorious for its poisonous properties. Natives of the South Seas and Indian Archipelago use the sap of this tree to poison their arrows, but there is no danger from contact with the tree itself.

Strychnine trees furnish curare, the poison which South American natives

FIG. 309. Stinging Nettle (*Urtica dioica*)   FIG. 310. *Jatropha urens* of Tropical America

apply to their spears and arrows. Treat poison arrow wounds as you would snake bites.

Plants with Stinging Hairs

Plants of this group contain fine hairs which produce a burning sensation when touched, followed by the appearance of small red welts. This sting, due to formic acid, is usually not dangerous. Contact with the stinging nettle found in waste lands of the United States and Europe will give you an idea of what to expect from tree nettles and this group of stinging plants in other parts of the world.

IMAGINARY DANGERS

To the man alone in strange surroundings, dangers which exist only in the imagination frequently are the chief source of worry unless he has trained himself in advance to know what the few real hazards are and to concentrate on surmounting them. Vast, desert wastes; endless snow or ice in the Arctic;

infinite expanses of ocean; rugged mountains, or dark confining jungles—all give rise to imaginary fears. Apparent silence, continuous wind, or unexplained noise will magnify the effect of strange surroundings.

If silence bothers you, tune your ear to pick up high-pitched insect voices. You may find that there are lots of small previously unheard noises. Cuss a little just to hear your own voice. If the loneliness is depressing, or starts you thinking on your insignificance in the vastness about you, remember such thoughts are normal in such a situation, and will help alleviate your fear of personal dangers.

Jungles are noisy day and night. Birds, such as parakeets, may flash through the treetops like a squadron of planes and be almost as noisy. Peacocks calling in the early morning or evening may sound like anything your imagination can conceive. Some birds will be noisy all night long. Mammals, such as cheetal or sambar, may bark at night. Tigers and leopards may roar or moan, and jackals howl. These and a thousand others are all natural sounds, and in some cases can be helpful. A prolonged quiet or unusual excitement indicates that something has disturbed the jungle life. Cheetal and sambar (deer) may bark nervously when tigers or leopards are near. Langurs and other monkeys give warning of the presence of large cats. Jays, crows, babblers and magpies scream excitedly at the approach of man or other enemies. Frogs usually stop croaking at the approach of man. Experience may enable you to utilize these noises in detecting the presence or approach of an enemy.

The eyes of numerous animals gleam at night in the presence of a light. Cats are among them, but the chances of seeing the eyes of a tiger, lion or leopard under such conditions are very slim. The eyes of spiders, land crabs, large insects and birds such as the goatsuckers also shine. Remember to rely on reason and knowledge. Don't let your imagination run riot.

DEALING WITH NATIVES

Native people throughout the world vary a great deal in their attitude toward strangers. At times it may be best to avoid them; but in most cases you can seek their aid with confidence. They will be friendly and will know the country well. The help and friendship they extend to you will be directly proportional to your own good will and good conduct toward them.

The following are a few general pointers to remember when dealing with native people:

(1) Approach natives with a smile and confident bearing. Attempt to make your wants known to the man who by appearance and action seems to be the chief.

(2) Never show fear, and don't threaten or order the natives around.

(3) Treat them as equals, be eager to learn, and show enthusiasm and

admiration for their skill and proficiency in guiding and supplying you with the necessities of life. With a little subtle praise, they will outdo themselves in your behalf.

(4) Observe the way the natives do things, then imitate them.

(5) "Actions speak louder than words." If you can outdo natives in feats of strength or skill, you will be held in esteem for this above all else.

(6) Try to learn and follow the customs and laws that govern the religious, social, and private lives of the natives. Be extremely cautious in your attitude toward native women.

(7) Insofar as it is possible, eat only hot food that has been boiled or otherwise thoroughly cooked, and fruits that have not been peeled or husked. Avoid eating raw greens handled by the natives. Boil your own drinking water and all milk, or make sure it is done. Insist on this.

(8) Sleep well-covered, and by all means use a mosquito netting if you have one,

(9) Among natives your problem of food, water, and shelter will be solved, but the danger of disease is greatly increased. So take all possible health precautions without giving offense to your hosts.

(10) Remember that not only your own fate but that of many other members of the Allied forces may depend on your treating native peoples well.

CHAPTER X

Survival Under Nuclear, Biological, and Chemical Warfare Attack

THE NATURE OF NBC WARFARE

A primary objective in any kind of warfare is to reduce the enemy to such a condition that he can no longer continue to fight. The destruction of his war machines and fighting forces, his industrial centers, and his centers of population are all factors in the achievement of this objective. The means by which targets are destroyed or casualties are produced may vary with the circumstances or with the strategy and tactics required by a particular situation. Nuclear, biological, and chemical weapons are some of these means.

An attack may be made with either nuclear, biological, or chemical weapons—or any combination of the three. An enemy could drop a nuclear bomb on a city, and then at the appropriate time follow through by dispersing chemical agents or biological agents along exit routes and at personnel collection stations in order to reduce further the number of survivors. Consequently, defensive measures must be both flexible enough to cover all three types of warfare and specific enough to counter the particular effects of each type.

Since the present-day concept of "total war" involves civilian centers and populations, as well as military targets and personnel, it is imperative that every one know what measures would most contribute to survival in an NBC (nuclear, biological, and chemical) attack. If we understand the nature of NBC warfare, the effects caused by NBC weapons, and the symptoms produced by NBC agents, we will be better able to escape the effects and minimize any injuries.

Nuclear Warfare (NW)

Nuclear weapons are primarily designed to cause destruction by blast or shock. In this respect the atomic bomb and the hydrogen bomb are similar to, but immensely more powerful than, the ordinary high-explosive bombs with which military men have long been familiar. As with TNT weapons, the explosion of a nuclear weapon is accompanied by blast and heat. Unlike TNT explosions, such an explosion is also accompanied by nuclear radiation. By means of special weapons, it is also possible to use radioactive materials or agents to produce casualties, without the heat and blast of an actual explosion. Such deliberate contamination of an area with radioactive materials or the purpose of contaminating personnel or equipment is known as Radiological Warfare. Destruction, death, and injury in nuclear warfare, then, are caused by blast, heat, and nuclear radiation.

Biological Warfare (BW)

Biological warfare is defined as the use of living agents, or their toxic products, to produce disease or death of personnel, animals, or plants. The chief objective of biological warfare is mass infection resulting in the incapacitation or death of large numbers of individuals or in the destruction of their sources of food, animal or plant, or perhaps in both. The weapons of biological warfare, unlike most other weapons, act on living matter only, and are limited in use to those objectives.

Chemical Warfare (CW)

In chemical warfare, death, injury, or irritating effects are produced by toxic chemical agents. Although commonly called gases, actually these agents may be found as solid particles, liquids, or gases. CW agents may be disseminated by aircraft spray, chemical projectiles, bombs, or grenades, smoke pots and candles, or by the use of chemical land mines or chemical cylinders. They attack the body and produce specific damages according to the nature of the particular agent. The following breakdown into six major groupings will indicate the primary action of each group on the body: nerve gases; blood gases; blister gases; choking gases; vomiting gases; and tear gases. The first four are classified as casualty agents; vomiting and tear gases are classified as harassing agents.

THE EFFECTS OF NBC ATTACKS

There are five over-all effects produced by NBC weapons: blast; thermal radiation or heat; nuclear radiation; disease; and chemical poisoning. The first three, the products of various nuclear weapons, occur simultaneously and instantaneously, with some possible lingering effects of the nuclear radiation. Blast and heat, of course, are anti-material as well as anti-personnel effects. Nuclear radiation is an anti-personnel effect, since materials and equipment are not affected in any visible manner by alpha, beta, or gamma radiation. Disease and chemical poisoning are chiefly anti-personnel effects.

Nuclear Attack

In discussing the general effects of nuclear weapons it is necessary to use some standard, typical weapon with which we have had experience. Since we have the most data on effects from the bombs dropped on Japan, we will consider such bombs as our standard weapon in the following pages.

You must realize that the size of the weapon and the manner in which it is exploded will have some bearing on the protective measures required In military operations a nuclear bomb may be exploded in one of four ways in the air, on the surface, underground, or underwater.

In the explosion of a standard atomic bomb in the air, the following event occur:

Immediately there is visible a ball of fire, which appears many time brighter than the sun at noon. As it cools the ball of fire increases in size and decreases in intensity. At the same time, it rises, like a hot-air balloon, and reaches its maximum size about one second after the explosion. (See Figure 376.) While the ball of fire is still visible, the temperature—at least in its interior—is so high that all substances present are in the form of vapor. As the temperature decreases, the vapor will condense to form a smoke. Depending on the height of the air burst and on the nature of the terrain a strong updraft with inflowing winds will occur in the immediate vicinity. These, together with the air burst created by the explosion, will suck up dust and other debris from the earth's surface, forming an expanding and rising column of smoke The column consists of very small radioactive particles of the fission products of "leftover" fissionable material, of dust, and, if the air is moist, of drop of water.

The rate at which this smoke column or cloud rises varies with the weather conditions. Generally, it will reach a height of one mile in 20 seconds, two

FIG. 376. H-bomb explosion at Bikini.

miles in 50 seconds, and three miles in a little over 90 seconds. When the cloud reaches the base of the stratosphere, five to eight miles above the earth, it stops rising and the top of the cloud spreads out, forming into the well-known mushroom-shaped cloud. This is what you see. In addition you might *feel* the terrific blast, which moves out from the point of explosion in all directions, and the heat given off by the explosion. You can neither *see* nor *feel* the nuclear radiation which is given off at the time of the explosion, and which is absorbed in the air, in the dust, and in any drops of water in the vicinity of the burst.

In a surface burst there will still be the blast, heat, and nuclear radiation, but the effects will differ in degree from an air burst. For instance, the heat developed in a surface burst will be about the same as that of an air burst, but since thermal radiation travels in a straight line, it will be easier to find shelter behind a building, wall, or hill, or any number of objects between you and the point of explosion, and so the danger from burns is less. In a surface burst, the over-all destruction by blast is somewhat lessened because part of the shock is absorbed by the ground and part of the energy is used up vaporizing the materials on the surface and in forming a crater. The targets close to ground zero (the spot immediately beneath the explosion) would be completely destroyed, but the effect of the blast would not be as great farther out as for an air burst. The over-all, immediate nuclear radiation would probably be about the same for a surface burst as for an air burst. There would be more nuclear radiation danger from falling radioactive dust, since there would be more dust sucked up in the cloud from a surface burst. Radioactive dust and drops of water which fall back to earth after the explosion are known as *fall-out*.

In the case of an underground or an underwater burst, the fall-out would be very great since the cloud would contain huge quantities of radioactive dirt or water. Therefore, there would be more danger from nuclear radiation in the area contaminated by this fall-out. The thermal radiation from an underground or underwater burst is of little concern since it would be completely absorbed by the earth or water immediately surrounding the point of explosion.

The effects of blast in an underground or underwater burst would be greater only at the point of explosion, for the shock wave travels faster but not as far in ground or water. In an underground burst, the blast creates a mild earthquake, the force of which will depend somewhat on the type of soil. If there are considerable rock layers near the point of explosion, the earthquake effect will be felt over a greater area.

Subsurface bursts have one characteristic which is either inconsequential or is not found in the air burst or the surface burst. At the base of the cloud column a mass of dust or water rolls out in great waves, much like ocean waves rolling toward a shore. This mass is called a *base surge*. The dust particles or drops of water making up a base-surge are very radioactive, and the areas over which a base surge rolls become dangerous due to the nuclear radiations. These types of bursts are called *contaminating bursts*, since both the base surge and the fall-out spread radioactive materials.

The atomic bomb was designed chiefly as a blast weapon, and since the air burst can cause the greatest blast damage, it is probable that air bursts would be used by an enemy to destroy our major military facilities. Naval vessels underway are less liable to such attack than military shore installations, vessels in port, or even civilian centers, because they offer no fixed target. If an enemy should want to preserve a facility or an industrial area for his own use later, he probably would use a contaminating burst, either underground or underwater, which would force evacuation but would leave most buildings and equipment intact.

Blast Effects

A building's resistance to blast depends primarily on its strength and, to a lesser degree, on its shape and on the number of openings which can serve to relieve the pressure on the outside walls. The strength is determined mainly by the type of construction. The effect of shape is not particularly marked, since most buildings are rectangular in form. A long narrow structure will be more resistant to blast striking it on the narrow end than on the long side. However, if struck on the long side, a rectangular building would probably suffer more damage than a square one. The effect of shape is more evident in circular structures such as smokestacks. Pressures equalize rapidly around them, which makes them surprisingly resistant to blast. They often remain standing when adjoining structures are leveled to the ground. On the other hand, flat surfaces, such as windows and doors in an extensive wall, will tend to give way very easily.

The instantaneous failure of window panes, light siding, and other flat, weak portions of a structure is often advantageous for it allows the pressure inside and the pressure outside to equalize. This reduces the destructive effect of the blast on the structure as a whole.

In an air burst, the blast striking a building near ground zero will be almost vertical. At a distance, however, the blast striking a building will be almost horizontal. Therefore, near ground zero the blast will be mainly from above; roof failures will be common. Farther away the pressure will be largely on the walls. (See Figure 377.) At ground zero there would be little possibility of a building being shielded by any feature of the terrain, such as a hill,

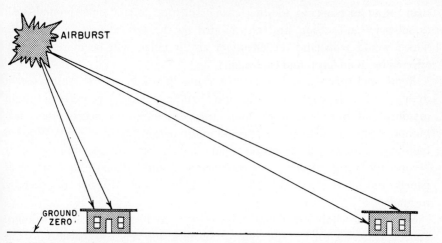

FIG. 377. In an airburst, the blast pressure on a building near ground zero is mainly on the roof; further from ground zero, the pressure is mainly on the walls.

because the blast is coming from a point almost directly above it. But at some distance from ground zero, hills can provide partial shelter. (See Figure 378.)

For moderately shallow underwater or underground bursts, about a quarter of the bomb's energy would appear as air blast. The range of damage from ground zero would be about half of that from an air burst. The over-all destruction near ground zero will be much greater for an underground burst

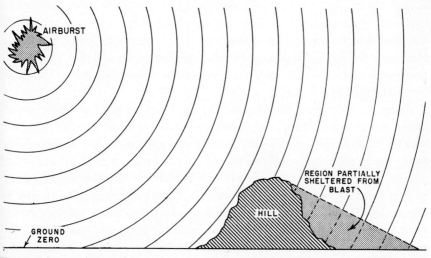

FIG. 378. At some distance from ground zero, a hill provides partial shelter from blast due to an airburst.

than for an air burst. In addition, many structures located underground, such as subways, and strong structures located on the surface near ground zero, which would withstand the effects of an air burst, will be more seriously affected by an underground explosion.

Reinforced concrete and heavy steel-frame buildings are the most resistant to blast. Heavily constructed masonry buildings stand up well, but light masonry and brick structures offer little resistance, and debris from such buildings provide missiles which could injure persons in the vicinity. Wooden buildings offer the least resistance and will either collapse quickly or, if beyond the range of severe destruction, will suffer damage to roofs, wall panels, and interior partitions. Bridges, highways and railroads are generally resistant.

Ships as a whole are remarkably resistant to blast damage. The design and the materials used in the construction of a ship are such that it can stand considerable stresses and strains. This is understandable when you consider that a good portion of the topside area of a combatant ship is built to withstand blast from the firing of its own guns and that the hull proper is required to withstand the impact of waves, as are portions of the superstructure. Furthermore, many important stations are protected by armor or splinter shields, which are strongly built.

The nature of the specific parts of ships and of the equipment on board will determine the effects that a nuclear blast will have on them. Some will probably be broken, bent, or twisted out of shape by the blast. Others will suffer no appreciable damage.

Both the course on which a ship is heading and its shape have considerable influence on damage. For example, a ship headed either toward or away from the blast will be damaged less than one which presents a broadside to the blast; and the more streamlined the ship, the better. In addition, the ship is floating in water and can "give" as a whole (by rolling or pitching) without being damaged by this motion.

Aircraft are designed to withstand the great stresses and loads experienced under actual flight conditions. Because of the nature of their mission, the smaller fighter-type planes—jet fighters, in particular—are designed for heavy loads and high accelerations with a minimum of surface area. Such aircraft will be much less susceptible to blast damage than the larger aircraft, such as bombers and cargo planes, with their greater surface area. Aircraft in flight normally will be above the altitude at which they might get some effects from the shock waves that are reflected from the ground. Consequently, the radius of damage due to air blast should be significantly less than for grounded aircraft.

Thermal Radiation Effects

Heat and fire are the second main cause of damage to structures and equipment due to the explosion of a nuclear bomb. The thermal radiation accompanying an air burst strikes everything within several miles that is not shielded. In the case of an air burst of our "standard" bomb, the intensity of radiation is sufficient to cause burns of the exposed skin as far as two miles away, on a moderately clear day. The warmth may be felt at a distance of 10 miles.

When thermal radiation hits an exposed surface, it is partially absorbed and is immediately converted into heat. Because nearly all the radiant energy from a nuclear explosion is delivered in less than three seconds, there is not sufficient time for the heat to spread from the surface into the body of the exposed object or material. Consequently, the thermal radiation from a nuclear bomb causes exceptionally high surface temperatures.

Due to these high temperatures, many substances will scorch, char, or even burst into flame. The actual effect will depend on the color and nature of the material and the amount of radiant heat received. Typical products which are easily charred or burned are paper, wood, cloth, rubber, paint, and asphalt. Dark colored or dark painted materials absorb a larger proportion of the thermal radiation and so will char or burn more easily than those having light color. The extent of the damage depends on the nature and color of the material. Textiles of various kinds are sensitive: nylon melts fairly easily; other fibers burn. Cotton materials—cotton twill, in particular—seem to be relatively resistant to heat. Loosely gathered materials, such as piles of paper or rags, thin black draperies and curtains, and canvas tarpaulins, may be set afire by the radiant heat from the bomb. Dry vegetation, such as dry grass or stubble, may also be ignited.

While thermal radiation may start many fires, a good proportion of these will be extinguished by the air blast wind which arrives a few seconds later. Material which is shielded from the blast by a transparent substance, such as glass, may catch fire and may well continue to burn, for the heat will pass through the glass, but the wind may not.

Fires accompanying a nuclear explosion may be classed as "primary" or "secondary," according to their origin. Primary fires are those caused directly by the thermal radiation igniting such materials as paper, thin cloth, rags, wood, and dry vegetation. Secondary fires are due to other causes, for which the blast is mainly responsible, such as upset stoves and furnaces, broken gas and other fuel lines, and electrical short circuits. The evidence from Hiroshima and Nagasaki indicated that the great majority of fires were secondary in nature.

No matter what the immediate cause, a nuclear air burst over a built-up area will result in many fires burning simultaneously and over a wide area. Once the fires have started, the chances of their spreading will depend on the combustibility and closeness of the buildings, the nature of the terrain, the weather conditions at the time of the attack, and the adequacy of the defense. In any event, by breaking glass windows and blowing in or damaging doors at stairways and elevators, and in firewall openings, the blast will make the interior of the building very vulnerable to the spread of fire. Burning debris blown or blasted through the air, can enter through windows, doors, and roofs and cause fire to spread from one structure to another.

When a large area is burning simultaneously, the phenomenon known as "fire storm" may develop. As a result of the huge masses of hot air and gases rising from the fire, air is sucked in with great force. Strong winds consequently blow from outside toward the center of the area on fire. The effect is similar to the draft that sucks up a chimney under which a fire is burning, except that it is on a much larger scale.

It should be understood that (1) a fire storm does *not always* accompany a nuclear explosion, and (2) it *could* occur with fires resulting from other causes, such as incendiary attacks or forest fires.

In a subsurface burst, either underwater or underground, the thermal radiation from the exploding bomb will be absorbed almost entirely in the water or by the earth. However, as in the case of an air burst, secondary fires may occur. The rupture of underground gas mains will probably cause fires in a built-up area. On the whole, the fire hazard in an underground explosion will be similar to that after an earthquake.

The effective range of the thermal radiation accompanying a surface explosion will depend on the nature of the terrain. In open terrain or at sea, where there is no protection from the radiant heat, the damage ranges will be as great or greater than those for an air burst. In a built-up area, however, large proportion of the radiation will be obstructed and its spread arrested. Even though few fires may be started by the *radiant* heat from a surface burst there will be many of the secondary type due indirectly to blast damage. Since the outbreak and spread of fires depends on such factors as the type of buildings and their contents, the weather conditions, and the nature of the terrain the fire-damage range will vary greatly. However, it may be expected, in general, that fire will spread to all structures which have suffered at least moderate blast or shock damage.

Reinforced concrete buildings are the most fire resistant, for the concrete protects the steel structural members from the heat. However, if the contents of the building are combustible and continue to burn intensely for some hours, the concrete can crumble and expose the reinforcing steel. This may then be weakened by the heat, and the building may collapse. Because the strength of the steel members decreases markedly at moderately high temperatures, steel-frame buildings of all types are susceptible to serious structural damage by fire.

Brick and masonry buildings with load-bearing walls, if close enough to ground zero, may be destroyed by the blast, and the question of structural damage by fire, then, is not important. However, fire can contribute to the damage independently, by weakening the remaining supports and thus contributing to the collapse of the building, and can add to the over-all destruction by consuming the contents.

Wooden buildings are obviously most susceptible to destruction by fire.

In zones of heavy damage, the fuel tanks of vehicles may rupture and the ignition of the gasoline may cause much fire damage. Thermal radiation may cause superficial damage to tires, paint, and upholstery, but it will not ignite gasoline unless the tank is ruptured.

The Bikini tests indicated that thermal radiation would not be an appreciable factor in producing damage at sea, since the exposed portions of naval vessels are practically fireproof. However, this does not exclude the possibility of secondary fires involving such combustibles as gasoline or explosives where there has been extensive blast damage.

Nuclear Radiation Effects

Nuclear radiations given off by radioactive elements consist of three types: "alpha" particles, "beta" particles, and "gamma" rays. Alpha particles are so large, relatively speaking, that they cannot travel more than one to three inches in air without being stopped, and they certainly cannot penetrate ordinary clothing. Beta particles travel several hundred times farther than alpha particles, but even with their greater speed they cannot penetrate a sheet of aluminum more than a few millimeters in thickness. Alpha and beta radiation danger is slight unless some of it manages to enter the body through any of the body openings, such as the mouth or the nose, or through open wounds.

Gamma rays are a form of electromagnetic radiation, very much like light rays or X-rays. Gamma rays move at the speed of light, 186,000 miles per second, and differ from light only in having a much higher frequency. Gamma rays have the greatest penetrating power of the three forms of nuclear radiation. To stop gamma rays originating from an atomic explosion, it is necessary to use concrete several feet in thickness, or lead. So your greatest radiation danger is from gamma rays.

Nuclear radiations do not affect materials in any visible manner. Thus the essential serviceability of any equipment (ship, vehicle, electronic equipment) is not impaired by this effect. However, radioactive contamination may be a danger to operating personnel.

There are two possible sources of radioactive contamination in a nuclear air burst: first, the neutrons that are flying about during the explosion could cause material close to the burst to become radioactive; and second, the residue from the bomb, the products of the fission and the uranium or plutonium that did not fission, will be present as radioactive dust in the cloud and the fall-out.

The fall-out from an air burst will be less hazardous than that from a surface or subsurface burst. In the surface burst of an H-bomb, for example, the cloud rises rapidly and spreads over hundreds of square miles in the first hours. (See Figure 379.) The prevailing winds carry the radioactive particles along, and although these particles lose some of their radioactivity while in the air, they can still be dangerously radioactive when they eventually reach the ground.

In an underwater burst, structures and equipment may become contaminated due to the radioactive particles that would be deposited by the base surge and the water fall-out. This type of contamination of a vessel or shore activity is serious chiefly because the radiological hazard to personnel may make their operation temporarily dangerous.

The degree to which a particular material or object will become contaminated depends on many variables that cannot be predicted in advance. Nevertheless, two factors have an important bearing on the problems of contamination and decontamination. First, a material with a rough finish is more susceptible to contamination than a smooth one, because the rough finish will give the particles greater surface area to which they can stick. Second, if the material is porous, the radioactive particles can penetrate under the surface and thus become difficult to remove.

Well-painted surfaces are smooth and nonporous and consequently are not so susceptible to contamination. If the painted surface is worn or weathered, however, it becomes relatively rough and porous and radioactive particles can then penetrate more deeply into the material. Similarly, clean smooth metal surfaces are not easily contaminated, but metals are likely to corrode and the corroded parts collect the contamination. Thus, rusty spots on metals, places where paint is chipped, cracked or roughened, and worn surfaces of wood are all areas which will become contaminated. Articles made of porous materials, such as manila line, nets, and canvas are especially susceptible to contamination.

Concrete, unglazed brick, unpainted wood, and asphalt are porous. Buildings or roads constructed of these materials are highly susceptible to contamination. Weathering and wearing will make it even easier for the particles to stick to these surfaces.

The extent of radioactive contamination of a ship will depend on certain external and so-called internal conditions. Among the external conditions which will have some effect are the distance of the ship from surface zero and the amount of time it spends in the base surge. The internal circumstances involve the securing of the ship against atomic attack. If the weather envelope of the ship is intact, with all openings secured, and if the ventilation system has been shut down while passing through the base surge, there should be little contamination below decks. On the other hand, if the base surge should get into the interior of the vessel, especially through the ventilation system, the consequences could be serious.

A secondary factor in determining the extent of contamination topside is the amount of cover available. In its early stages, the base surge is a mist or

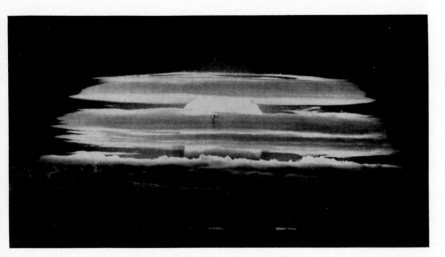

FIG. 379. H-bomb explosion at Bikini.

fog which moves outward and which can envelop everything in its path. However, radioactive fall-out and rain descend vertically, and objects and equipment protected from above will thus be somewhat less contaminated than those having no protection, or which are protected from the sides only.

The water from the fall-out and rain will continue after the base surge has thinned out and will cover all topside surfaces. If there is good drainage, a large amount may run off the vessel and carry away some of the radioactive particles. If any of this water penetrates below decks, it will, of course, contaminate the interior of the ship.

Water waves which might wash over ships will probably tend to *decrease* the contamination rather than increase it. This water will be considerably less radioactive than the water from the base surge or fall-out and therefore it will wash away much of the contamination already deposited. A good part of the contamination from the base surge and fall-out will be deposited after the waves have washed over the ship. Since the surface is wet prior to contamination, the radioactive particles will not stick as firmly as they would to a dry surface. Thus the waves produced by an underwater explosion may help to reduce the amount of contamination. Furthermore, since washing down with fire hoses is one of the most effective methods of removing radioactive contamination, and since there is an abundance of uncontaminated sea water available, the problem of decontaminating the exterior of a ship is not a very difficult one.

A recent development for the protection of ships from radioactive contamination is a sprinkler system which envelops the ship in a fountain of water. (See Figure 380.) Turned on at the first warning of an atomic attack, the system serves to prevent heavy contamination of a ship by "coating" the weather surfaces with a flowing stream of water. The flowing water carries away the radioactive particles as they fall on the ship and at the same time fills in the cracks and crevices so that these particles cannot settle into them.

The sprinkler system can be used at any time to reduce radiation intensities. However, if portions of the ship are heavily contaminated, the sprinkler system may not reduce the radioactivity sufficiently because the water flowing over the surfaces will not have the force to wash away enough of the particles. These areas of heavy contamination can be vigorously hosed down with sea water under pressure. Disposal of waste is not a serious problem, for it can be allowed to run over the side where it is diluted with large quantities of sea water.

Since it is somewhat more difficult to decontaminate the interior of a ship while it is still at sea, it is most important to try to prevent or restrict radioactive contamination below decks. Even some time after the explosion, the interior of a ship could be contaminated by the lack of precautions on the part of personnel whose clothing had become contaminated. Tracking of water below decks from the topside will contribute to the spread of contamination.

The radiological effects of an underground burst will be similar, in many respects, to those of an underwater explosion. A base surge of dust particles, if formed, will contaminate everything in its path.

Although the contamination due to fall-out will be very great in and around the crater area, all structures and equipment in this region will already be made useless by the blast and the thermal radiation, so the radioactive contamination will not be of immediate concern. You will not be able to go into the crater region for days.

While many of the finer dust particles will remain in the air for some time, the larger ones in the fall-out will descend and contaminate the area near the explosion center. Since the particles can be carried by wind, the total area

FIG. 380. The USS *Worcester* steaming under a protective water screen during nuclear defense maneuvers.

covered by the fall-out from an underground explosion may be greater than for an underwater explosion.

There is little difference between the contamination by the base surge and fall-out from an underwater explosion and that from an underground explosion. The only important variation is that while contaminated water will drain from higher to lower regions, and may in some cases largely drain away altogether, contaminated dust will tend to stay where it settles, unless carried away by the wind.

In addition to the spread of contamination by wind, there is the possibility that it may be spread by personnel, unless special precautions are taken. Persons moving out of a contaminated area could carry radioactive particles with them on clothing and other articles. Tracking—especially by vehicles—could also spread contamination. Heavy traffic would press the particles into the road surfaces, making subsequent decontamination difficult, if not impossible.

The radiological contamination from a surface burst will generally have the same characteristics as that from a subsurface explosion. The base surge may be less pronounced in a surface burst, but there will be considerable fall-out.

Unpackaged food which has been in direct contact with the base surge or with the fall-out will be unfit for use. However, if there is no actual contact with the food itself, it will not be affected. Nuclear radiations as such can do no harm to food. It is only when the radioactive particles are on the food and can enter the body that there is real danger. Canned and packaged foods are not affected in any way, and the contents may be considered safe to eat, provided the contamination can be washed off the outside of the container without risk and that the hands are clean.

Drinking water supplies will be safe for use if stored in closed tanks. Care must be taken to prevent the water from becoming contaminated by handling.

Disease

We have said that biological warfare (BW) is the use of living organisms or their toxic products to cause disease or death in humans, animals, or plants. Agents of biological warfare may be selected from several large groups of microorganisms such as bacteria, rickettsiae, viruses, fungi, and protozoa. Representatives of all of these groups are found everywhere in nature, but relatively few members of each are capable of producing disease in man and animals. In most cases, those that produce disease do so by invading the body of the host and growing in its tissues; this is known as "infection." Bacteria do not have to invade the living body to cause their effects. They may produce very potent toxins in food or other organic materials.

Most microorganisms are non-pathogenic; that is, they do not cause diseases. In fact, many of them are helpful to man in the production of antibiotics such as penicillin, in the production of vinegar, in cheese-curing, or in improving soil fertility. Militarily, BW agents can be classified on the basis of persistency, contagion, and potency or virulence. An agent able to resist unfavorable conditions of environment for long periods of time is classed as a *persistent* agent. Most organisms, however, are rather sensitive to changes from their normal living conditions and will be affected adversely by changes in temperature, nutrition, moisture, light, or exposure to air. Such organisms are classed as *nonpersistent* agents. Certain diseases spread rapidly from one person to another by direct or indirect contact. These are known as *contagious* diseases. Others are rarely transmitted by contact. Microorganisms vary considerably in *potency* or *virulence* and consequently in the degree of illness they are able to produce. In fact, the effects of different strains of the same organism may vary from mild infection to fatal illness.

Since man has not yet created a new pathogenic organism, it is probable that an enemy conducting biological warfare would use some form of a known microorganism from one of the groups mentioned above. The bacteria are probably the most numerous of possible organisms. There are many types which can cause infection, and the powerful toxins produced by some could be used alone for biological warfare. Examples of diseases caused by bacteria are typhoid fever, meningitis, and tuberculosis.

Rickettsiae are potent disease-producers in man and animals, and many of them are transmitted by insect bites. Diseases caused by rickettsiae include rocky mountain spotted fever and typhus. The viruses, like rickettsiae, are probably less well distributed than bacteria because of their fastidious growth requirements, but it is known that they can survive for short periods in air. Mumps, smallpox, psittacosis ("parrot fever"), polio, and influenza are examples of virus diseases.

Fungi include such plants as the yeast, molds, and mildews. These organisms are well-known for their ability to cause spoilage of foods and fabrics. Generally speaking, diseases caused by fungi in humans are less severe than those produced by other microorganisms. They usually produce low-grade, mild, and often chronic diseases such as ringworm and athlete's foot. A few fungi are capable of producing serious diseases, such as "lumpy jaw" in cattle and blastomycosis in humans. Several of the plant diseases, such as potato blight, cotton root rot, corn smut, and wheat rust, are caused by fungi.

Finally, there are the single-celled animal-like forms called protozoa, which occur in a great variety of shapes and many of which have complicated life cycles. Examples of protozoal infections of man are amoebic dysentery and malaria.

Toxins, which are poisons produced by certain microorganisms, might be used in biological warfare in two ways: either they could be produced outside the body and introduced into foods or wounds, or the organisms producing them could be used as agents. In the case of botulism, a form of food poisoning, the toxin is produced outside the body and is eaten. The toxin produced by the botulism organism is the most potent known to be produced in nature. It is hundreds of times more poisonous than mustard gas or cyanide and several times more toxic than rattlesnake or cobra venom.

By strict definition, synthetic chemical compounds are not biological agents. They do not have the power to spread their effects beyond the original area of dispersion, but they are easily produced and stored. They are classed with the BW agents because of their importance in destroying food and industrial crops. Among the recently developed compounds are the plant growth regulators and the defoliants. The plant growth regulators may inhibit growth or cause death of the plant at very low concentrations. They also hinder the germination of seeds, and if present in the soil, may prevent establishment of seedlings. Defoliants are chemical compounds which cause trees and shrubs to drop their leaves.

Chemical Poisoning

Chemical warfare (CW) agents, like the BW agents, are used chiefly for their effects on personnel. These agents produce a harmful physiological reaction when applied to the body externally, when breathed, or when taken internally. Most CW agents cause disorganization of the functioning or of the metabolism of the body. The physiological effects of CW agents, such as choking gases, nerve gases, blood gases, and blister gases, vary widely.

Choking gases will cause injury chiefly in the respiratory tract; that is, in the nose, throat, and particularly the lungs. In extreme cases, the membranes swell, the lungs become filled with liquid, and death results from lack of oxygen; thus these gases "choke" an unprotected man.

The nerve gases, or G-agents, effect their results by a radical disturbance of the chemical processes of the nervous system. Briefly, the action is as follows: The operation of the nervous system involves the production and almost simultaneous destruction of a substance called acetylcholine. The inhibition of acetylcholine is normally accomplished through the working of an enzyme known as cholinesterase. In the presence of nerve gases, the cholinesterase does not act and the accumulated acetylcholine causes the symptoms of nerve gas poisoning, which include constriction of the pupils of the eyes, headache, and tightness in the chest.

The blood gases are absorbed in the body and produce their effects by interfering with respiration and other body functions. Some of these agents act by interfering with the utilization of oxygen by the body tissues or the hemoglobin. They also poison the central nervous system. Others interfere with the functioning of the blood and damage the liver and kidneys.

In contrast to the choking gases, the nerve gases, and the blood gases, blister gases are particularly effective because they may attack any part of the body. Whereas the choking gases affect chiefly the lungs, blister gases affect the eyes and all accessible body parts as well as the lungs.

The effects of the class of agents known as "harassing" agents are temporary and usually are not very serious. Vomiting gases, for instance, will cause violent coughing and sneezing, nausea, and vomiting. Tear gases attack the eyes and induce a considerable flow of tears. Militarily, the primary purpose in using a vomiting gas is to force the victim to *remove* his gas mask so that he could then become a casualty of the more deadly agents; the primary purpose in using tear gases is to force the victim to *wear* a mask, thereby reducing his efficiency.

SYMPTOMS FROM NBC ATTACKS

The blast and heat injuries suffered in a nuclear explosion will not differ greatly in character from those caused by ordinary high explosive and incendiary bombs. An important aspect of injuries in nuclear explosions is the combined effects of blast, heat, and nuclear radiation. In this respect, nuclear radiation injury may be a complicating factor.

Blast and Shock Wave Injuries

Injuries caused by blast can be divided into primary, or direct blast injuries, and secondary, or indirect blast or mechanical injuries. Primary blast injuries are those which result from the direct action of the air shock wave on the human body. The amount of blast pressure that the human body can stand is sufficiently great that a "standard" bomb will cause no primary blast injuries; the greater blast power of the H-bombs however, might cause some injuries.

Secondary blast injuries are caused mainly by collapsing buildings, and by timber and other debris flung about by the blast. Persons may also be hurled against stationary objects or thrown to the ground by the high winds accompanying the explosion. The injuries sustained are thus similar to those due to a mechanical accident: bruises, concussions, cuts, fractures, and internal injuries.

At sea the shock wave accompanying an underwater burst will produce various mechanical injuries. The casualties will resemble those caused by more conventional underwater weapons, such as non-contact mines and depth charges, but instead of being localized, they will extend over the entire ship. Fracture of the legs due to the severe jarring of the ship by the underwater shock, may occur. There will also be mechanical injuries resulting from personnel being thrown against fixed objects and structures. Equipment, furniture, boxes, and similar gear, which are not properly secured can act as missiles and cause many injuries.

Hemorrhage and shock frequently are serious complications of blast injuries. The importance of shock cannot be over-emphasized, since it is often the main factor in determining the fate of the patient suffering mechanical injury.

The nuclear bomb does not present anything especially new in respect to the types of blast injuries. Both primary and secondary blast injuries have occurred with ordinary high-explosive attacks. However, with these bombs there will be an enormous number of injuries occurring in a limited area in a very short time.

Burn Injuries

Burns due to a nuclear explosion can be classed as primary burns, which are a direct result of the thermal radiation from the bomb, and secondary burns, which are the result of fires caused by the explosion. From the point of view of their effects on the body and of their treatment, both types of burns appear to be similar to each other and to burns produced in other ways.

Burns are generally classified according to their severity, in terms of the degree (or depth) of the injury. First degree burns cause redness of the skin, they heal without treatment and they leave no scar. Second degree burns are deeper and more severe; they cause blisters, they are slower to heal, and they leave no scars. Third degree burn injuries extend through the skin to the deeper tissues; they heal slowly and may result in scars.

The depth of a burn is not the only factor in determining its severity. The extent of the area of the skin which has been affected is also important. Thus, a first degree burn involving the entire body may be much more serious than a third degree burn of limited area.

As with mechanical injuries, shock is commonly associated with extensive burns. In many instances the occurrence and treatment of shock are important in determining whether the injured person will recover or not. Burns are also subject to infection, and this may have serious consequences. A late and serious complication of extensive burns is anemia.

Flash burns (primary burns) are likely to occur on a large scale as a result of a nuclear explosion in the air or on the surface. About one-third of the energy of fission appears as thermal radiation or radiant heat, and most of it is given off during the first second after the explosion. The high temperatures of the skin produced by this radiation result in burns of exposed personnel. Since thermal radiation travels in straight lines, it burns primarily on the side facing the explosion, but it also produces shadow effects, like sunlight. The burn injuries from such an explosion may vary considerably, since the effects of thermal radiation are modified by distance from ground zero, and by weather, clothing, and shelter.

Temporary blindness resulting from the intense flash of light from a nuclear bomb may occur, but usually this blindness will not last more than half an hour.

Nuclear Radiation Symptoms

There are a number of factors involved in determining nuclear radiation injury: distance, time, protection, type of burst, the size of the bomb, and the area of the body affected. The amount or dosage of immediate nuclear radiation you would receive from an atomic air burst decreases the farther away you are from the explosion. The closer you are, the greater the dosage. In a surface or subsurface burst, if you are exposed, you might also receive a large dosage of radiation from the base surge and the fall-out. These large dosages, if received over the whole body within a short time—24 hours, or less—would be fatal. Smaller dosages received continuously over a longer period of time could also be fatal. Nuclear radiation collects in the body, and if it collects faster than the body can recover from it, the result will finally be the same as if you had received a large dosage in a short time. It must be remembered, too, that the area of the body affected by radiation is also important.

Nuclear radiation dosages are expressed in terms of a unit called the roentgen, which gives an indication of the extent of possible radiation injury to personnel. You can actually take thousands of roentgens of radioactivity over a very small area of body without suffering any ill effects. Generally speaking, if the radiation is received over the whole body at one time, 600 roentgens would be lethal to most persons. In a group of persons receiving 450 roentgens, about half of them would die as a result of the radiation; a dosage of 300 roentgens will be lethal to about 20 percent of the personnel. So taking an average, it can be said that the average lethal dosage is 450 roentgens. When the dosage is 200 roentgens or less, no deaths are expected.

For any dosages of 100 roentgens or more received at one time, the symptoms are the same—nausea and vomiting. These symptoms are the first indication you will get that you have been exposed to nuclear radiation, and they probably will not show up for several hours. When nausea and vomiting do occur, you will probably be checked with a radiac instrument to determine what dosage you have received, and you will be treated accordingly. Depending on the dosage and the individual, other symptoms which occur from a few days to a few weeks are diarrhea, inflammation of the mouth and throat, fever, skin hemorrhages, loss of hair, and loss of weight. However, you will probably be under medical care long before these symptoms appear.

There has been some publicity about *sterility* (the inability to have children) and *impotency* (the inability to perform sexual intercouse), in connection with nuclear radiation. If you were close enough to an atomic explosion to receive a radiation dosage which would make you permanently sterile, that dosage would also be great enough to kill you. You may get enough radiation to make you temporarily sterile, but this condition does not last for long. As to impotency, there is *no* evidence that it can result from nuclear radiation.

Disease Symptoms

Agents of biological warfare may be selected to produce many strategic and certain tactical goals, ranging from a brief but crippling disease to widespread serious illness with many deaths. The effectiveness would depend largely on the agent selected. The basic principles of infection and resistance to infection remain the same whether the disease is spread by natural or artificial means.

The route by which an infecting organism enters the body (portal of entry) may determine whether disease will result. Many microorganisms require a specific portal of entry in order to produce infection, while others are less

exacting and can cause disease when they enter by any of several routes. Th
type of disease may vary depending on the portal of entry. For example, th
tuberculosis organism may cause disease of the lungs if it is inhaled, bu
may cause intestinal disease if it is swallowed. The organisms of gas gangren
may cause no disease if swallowed, but may induce fatal infection if th
enter a wound.

Under natural conditions, diseases of different types enter and leave th
body by specific routes. Diseases of the respiratory tract are usually tran
mitted by droplet infection. The organisms are sprayed into the air durin
talking, sneezing, or coughing, and are of such small particle size that the
remain suspended in the air and may be inhaled, causing infection. Disease
of this group are difficult to control, particularly under crowded condition
The diseases of the intestinal tract result from swallowing of the organism
Contaminated food, water, and milk are the usual carriers. Diseases of th
group may be controlled by strict sanitary measures.

Another means of transmission is by direct contact, such as the physic;
contact which results in venereal disease, or mechanical contact with cor
taminated objects and surfaces. Malaria results from the bite of a mosquit
carrying the malarial parasite; other diseases transmitted by biting insects ar
typhus fever, carried by body lice; rocky mountain spotted fever carried b
ticks; and bubonic plague, which is carried from rat to man by the rat flea.

Infection may be defined as the multiplication of the microorganism withi
the body of a host, with resultant damage to the host. The mere presence c
a disease-producing organism on or in the body of a host does not guarante
that infection will result. In fact, such organisms are frequently present in th
human body for long periods and cause no harm to the person carrying then
The factors which determine whether infection will result from contact be
tween a pathogen and a host are not completely understood, but among thos
which are known to be important are the general state of health of the ind
vidual, his state of immunity, the number of organisms to which he is e
posed, and the pathogenicity of the organisms.

The individual who becomes infected never shows symptoms of the diseas
immediately. The time between the entrance of the microorganism into th
body and the appearance of symptoms (the incubation period) may vary fro
a few hours to several weeks, depending on the nature and the number c
infecting organisms, and the ability of the host to resist. After this perio
comes the acute stage of the disease during which the individual is ver
ill, with symptoms of the particular disease with which he is infected. Durin
this stage, the defense mechanisms of the host are mobilized and the outcom
of the disease depends on whether these are sufficient to repel the infectior
The individual may recover; if not, he may either die or be disabled for yea

ith a chronic infection. The duration of the acute stage varies with the indi-
idual disease as well as the resistance powers of the host.

In the early stages of disease, a few general symptoms usually appear which
idicate that infection has been established. These are *fever, malaise,* and
iflammation.

Fever is an abnormal rise in temperature. The degree of fever varies in
ifferent diseases, but may serve as a rough guide to the severity of the in-
:ction. As a rule, the individual with fever feels quite warm and his skin is
kely to be flushed. The onset of fever may be preceded by a chill which
iuses him to shiver, sometimes violently. Fever, whether preceded by a
iill or not, is usually one of the earliest symptoms of infection and is indica-
ve of illness.

Malaise, another early symptom of infection, is characterized by a vague
:eling of bodily discomfort, weakness, and exhaustion. It may be accom-
anied by nausea, dizziness, loss of appetite, and generalized aches; there
iay be pains in the back, arms, legs, and head. These symptoms may increase
i severity as the disease develops, or they may be overshadowed by other
)ecific symptoms.

Inflammation is a reaction of certain body tissues to injury and is char-
:terized by pain, heat, redness, and swelling. Certain kinds of infection are
idicated by inflammation of the skin, the mucous membranes, or the glands,
; the body defenses are mobilized to combat the invader and seal off the
ifection. Some infections are accompanied by a characteristic eruption or
ish of the skin, by means of which it is often possible to make an early
iagnosis.

The above general symptoms of disease apply to animals as well as to
umans. Deviation in the normal behavior of animals, such as undue drowsi-
ess or restlessness, might also indicate infection, even though the general
·mptoms are either not immediately discernible or are entirely absent. Other
·mptoms which might appear with specific diseases in animals include lame-
ess, diminished milk secretion, ulcers, marked and rapid weight loss, se-
erely lowered reproductive capacity, bloody diarrhea, erosion or eruptions of
ie mucous membranes of the mouth, discharges from the eyes, and hemor-
iages and paralysis.

Plant disease agents attack food, feed, fiber, oil, medicinal, or industrial
rops in a number of ways. They may attack the conducting tissues of plants and
iterfere with water movement, or they may invade the soft tissues of leaves and
)ots. They may inhibit growth, or they may cause lesions, rusts, or galls on
)ecific parts of the plants. In addition, plants may be damaged by insects which
:ed on the leaves and fruits.

The symptoms which indicate that a crop has been attacked or infected will vary with the type of pest or the specific disease. Some of these symptoms might include water-soaked lesions on the foliage; shriveled and blighted kernels; lesions of the leave sheaths and stems; orange-colored pustules on stems and leaves; galls on stems, leaves, buds and ears; mottled and wrinkled leaves; yellowing of leaves and blackening of the veins; and general wilting and rotting.

Symptoms Produced by CW Agents

There is a wide variation of reaction to the toxic CW agents—even to those of similar physiological classifications. For example, among the blister gases distilled mustard causes no immediate sensation on the skin and causes no effect for several hours or, even, in a few cases, for ten to twelve days. On the contrary, lewisite produces an immediate burning sensation on the skin upon contact, and blistering in about half an hour. None of the other blister gases are as delayed as distilled mustard in their effects. The nerve gases and blood gases, with the single exception of arsine, are characterized by the great rapidity with which they act. First aid measures, such as administering anti dotes, must be carried out within two minutes after lethal dosages of these gases have been absorbed if death is to be averted. The vomiting gases also exert their effects within a short time after being inhaled and are effective only by inhalation.

Since some CW agents are fast-acting, any measures to counter their effect must be taken quickly; if possible, even before symptoms of chemical poison ing appear. A knowledge of these symptoms, however, will help you to ad minister self-aid while you are waiting for medical aid.

Nerve gases are quick killers. Very small amounts result in dimmed vision headache, dizziness, and nausea. Upon entering your body through the nose skin, or mouth, nerve gases interfere with breathing and may cause convul sions, paralysis, and death. The first effect is the contraction of the eye pupil to pinpoint size, thus dimming the vision. This effect is a vital tip-off and is a warning not to be ignored. This is usually followed by a running nose nausea, stomach cramps, rapid breathing, tightness of the chest, and twitching muscles.

When a large amount of a *blood gas* is inhaled, the main symptoms are rapid breathing followed by violent convulsions. A mild exposure may pro duce headache, dizziness, and nausea. Blood gases will either cause a speedy death, or else complete recovery will probably take place within a few hours

Blister gases cause blisters of the skin, and the result can be far worse than a severe case of sunburn. These agents, in either liquid or vapor form, irri tate and blister any part of your body that they touch, and can be effective even in small amounts. A drop the size of a pinhead will produce a blister the size of a quarter. These gases are more effective in hot weather than in cold eather, and they first affect the moist parts of the body, such as the bend of ms and knees, the armpits, and the crotch. If you are exposed to blister gas, othing will happen immediately. One to several hours will pass before your kin starts to turn red, and it will be hours or even days later before the listers appear. However, the damage is done during the first few minutes of xposure. That is why speed in administering self-aid is essential.

The damage to the eyes may be worse than the effects on the skin. Gases, ven liquids, may only mildly irritate the eyes at first, or there may be no pain t all. In a few hours, however, your eyes will smart, become inflamed, and be ensitive to light. Tears and great pain will follow, and permanent injury may esult. Some blister gases will cause immediate pain to the eyes. If breathed ato your lungs, blister gases will inflame the throat and windpipe and will roduce a harsh cough. In serious exposure this may result in pneumonia and eath.

As the name implies, *choking gases* cause a choking effect by attacking the ungs, If large amounts enter the lungs, they will became filled with liquid nd death may result from a lack of oxygen.

The general symptoms of *vomiting gas* poisoning include a sense of full-ess in the nose, a severe headache, intense burning in the throat, and tight-ess and pain in the chest. These are followed by uncontrollable coughing, iolent sneezing, nausea, and finally vomiting.

The *tear gases* are the least toxic of the war gases. The vapors of tear gases roduce sharp, irritating pain in the eyes, resulting in an abundant flow of ears. There is usually no permanent damage to the eyes, and the effects wear ff quickly. For a short time you may not be able to see.

INDIVIDUAL PROTECTION IN NBC WARFARE

Protection of personnel in NBC warfare involves both collective and indi-idual measures. Collective protection of civilians is prescribed by the Federal Civil Defense Administration. The collective protection of military personnel ; the responsibility of the military services. Instructions concerning such roup protection have been issued by each of these organizations.

Individual protection is of more immediate concern, for what each indi-idual does in the first few moments after an NBC attack may determine /hether or not he will survive. The most important items to the individual re cover and shelters, clothing, food and drink, and self-aid against NBC gents and their effects.

Cover and Shelters

If there is sufficient warning in advance of an attack, make for the best helter that is available, as quickly as possible. If you are on military duty, our action of course must be determined by the circumstances existing at the time. In general, this will be the same as that prescribed for an attack by ordinary high explosive bombs. At the sound of the alarm, get your protective mask ready and proceed to your station or to a shelter as ordered. If you are a civilian, proceed to the nearest area designated as a shelter by Civil Defense authorities. Remain there until the "all clear" signal is given.

During a nuclear attack ashore, in the absence of specially constructed shelters you can get some protection in a foxhole, a dugout, or in the lowest floor or basement of a reinforced concrete or strong, steel-framed building. Generally, the safest place is in the basement, near walls; the next best place is on the lowest floor in an interior room, passage or hall, away from windows, and, if possible, near a supporting column. Avoid wooden buildings, if at all possible; if you have no choice, take shelter under a table or bed rather than to go out into the open. If you have time, draw the shades and blinds to keep out most of the heat from the blast and to help shield you from broken window glass. Tunnels, storm drains, and subways provide effective shelter except in the case of a nearby underground explosion.

In the event of a surprise attack, no matter where you are, out in the open on the deck of a ship, in a ship compartment, out in the open ashore, or inside a building, drop to a prone position, face down, in a doorway or against a bulkhead or wall. If you have a protective mask with you, put it on. Otherwise, hold or tie a handkerchief over your mouth and nose. Cover yourself with anything on hand, making especially sure to cover the exposed portions of the skin such as the face, neck, and hands. If this can be done within a second of seeing the bright light of a nuclear explosion, some of the heat radiation may be avoided. Ducking under a table, desk or bench indoors, or into a trench, ditch or vehicle outdoors, with the face away from the light, will provide added protection.

If you can reach some kind of shelter within a second, you might possibly avoid about half of the immediate nuclear radiation. Shielding from nuclear radiation requires a considerable thickness of material, and this is not generally available in the open. Besides, *gamma* radiation is scattered by air molecules, so that a shield in front of you does not provide complete protection shielding from *all directions* is necessary. (See Figures 381 and 382.) By dropping to the ground or deck, you may secure some shielding from the terrain, buildings, or surrounding structures and equipment. However, since radiations continue to reach the earth from the resulting cloud for a short time as it rises, the protection will be only partial.

Stay down for at least 10 seconds or longer if heavy objects such as large pieces of superstructure, parts of roofs, or other heavy debris are still falling. This will allow time for the blast wave to pass and lessen the danger from flying objects. Hold tight to some solid object.

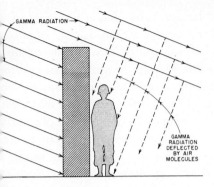

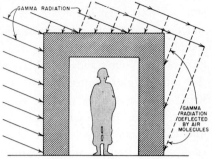

FIG. 381. Gamma radiation is scattered by air molecules; a shield in front does not provide complete protection.

FIG. 382. Shielding from *all* directions is necessary for complete protection from gamma rays.

Although you may feel the effects of blast and shock before you fully realize that a subsurface nuclear explosion has occurred, you may still have time to obtain some shelter from the base surge and fall-out. You should remember that the base surge is like a fog or mist, and envelops everything over which it passes. Consequently, adequate shelter can be obtained only in closed space which the radioactive fog cannot penetrate. The fall-out, on the other hand, descends almost vertically, and protection against it is much easier to obtain. If you can't find shelter from both base surge and fall-out, then you should at least seek protection from the fall-out.

The gas clouds of a CW attack and the aerosol sprays carrying BW agents can be as enveloping and penetrating as radioactive fog; consequently, adequate shelters against these must be gas-proof and leak-proof.

Clothing

Clothing of any kind will offer partial protection against some of the effects of an atomic explosion. Clothing is no protection against the blast effects of an atomic bomb and the resulting flying debris and falling buildings, but any type of clothing will help reduce the effects of the terrific heat that is given off. It will even help to keep the radioactive dust, mist, fog, or spray from coming into actual contact with your skin.

Military uniforms and civilian clothing both provide good protection against the heat given off at the time of an atomic explosion. Heavy clothing is better than thin material; light colors are better than dark. Light colored materials reflect more of the thermal radiation, while dark colored clothes tend to absorb it. Thus, dark colored clothes are more likely to scorch and to cause burns on the skin beneath them, especially where they fit tightly. Loose garments are desirable because they leave an insulating airspace between the material and the skin.

Thermal radiation has the greatest damage range. So, in the event of an atomic attack, even if you are beyond the zone of serious damage from blast and from immediate nuclear radiation, you should make sure that you are completely covered by clothing as possible in order to protect yourself from flash burns. Your standard military clothing, combat fatigues, or any clothing that can be tightly buttoned at the neck and tied at the wrists and ankles with string will serve very well. It will also offer some protection against BW agents. If you are wearing combat boots, stuff the bottoms of your trousers into your boots. Any form of gloves available will protect your hands. possible, use long gloves that will overlap your sleeves. Complete the outfit by wearing a protective mask, if available, and any type of head covering preferably tight fitting. Make sure that the facepiece of the mask fits proper against the skin.

For greater protection against BW agents, a more effective combination of ordinary clothing consists of two layers of clothing (underwear and coveralls) with gloves, socks, shoes, hood, and mask. The hood should cover the head, face, and neck and have openings for the eyes.

Ordinary clothing offers little protection against the penetration of war gases either in the form of vapor or liquid.

In order to prevent spreading of contamination, extreme caution must be exercised in removing clothing that may be contaminated. Such clothing should either be buried or be decontaminated by washing with soap and water and then dried in the sun.

Food

If you must remain in a contaminated area for some time, eat only food approved by medical authorities. If this is not possible, any foods or field rations with the outer wrappers intact, especially those in cans and glass containers, can be considered safe *if* you decontaminate the outside before you use them. If you suspect radiological contamination, wash the containers with soap and water; if they are likely to be contaminated with biological or chemical agents, wash the outside with a chlorine solution (a handful of bleach in a half-gallon of water). Unpackaged foods or those whose packaging has been torn or opened are considered unsafe. Don't use these without the approval of medical authorities. Bury food which cannot be decontaminated.

Self-aid

If you should sustain injuries or become contaminated with radiological, biological, or chemical agents during an attack, you can increase your chances of survival by immediately administering certain self-aid measures.

The blast and heat injuries from an atomic explosion are treated in the ame manner as those resulting from high explosive bombs, incendiary weapons, and mechanical accidents. Fractures, concussions, lacerations, contusions, emorrhages, and burns are treated in accordance with standard self-aid and rst-aid measures.

There is nothing that needs to be done immediately for nuclear radiation ckness. If there is any possibility that you have received a dosage of radiaon, you will be checked by medical personnel and treated accordingly. By king off your clothes you may remove most of the contamination, since uter clothing will serve as a trap for most radioactive particles. Within a ontaminated area, do *not* eat, drink, smoke, chew gum, or do anything which :quires putting your hand to your mouth. This will help prevent the entry f radioactive particles into your body. Do not stir up dust or step into pudles. Do not brush against shrubbery and trees or touch buildings, structures, nd objects in the contaminated area. Do *not* pick up "souvenirs."

If directed, you will proceed to a personnel decontamination station where ou will discard your clothing and equipment and take a shower, using plenty f soap and warm water. In washing, pay close attention to the hairy parts of our body, body creases, and fingernails, where dirt tends to gather. If a apply of water is lacking, wiping yourself with any *clean* material at hand, ach as paper, straw, grass, leaves, or sand will remove some of the radioactive ontamination from the skin. But the material used for wiping must be unontaminated or it may do more harm than good. Take care to prevent tearing ae skin or forcing contamination into wounds, body openings, or skin folds.

Do not hesitate to give first-aid to anyone else who has received a dosage f radiation; it is *not* contagious and he will *not* be sufficiently radioactive ɔ affect you.

Since symptoms caused by BW agents may not appear for several days, you nay not be aware that a BW attack has occurred. However, should you suspect aat BW contamination has taken place, observe the basic principles of preentive medicine, which include individual hygiene, sanitation, and physical heck-ups. Scrub all areas of your living quarters and clean all household and ersonal effects. Report any illness to medical authorities immediately.

If there is a possibility that you have been contaminated by BW agents, arefully remove your clothes to avoid spreading any contamination, and take thorough soap and water shower as soon as possible. Pay careful attention to our face and hands. Use a fingernail brush to remove dirt under your nails. ¡rush your teeth and gums frequently, as well as the roof of your mouth and our tongue. If you are unable to take a shower, use some means such as oil og, to seal the germs to the clothes. Change your clothes, and at the first pportunity boil and scrub contaminated clothing.

The speed with which the deadly effects of some CW agents take place will require you to take immediate self-aid measures. At the first signs o symptoms of CW attack, you should put on a protective mask if one is avail able.

You may have to rely on whatever you have on hand to remove war gase from your skin, eyes, or equipment. If liquid nerve or blister gases touch an part of your body, wash the effected parts as fast as you can. If soap an water or the ointments provided for military personnel are not available, us anything on hand—mud, oil, urine, etc. It will be better than nothing.

Generally, the following standard procedures must be used to preven injury from liquid nerve or blister gases:

1. Decontaminate the eyes and face by washing with water.
2. Put on your mask if you have been provided with one.
3. Rinse any other contaminated areas with water.
4. Remove contaminated clothing as quickly as possible.
5. Blot off any remaining liquid agent; use a pinch-blot action rather tha a wiping action, to avoid spreading the contamination.
6. If you have been provided with protective ointment, apply as directed— to remove blister gases only.
7. If you have been supplied an atropine injection device, use it *only* if th effects of nerve gases begin.

Besides masking, the chief action you need to take against blood gases an choking gases is to avoid unnecessary movements; rest is essential. If yo have received a large dose of blood gas, you may need medical aid.

In the case of vomiting gas contamination, wear the mask, lifting it briefl from the face only to permit vomiting or to drain saliva from the facepiece Carry on your duties as vigorously as possible; this will help to lessen an shorten the symptoms.

If tear gases have been released, put on the mask and keep your eyes ope as much as possible. When it is safe to remove the mask, blot away the tears but do not rub your eyes; face the wind and loosen your clothing.

Remember that soap and water are still the best means of removing N W BW, or CW contamination.

Most of these self-aid measures can be carried out by both military an civilian personnel. Some of them require special equipment or medicatio available only to military personnel. Specific instructions relating to the use o such items can be found in publications issued by the military services.

The United States Naval Aviation Survival Training Program

The United States Naval Aviation
Survival Training Program

In the early days of World War II Survival Training consisted essentially of land survival training and water survival training. During the course of the war the value of such training became more and more apparent and the scope was broadened to include all subjects that pertained to the safety and survival of an airman after he had abandoned his plane, whether on land or sea. At the close of the war the various phases of survival training were being organized and consolidated into an integrated training program throughout Naval Aviation. These included the following broad categories: Land Survival, Water Survival, Survival Equipment, Personnel Health and First Aid, Ditching and Bailing-out Procedures, and Air-Sea Rescue. The following program is concerned primarily with the Land Survival phase of training and secondarily with Water Survival and Emergency Equipment in so far as they are all interrelated and cannot be treated wholly independently of one another.

Land Survival Training falls naturally into two phases of training:

1. General or primary survival training which consists of basic skills that can be utilized and adapted anywhere.

2. Special area or advanced base survival training which consists of specific knowledge and skills particularly applicable to special areas of the world.

Courses in basic survival training were conducted in the United States, and the training syllabi presented here illustrate the type of training given. The syllabi for special area training are based on the information and experience derived during World War II, and though never put into actual operation are recommended as part of the training program for the future.

Basic Training

(In operation during World War II)

PRE-FLIGHT TRAINING

The United States Naval Aviation Survival Training Program has been designed to impart a wide range of knowledge and experience to large groups of men in a limited time. In a training program it is impossible for great numbers of men actually to live off the land, but it is possible to teach the fundamentals of how to do it and to show how these fundamental principles can be applied to any region of the world.

The programs operated in the U. S. Navy Pre-Flight Schools were designed to teach basic skills and principles of outdoor living that are a necessary background of knowledge and experience for surviving under adverse conditions. They also served as a preliminary training, necessary as a prerequisite for later, more specialized instruction.

This Pre-Flight Training was accomplished by means of:

1. The use and study of this manual as a basic text
2. Illustrated classroom lectures
3. Field trips planned to impart experience or to simulate emergency situations
4. Demonstration areas

CLASSROOM LECTURES

The classroom lectures include Chapters I, III, IV, V, VIII, and IX. Information in Chapters II, VI and VII can be adequately covered on the field trips. Instructors should closely coordinate classroom instruction with the field work. Wherever possible the classroom lectures should be given by officers who instruct in the field. Reading assignments should be made before each lecture period, and the instructor should confine his discussion to emphasizing and clarifying the most important information and answering questions. Colored slides, colored movies and demonstrations have been prepared for each lecture to emphasize important information and technics and to add interest and inspiration.

The following plan is recommended but may not always be practical because of time. However, where the complete lecture and hiking plan is not possible at the Pre-Flight Schools every effort should be made to cover the omitted material at subsequent stages of training.

· LECTURE I

ASSIGNED READING: Chapter I—General Survival Hints
The instructor should emphasize:
1. The importance of being prepared for an emergency and thinking a situation through
2. Individual emergency equipment
3. How to search intelligently for food
4. The association of plants and animals and their distribution throughout the world
5. Careful study and explanation of World Map showing land areas where living off the land is essentially the same

LECTURE II

ASSIGNED READING: Chapter III—Water
The instructor should emphasize:
1. Importance of water and its use in an emergency
2. Methods of locating water
3. Principle of the water table
4. Plants as a source of water
5. Water-borne diseases

LECTURE III

ASSIGNED READING: Chapter IV—Wild Plant Food
The instructor should emphasize:
1. General information concerning plant food
2. The importance of plant habitats in locating plant food
3. The similarity of species of plants of the same group (Genus)
4. The value of knowing a few edible plants of the U.S. found elsewhere in the world
5. The importance of learning food plants of an area from natives or authorities before an emergency arises

LECTURE IV

ASSIGNED READING: Chapter V—Wild Animal Food
The instructor should emphasize:
1. That a great variety of wild, easily available foods are to be found in or near streams, lakes and rivers
2. That the small forms of life such as insects, clams and crustaceans are in general the most available source of animal food
3. Fishing methods and technics

FIG. 311. Lay Out Cross Country Hikes so as to Encounter Natural Obstacles

4. Why all freshwater food should be thoroughly cooked
5. That birds and mammals have definite habits that can be utilized in their capture
6. Trapping and stalking principles

LECTURE V

ASSIGNED READING: Chapter VIII—Survival in Special Areas (Survival at Sea and Along the Seashore)

The instructor should emphasize:

1. How to conserve energy on a life raft
2. The danger of drinking sea water
3. Methods of getting fresh water at sea
4. The importance of knowing how to fish and how to improvise fishing tackle (Demonstrate)
5. That animal seashore food is quite similar in appearance and habitat throughout the world
6. That poisonous seashore foods are relatively few and rather easily identified

LECTURE VI

ASSIGNED READING: Chapter VIII—Survival in Special Areas (The Far North and Tropical Plant Foods)

The instructor should emphasize:

1. That living off the land in the north is difficult but there are few serious diseases to worry about
2. Animal foods that will be found in the far north
3. That there are no seriously poisonous plants in the far north with the possible exception of the Amanita and water hemlock.
4. Importance of eating fat in a cold climate
5. Palms as an excellent source of emergency foods
6. That many tropical plants must be specifically identified to be eaten with safety, and therefore the cadet should familiarize himself with some of the more common ones

LECTURE VII

ASSIGNED READING: Chapter IX—Environmental Hazards

The instructor should emphasize:

1. Physical effects of heat—precautions
2. Physical effects of cold—precautions
3. The great danger of malaria in the tropics
4. Methods of avoiding insect-transmitted diseases
5. General information to dispel imaginary fears of poisonous snakes

6. What to do in case of snake bite
7. That some aquatic animals can be seriously dangerous, but as a rule such dangers can be rather easily avoided
8. That poisonous plants are not generally a serious hazard, and a general knowledge of American species will be of help in recognizing such plants anywhere in the world
9. Instructions on how to deal and live with native people

FIELD TRIPS

The purpose of the field trips is to impart the information, technics and experiences deemed necessary for surviving in wilderness areas.

It is not practical to follow a hard and fast syllabus in conducting survival hikes or field trips as the information and technics to be included in any one field period will vary with the season of the year, topography, vegetation, weather conditions, and such local factors as length of instruction period, and distance to suitable terrain.

This manual contains the basic information and technics that should be worked into the trips. Use it as a guide and reference in planning and executing field trips.

The success of these hikes and the value of them to the cadets will thus, to a large extent, depend upon how thoroughly they are conceived, arranged and organized by the officers conducting the Survival Program at each Pre-Flight School.

Several proposed field trips are included in this syllabus to serve as a guide. It is not expected that they can be rigidly followed and details of instruction and procedure have purposely been omitted. Neither have they been designed for a definite time period. Officers will have to experiment and fit into each field trip as much information and as many technics as possible.

Take advantage of all natural facilities at the station, such as streams, swamps, rough and wooded country or cliffs, in planning the field exercises.

Each field trip should be planned to include a maximum of physical exercise with specific instruction on some phase of survival. A definite subject such as orientation methods, shelter construction, fire-making, etc., should serve as a basis for each field trip and if the hike is properly planned and conducted, much additional information can be imparted en route. For example, edible plants and animals should be continuously pointed out on all field trips. Poison ivy, poison oak and poison sumac should be noted and their relationship to similar plants in the tropics made clear to the cadets. Every possible phase of survival should be integrated into each field trip so that previously imparted information and technics are repeated. In this way the cadets constantly learn new information and at the same time review things taught on earlier hikes.

Wherever and whenever possible the cadet should be allowed to learn by doing. In many cases demonstrations by the officer-in-charge will have to suffice, but it is most important that the cadet be put *on his own,* as much and as often as possible.

GENERAL INSTRUCTIONS FOR FIELD TRIPS

1. At least three officers well qualified in woodcraft and survival technics should accompany a battalion on every hike.
2. Platoon officers should accompany their platoons on the field trips and act as instructors.
3. For demonstrations, the battalion should be broken down into platoons and the demonstrations be conducted by the platoon officers. The survival officers should check and assist the platoon officers in these demonstrations.
4. Whenever possible each cadet should be allowed to participate as an individual; so that he has actual experiences sighting a compass, building a fire, cooking a meal, etc. When this is not practical, use the smallest unit possible so that a maximum number of men participate.
5. Plan all field trips using topographic or aerial maps as a basis. (Pages 262-263.)
6. When issuing equipment, have it available so there is no delay, and make each cadet, as well as officers, responsible for its safe return.
7. Use K rations for all meals. Acquaint cadets with the use of D ration and pemmican.
8. Carry packs, canteens, knives, rations and first-aid kits on field trips.
9. Be prepared for all weather and carry through an outdoor exercise regardless of weather conditions.
10. Inform cadets as to type of clothing to be worn and extra clothing to be carried.
11. Advise cadets to read material in manual relating to field trip.
12. Caution cadets concerning property rights.
13. Caution cadets concerning any poisonous snakes, plants or other natural hazards in the area.
14. Explain the purpose of each field trip and any details of procedure.
15. Instruct and question cadets at every opportunity en route and during stops.

Suggested Field Trips

HIKE I—ORIENTATION AND TRAVELING

Purpose

To instruct cadets in the use of a compass in densely wooded or jungle country, methods of orienting themselves, and technics of traveling in such country. (See Figure 311.)

Procedure

1. Hike battalion to rough wooded area.
2. Explain how to hike in wooded country.
3. Supply each cadet with an aerial map and compass, and hike by platoons or smaller units across country on a given course to a definite objective. Follow compass readings regardless of obstacles.
4. Hike back to starting point using compass to circumvent swamps, ridges, river bends or other obstacles. Average compass readings to maintain course. Explain use of a baseline.
5. Point out and explain the use of landmarks, sun, and bushmarks in keeping a course. Emphasize the value of constant observation.
6. Demonstrate method of telling direction with a watch.
7. Suggestions for similar but more advanced hikes:
    (a) If time and circumstances permit, a hike may be arranged for a small number of hold-over cadets.
    (b) Drop cadets from a bus or truck in small groups. Supply them with a topographic map and compass. Locate their position on a map and instruct them to set a course for the base ten miles away. Select rough country for the hike. Instead of a direct course to the base, several bearings intersecting various landmarks on the map can be given. (See pages 262-263.)
8. A still more difficult test can be arranged by placing previously blindfolded cadets at an unfamiliar point with map and compass. Do not orient them, but instruct them to hike until they can recognize a landmark on the map, and then set a course for the station.

Reference—Chapter II.

HIKE II—WILD FOODS AND WATER

Purpose

To acquaint cadets with the use of wild edible plants, to give them general instructions on how to look for plant and animal food, and to show technics of finding and obtaining drinking water. (Figures 313, 314 and 323.)

Procedure

1. Officers in charge of program should, in prior reconnaissance, locate areas where particular species of wild food plants are abundant. This will prevent loss of time and give a definite destination for the hike. One such selected area should be in the vicinity of a creek, river, lake or shore where edible water plants grow. When particular berries, fruits, or nuts are in season the hike should be planned to pass through regions where these wild foods are found.

2. Demonstrate methods of searching for food emphasizing observation, the value of habitat recognition, and plant and animal indicators.

   (a) At least some widely distributed food plants found both in the vicinity and in other parts of the world should be pointed out. (See pages 61-74)

   (b) Demonstrate with the proper plants that leaves, sap, stems, buds, roots and fruits are all potential food sources.

   (c) Let the cadets taste and eat the wild foods, but don't encourage this if demonstration plants are scarce.

3. Show cadets where to look for mussels, crayfish, salamanders, frogs, water snakes and insect grubs.

4. Instruct cadets in methods of obtaining water. One or more of the following can usually be demonstrated.

   (a) How to tell whether water from streams is relatively safe to drink.

   (b) Water from grape and other vines.

   (c) Water from desert plants.

   (d) Water along the seashore and low river flood plains (digging).

   (e) Water reservoirs—plants.

   (f) Demonstrate how the presence of certain plants and animals indicates the nearness of water.

5. Include information on boiling, filtering and deodorizing water when practical to do so.

6. Additional compass and orientation practice can easily be worked into such a hike.

References—Chapters III, IV and V.

HIKE III—SHELTER

Purpose

To demonstrate methods of making shelters and beds.

Procedure

1. Various types of overnight shelters, beds, reflector fires and fireplaces should be constructed at a given place and used for demonstration purposes.

N.

296°   CAMP AND   249°
DEMONSTRATION
AREA

ROAD BASE LINE

3

170°

310°

341°

16°

34°

Method of Planning Field Trips

1 —— Instruction hike in the use of map and compass.

2 —— Hike to base from a drop-off point.

3 —— Night hike from camp area.

2. Hike battalion to demonstration area, pointing out any natural shelters encountered en route.

3. Explain construction of shelters, beds, and fireplaces, and demonstrate various types of shelter, and signal fires.

4. Demonstrate how a parachute can be used as a tent, hammock, sleeping bag, and pack sack.

5. Demonstrate how a fire should be made with matches in dry and wet weather, then let platoons compete. Make certain that all fires are thoroughly extinguished.

6. On return hike let each platoon select a camp site; considering their selection in regard to one limiting factor that must be met in order to get a good night's sleep. That is: Instruct one platoon to select a site because it would be relatively free of mosquitoes, another one to make a selection with regard to protection from cold, or because bedding or shelter material is at hand, or because drinking water is available. Explain to the platoon why their selection is good or bad.

References—Chapter VI, pages 106-108; Chapter VII; Chapter IX, pages 187-188.

HIKE IV—FIREMAKING AND COOKING

Purpose

To give cadets the experience of making a fire and cooking a meal.

Procedure

1. Issue available equipment deemed necessary for hike and carry food for one meal. If possible take foods that can be cooked without cooking utensils, as would be the case with most wild foods utilized in an emergency.

2. Hike to demonstration area. Let each cadet make a fire and roast a half fowl and bake potatoes in mud or stone-lined pit ovens. Cook a few samples of wild foods, such as cattail roots, arrowhead bulbs or potherbs.

3. If green bamboo, coconut shells or sea shells can be obtained, demonstrate cooking in these utensils.

4. While food is cooking, point out and gather various tinders which can be used to start a fire with a lens from a flashlight, camera or binoculars. Demonstrate how such a fire is made. At a given signal, let several cadets from each platoon produce blazing tinder.

5. Construct various types of cooking fires for demonstration purposes.

Reference—Chapter VI.

FIG. 313. Cadets Sample the Starchy Root of the Cattail. Edible Plants Should Be Pointed Out on All Hikes.

FIG. 314. Demonstrating How Water Can Be Obtained from a Vine

HIKE V—CLIMBING TECHNICS
(A)—(ROPE WORK)

Purpose

To instruct the cadets in rope technics necessary for getting out of rough, canyon, or mountainous country, and useful in abandoning ship. (Figure 324.)

Procedure

1. Hike to cliff, quarry, canyon or high wall where there is a steep or perpendicular drop of 20 or 30 feet.
2. Divide the battalion into platoons and demonstrate rappelling and climbing in a Spanish bowline.
3. Let each cadet rappell down the drop.
4. Instruct cadets concerning the dangers and necessary precautions that must be observed in rock climbing.
5. Demonstrate how a rope can be made from parachute shroud lines.
6. Demonstrate and practice useful knots.

Reference—Chapter II, pages 31-37.

HIKE V(B)—(TREE CLIMBING)

Purpose

To instruct the cadets in the various methods of climbing trees.

Procedure

1. Hike to wooded area.
2. Platoon officers demonstrate the following methods of climbing trees.
   (a) Shinnying.
   (b) Use of low limbs or vines.
   (c) Use of a rope.
   (d) Native method for climbing palms.
3. Demonstrate precautions that should be taken when climbing trees.
4. At given signal let each cadet attempt to climb a tree to a height of 25 ft. and take a compass reading on a distant landmark.
5. Order cadets to change trees and repeat performance.

Reference—Chapter II, pages 38-39.

HIKE VI—TRAVEL HAZARDS
(A) (RAFT CONSTRUCTION)

Purpose

To demonstrate construction of a raft and impart information and give practical instruction on inland water travel.

Procedure

1. Hike battalion along wooded creek or river bottom, fording the stream at several points. Demonstrate technics of fording streams under various water conditions.

2. Point out trees whose bark can be used for cord or lashing.

3. Using logs previously gathered for the purpose, construct a raft with bark lashing.

4. Practice poling the raft and give instructions on inland water travel.

References—Chapter II, pages 17-37; Chapter IV, pages 104-105.

HIKE VI(B)—(SWIMMING IN SURF AND DEEP OR SHALLOW RAPIDS)

Purpose

To give cadets the experience of swimming in swift or rough water such as is likely to be encountered in traveling any distance back to a base.

Note

This exercise must be carried out with careful supervision and caution.

Procedure

1. When rapids are conveniently close, demonstrate how to swim down shallow and deep rapids. Demonstrate how to swim in a current. Let each cadet practice when possible. Swim in clothes.

2. If near the seashore, locate a rip current and show cadets how to swim out of it. Let them practice this and practice going in and out through a moderate surf.

3. If there are lakes, ponds, or lagoons containing aquatic vegetation, plan an exercise to acquaint cadets with methods of swimming through such water. Don't avoid mud.

Reference—Chapter II, pages 20-28.

HIKE VI(C)—(TRAVELING THROUGH SWAMPS, BOGS OR QUICKSAND)

Purpose

To eliminate fear of these hazards by showing cadets what they can do when such hazards are encountered.

Note

The greatest value of this exercise and the preceding one is the confidence a cadet attains from the experience.

Procedure

1. If a swamp, bog, or quicksand is located near the base, plan a hike to this area and show the cadets how to swim or work their way through the mud, water and vegetation. Explain and demonstrate what to do if caught in a bog.

2. Take ropes along to encourage those who are poor swimmers, and instruct men to wear fatigue clothes

3. See that each cadet actually goes through the exercise

FIG. 315. Instructing Cadets Concerning the Poisonous Snakes Found Near the Base

4. If there is no treacherous bog or sand, hike the cadets through several miles of swamp or marsh land or along a river bottom. Follow a compass bearing, and don't detour natural obstacles.

5. Plan a platoon race over part of the distance.

6. Explain possible dangers from snakes, crocodiles, leeches and flukes that might be encountered in such places in other parts of the world.

References—Chapter II, pages 28-31; Chapter IX, pages 199-213.

HIKE VI(D)—(NIGHT HIKE)

Purpose

To instruct the cadets how to travel alone at night in unfamiliar country using a map and compass. (See Figure 321.)

Procedure

1. Map a route that will intersect wooded and open country, and if possible, include a stream, swamp, or ridge. It is well to have each change of course begin and end with a definite landmark.

2. Issue compasses to each cadet and maps to at least every five men.

3. Do not use lights except when absolutely necessary.

4. Plan the route so several different bearings must be followed.

5. When following one of these bearings, use only stars and skyline to keep the course, and do not use compass after once determining the direction of travel except occasionally to check bearing.

6. Point out the Big and Little Dipper, North Star and any constellations that may be of interest. Show cadets how to keep a course using compass and stars in combination.

7. Emphasize traveling quietly. This can be demonstrated by starting half of the men hiking toward the other half from the end of the course. Let these men stop and ambush oncoming ones.

8. Wear mosquito head nets for part of the hike, or if necessary, for the entire hike.

9. In rough country a hike of three or four miles will be sufficient. (See pages 262-263)

Reference—Chapter II, pages 9-17.

HIKE VII—TRAPPING AND FISHING

Purpose

To acquaint cadets with the principles of stalking and to demonstrate the construction of a few simple snares, fishing lines and hooks. (Figure 325.)

Procedure

1. At demonstration area explain construction and use of hanging snares, bird snares and deadfalls.

FIG. 316. Training Equipment for One Man.

FIG. 317. Equipment Should Be Stored so as to Be Quickly Available and Easily Checked

2. Point out animal signs such as: tracks, feces, feeding areas and beds that indicate where to hunt or trap.
3. On an overnight hike set a few rabbit snares.
4. Demonstrate how fishing lines can be made from bark. Fashion make-shift hooks and where possible allow cadets to fish with lines and hooks of their own construction.

References—Chapter V; Chapter VIII, pages 136-138.

HIKE VIII—OVERNIGHT HIKE

Purpose

To give cadets practical camping experience.

Note

Two or more overnight hikes or camping trips are strongly recommended, and where possible, should wind up the instruction period, affording both a review and a chance to impart additional experiences. (Figure 320.)

Procedure

1. It is suggested that overnight trips be planned on week-ends and whenever there is a period of inactivity following completion of the Pre-Flight Training, such as occurs when cadets are held over awaiting future assignment.
2. Issue K rations and complete equipment.
3. Select a suitable campsite as a destination. It should be a clearing near a body of water and make certain that suitable drinking water is available, or is carried along.
4. Hike to camping area and prepare camp, beds and evening meal.
5. Conduct a two-hour night hike. (See pages 262-263.)
6. Prepare breakfast.
7. Hike in small units to a designated area, using maps and compass.
8. Follow compass bearing back to base. If time and facilities are available incorporate the following exercises.
   (a) Practice raft construction and poling.
   (b) Give additional rope work.
   (c) Plan competitive exercises in firemaking and shelter construction.
   (d) Practice with emergency signalling mirrors.

Reference—Chapter II.

HIKE IX—COLD WEATHER HIKE

Purpose

To give cadets the experience of preparing a shelter and a meal in cold weather, and to impress on them the necessity for being dressed and prepared for such weather. (See Figures 326 and 327.)

FIG. 318. Adjusting Packs to Fit the Individual

FIG. 319. A Battalion of Cadets Starting an Overnight Hike

Procedure

1. Instruct cadets in proper cold weather attire before taking hike.
2. When winter weather conditions exist, hike cadets to a wooded are and point out the most protected camp sites.
3. Demonstrate the construction of snow or combination snow and boug bivouac as illustrated in manual.
4. Build a windbreak and impress on the cadets the necessity of sleepir out of the wind.
5. Construct a demonstration bough bed and reflector fire.
6. If possible, let each cadet cook a meal and melt snow for cooking an drinking purposes.
7. Instruct cadets how to keep warm with a minimum of equipment. Wai them of the danger of sweating in cold weather, and how to prevent i
8. Point out animal tracks in the snow, and show where snares could l set effectively, and where to look for winter food.
9. Many of the hikes already outlined can be and should be adapted to co weather. Make an overnight hike when possible, using equipment.

References—Chapter VII; Chapter IX, pages 183-188.

HIKE X—CROSS-COUNTRY OVERNIGHT TEST HIKE

Purpose

To test the speed, endurance and skill of cadets in traveling over roug country.

Note

The best possible training for an emergency is to have had previous e perience in a similar predicament and to have worked a way out. Therefo a planned exercise, simulating as nearly as possible the conditions as pilot w encounter and the activities he must perform when stranded in a wilde ness area, will be of great value in enabling him to automatically do the righ thing in the real pinch.

Procedure

1. Lay out on an aerial map a 10 or 20 mile course that will interse streams, swamps, hills, and wooded country.
2. Furnish each cadet with a map and have them carry only emergen equipment and K rations.
3. Instruct them to dress adequately for any weather conditions that mig arise and to carry a change of clothes.
4. Caution against fire hazards.
5. Drop cadets from busses in pairs or small units with instructions to hil until dark, make camp, and to arrive at the base at a designated time t following day.

FIG. 320. Sleeping Out

FIG. 321. Instruction for a Night Hike.

EXTENDED TRAINING PERIOD

The ideal method for imparting survival experience and training is to arrange a full week of continuous field work. At times this will be possible among holdover groups. For such occasions prepare an aerial map with a marked route of travel. Follow a roughly circular course (40 to 50 miles long) through wooded country, and along streams and river bottoms. Previously determine the camp site for each night. Carry full packs with food for several days. Additional food may be picked up where the route of travel crosses highways. Exercises already outlined should be modified to fit into each day's instruction. In practice it was found that four to five half-day field trips culminating with a three to five day trip best fitted the time allotment and instruction needs at the various Pre-Flight Schools.

DEMONSTRATION AREA

A demonstration camp site should be established and should be located near the base and have the following facilities:

1. Drinking water.
2. Adequate space for a battalion of men to camp.
3. Fireplaces.
4. Trench latrines.
5. Incinerator.
6. Large hot water containers for washing mess gear.
7. Demonstration units containing:
    (a) Various types of fireplaces and fires.
    (b) Stone-lined pit ovens.
    (c) Types of bough beds.
    (d) Framework for smoking or drying meat.
    (e) Types of shelters.
    (f) Types of snares.
    (g) Parachute used as a tent, hammock, sleeping bag and back pack.
    (h) Common snakes of the area.
    (i) Permanent shelter for equipment.

The purpose of the demonstration area is to enable instructors to impart certain information and technics to the men quickly. It should not take the place of field trips but should be included as part of the over-all survival program and be used in connection with the field exercises whenever demonstration procedures are most practical.

EQUIPMENT

The following equipment has been carefully selected and is adequate for carrying out the Survival Program in a Pre-Flight School.

Equipment for a Battalion of 300 Men and Officers

175 Tents—(preferable design—Masland survival tent.) 45 surveyed parachutes for making paratepees

350 Rucksacks

350 Canteens

350 Compasses

350 Rocket Knives

350 Individual mess kits, including knives, forks and spoons

350 12″ blade machetes and 50 18″ blade machetes

175 Axes

350 Sleeping bags with water-repellent covering. These bags may be wool or kapok but should preferably be the Army down sleeping bags. This is almost essential if winter camping trips are conducted.

350 Jungle hammocks

350 Mosquito head nets

350 Emergency signalling mirrors

350 Emergency fishing kits or individual survival kits containing fishing gear. Gill nets

10 100-foot lengths of ½-inch rope

Supply of K or C rations, or preferably pemmican if available

Supply of waterproof matches, preferably with 350 individual containers

Topographic and aerial maps of the base and vicinity covering a radius of 10 or 20 miles

For cold weather camping additional equipment should include:

350 Combat jackets with hoods or Army parkas

700 heavy wool Army sweaters

700 pairs of wool or Army ski trousers

1500 heavy wool Army socks

700 Army wool mittens and mitten covers

700 one piece heavy winter underwear

350 Army shoe pacs with felt innersoles

350 Army mukluks, innersoles, and felt socks

350 ski goggles

100 Army cooking outfits, aluminum utensils and gasoline stoves

If snow conditions require snowshoes and skis the following equipment will be necessary:

FIG. 322. Cleaning Mess Gear at Camping and Demonstration Area

350 pairs of cross country skis and bindings
350 pairs of Army snowshoes with bindings
700 ski poles
400 pairs of ski boots of assorted sizes

Liaison should be maintained with the Special Forces Section, Office of the Quartermaster General, to keep abreast of new designs in this basic equipment. Whenever possible, improved or new equipment should be ordered. There is a marked advantage in training with equipment that will be issued in combat areas.

CARE OF EQUIPMENT

A single man-unit of equipment should contain all individual units, such as sleeping bag, canteen, and compass (in the pack) and each piece should be numbered to correspond to the number on the pack. (Fig. 316 and 317.)

Wet sleeping bags, tents, and packs must be spread out and thoroughly dried before repacking. Mess gear must be kept clean and dry.

SURVIVAL USES OF THE PARACHUTE

The parachute is a piece of equipment that a downed airman generally has with him and can use to improvise shelters, bedding, clothing, back packs, footgear, rope, signals, and numerous other emergency items. The following uses should be taught and incorporated into the basic training courses through the medium of display rooms and field trips.

1. Paratepee, Lean-to, and other emergency shelters.
2. Parahammock
3. Pack-assembly
   a. Chest strap
   b. Pack cover
   c. Tump line
4. Footgear and clothing
   a. Mukluks
   b. Foot wrappings
   c. Protective head and body coverings
   d. Bed roll
5. Rope, fishing line, cordage and snares
6. First aid bandages

A parachute consists of the following parts, all of which have varied uses:
a. Nylon or silk panels
b. Parachute harness
c. Shroudlines

   d. Seat-pack cushion

   e. Harness buckles

   f. Ripcord pins and wire

   g. Rubber bungee cord

For further details see Bibliography; Army Air Forces—Emergency Uses of the Parachute.

Intermediate Training
(In Operation During World War II)

Training at intermediate bases was designed to impart additional basic knowledge and technics not treated at the Pre-Flight stage and to impart information on survival in special areas of the globe. The lectures were briefed in accordance with the decreased time allowance, and field trips necessarily had to conform to the climatic and topographic features in the vicinity of the bases. The training conducted at The Naval Air Station, Pensacola, will serve as an example of this phase of training.

Survival museums with exhibits illustrating all phases of survival are beneficial for quickly imparting a wide range of information (Figure 328).

At the Pensacola Survival Museum, a tropical and an arctic exhibit on land survival (Figures 329 and 330) fitted well into this stage of training.

Lectures were based on Chapters VIII and IX of this text, and material from Emory's *South Sea Lore* and Stefansson's *Arctic Manual.*

Field trips emphasized seashore survival, a phase of training not practical at Pre-Flight Schools.

CLASSROOM LECTURES

At least five hours should be allocated for lectures on land and sea survival. The text material for these lectures is indicated in the syllabus, and additional material can be obtained from references in the bibliography. Full use should be made of museum displays or prepared demonstrations (Figure 331). Suitable movies may well be substituted for the prepared lectures or used in conjunction with them. They include such films as MG-2063—Swimming Through Burning Oil and Surf, 10 minutes; MA-3854—Land and Live in the Desert, 60 Minutes; and TFI-3347—Land and Live in the Jungle, 60 minutes.

LECTURE 1   OCEAN SURVIVAL—1 hour.

Individual emergency equipment p. 5
Preparation for emergencies
Case histories of wartime survivors
Problems of cold and warm ocean survival—132
Living without food or water—134
Water at sea, food getting—135
Fish, makeshift fishing lines and hooks—136
Bait grapple—137

Bait, and containers—139
Fishing at sea—140
Seaweed, snaring birds for food—141
Indicators of land—142
Poisonous and dangerous aquatic animals—208
  Sharks
  Barracudas
  Electric ray
  Portuguese Men-of-War
  Exposure to water—186
  Morale—144

LECTURE 2   SEASHORE SURVIVAL—1 hour.

Landing in surf or coral—31
Types of seashores and similarity of foods—144
Where and what to hunt—144
  Shellfish crabs, lobsters, shrimp, prawns, turtles, fish, sea cucumbers
  birds and bird eggs
Methods of crabbing and fishing, dangerous mollusks—150
Poisonous fish—152
Obtaining water along the seashore—42
Seashore food plants
Shelter and beds
Steaming seashore foods—144
Insect pests
Protection from sun and heat—183
Stingrays—209
Sea snakes—205
Scorpion, stone and toad fishes, sea anemones and sea urchins—211
Morays and conger eel, shell, coral, crocodiles—211
When and how to travel—28
Discussion of seashore field trip and specific information concerning Gulf
  Coast

LECTURE 3   THE TROPICS—1 hour.

Tropical plant foods—153
Palms—156
Coconut palm, Nipa palm—156
Sago palm—158
Rattan palm—163
Bamboo shoots, sugar cane, bananas and plantains—164

FIG. 323. Aviation Cadets foraging for the potato-like tubers of the Arrowhead plant while in training at Iowa Pre-Flight School. (See Arrowhead page 65).

FIG. 324. Cadets at St. Mary's Pre-Flight rapelling down an escapement.

LECTURE 4 SURVIVAL MUSEUM TOUR AND LECTURE—2 hours.

Lobby Instruction

Discussion of world vegetation regions and the similarity of survival problems over large areas of the world.

Inspection of maps showing the distribution of various native peoples in relation to active war fronts.

Advice on the best procedure of dealing with natives.

Float Room Instruction

Explanation of the following exhibits:
Birds which indicate nearness to land
Lagoon glare
Snaring sea birds
Water and food at sea

Aquarium containing edible and poisonous fishes
Makeshift tackle from shoe laces, pins, canvas, etc.
Sea and seashore foods; preparation and cleaning of fish

Arctic Exhibit and Instruction (Fig. 330)

Building and use of a snow cave above timber line
Survival without equipment in below-zero weather
Parachutes as blankets
Making emergency snowshoes
Setting snowshoe rabbit snares
Bird snares
Timberline lean-to
Use of reflector fire
Fuels and tinder
Bough bed
Care of feet
Snow goggles
Preparation of meat
Arctic food plants
Equipment

Tropical Exhibit and Instruction (Greenhouse, Fig. 329)

Instruction in building shelters, hammocks
Use of mosquito head nets, mosquito repellents, and tabrin
Making bamboo cooking utensils, canteens, and plantain or banana leaf
    cooking vessels
Shoes of coconut husk or coconut cloth
Obtaining water from tropical vines
Instruction in the recognition of tropical plants; their preparation and uses
Keying of several plants using prepared pamphlets
Tidal pool containing common edible crustacean and shell fish
Snare for catching jungle fowl
Bamboo fish spears
Jungle beds

Field Exhibit Instruction

Discussion of field living conditions in the tropics
Material on hand for fashioning lines from palm; for making fish spears;
    snares; water containers; coconut shoes; nets and other articles
The exhibit lecture does not attempt to cover all material in the museum,
but only that dealing with "Living on Land and Sea" and only those subjects
not already treated in detail in the Pre-Flight Training.

FIG. 326. Winter survival trips were conducted at Iowa Pre-Flight, and a great variety of shelters were devised and used.

FIG. 325. Trapping, cleaning, and cooking wild game (cottontail rabbit), Iowa Pre-Flight.

SEASHORE FIELD TRIP

Pensacola, located on the Gulf Coast, is an ideal base from which to conduct sea and seashore field trips (Figures 332 and 333). Such experience acquaints cadets and pilots with survival problems that many of them will eventually face in other parts of the world.

A period of a day and a half is recommended for such a trip. Santa Rosa Island offers an ideal location for this exercise. Men should be dropped off a quarter mile from shore in groups of 25 to 50 and given an opportunity to paddle ashore in rubber rafts. The following outline illustrates a very effective trip conducted at Pensacola:

Personal gear required:

Jacket	Matches in waterproof container
Hat	Machete
Dark glasses	Flashlight
Keds	Mosquito dope (issued)
Headnet	Fishing kit (issued)
Knife	Socks (extra)
Bathing suit	
Rations (issued)	

Clothing required:

Wear: T-shirt and Khaki shirt; bathing suit under trousers
DO NOT bring wallet, watches, or cameras
Bundle gear together and wrap it in your jacket.

First Day

1530: Boat leaves the wet basin south of building No. 45.

1630: Arrive off Santa Rosa Island (one quarter mile out). Issue "Mae Wests," rafts, fish kits, and rations. Strip off clothing and wear swimming suit. Inflate "Mae Wests" in water. Inflate parachute raft. Paddle raft to shore and assemble at designated spot.

1730: Demonstration by instructor:
1. Digging beach well for fresh water (Figure 334)
2. Make steaming pit for cooking crabs and fish (Figure 335)
3. Collecting clams
4. Methods of catching crabs
5. Finding bait and fishing in surf with hand lines
6. Fashioning of a crude spear from driftwood material
7. Setting snares (Figure 336)
8. Use of life raft as a bed

1830: Divide into groups of four men. Select a camp site along the beach and practice technics demonstrated. Each group dig a beach well, make a steam pit, catch and cook a meal of crabs, gather bait and set lines, gather and cook small clams.

2100: Muster at instructor's camp for instruction in spearing flounders. Carry flashlights, spears, and mosquito dope. Come fully clothed.

2115: Spear flounders along the sea shore. Look for crabs with lights, set nights lines.

Second Day

0700–0800—Breakfast.

0800–0830—Muster.

Inspection of beach wells and tally of emergency food obtained.

0830–1000—Practice going in and out of surf with rubber raft. Fishing from raft and shore. Erect sun shelter (Figure 333).

1000–1200—Instruction in food plants and animal signs. Gather three food plants found on island and check with instructor.

1200–1400—Chow of K rations, fish, and crabs. Check with instructors. Cook fish and crabs in a steam pit.

1400–1600—Carry rafts and gear to bay shore. Travel along shore, looking for blue crabs, hermit crabs, conchs, and sting-rays. Muster at departure point.

1600–1700—Deflate and pack rafts; bundle gear and prepare to board.

1700–   Leave Santa Rosa for Naval Air Station.

Operational Training
(In Operation During World War II)

The aim of the survival training given at Operational bases was, and should be, to introduce men to specialized survival technics and information. Again this training is to a large extent determined by the location of the base. At this stage the instruction of aircrewmen as well as pilots must be considered together. The integration of land survival, water survival, and the use of survival equipment is usually both feasible and desirable. The following outline of a course conducted at Naval Air Station, Miami, will serve as an example.

TRAINING SYLLABUS

I. Tropical Garden Instruction—Arrive at Fairchild Tropical Gardens—0815–1100

1. Lecture on the uses, distribution, and recognition of tropical plant foods. These are gathered beforehand and displayed so the men can handle, see, and taste them. Special emphasis should be placed upon the wild foods of the Pacific Islands (Figure 337).
2. An exhibit of native handicrafts of the tropics, showing ingenuity of primitive peoples
3. A trip through the gardens pointing out the growing plants that are of value to a survivor. The uses, habitat, and identifying characteristics are emphasized.

II. A hike through the Mangrove Swamps near Matheson Hammock (1100-1230)

Instructor stresses the wide distribution of mangrove swamps along tropical shores and the necessity of the pilot or aircrewman to know how to travel through them, what to look for in the way of food and what to expect in the way of such dangers as crocodiles, snakes, deep mud, mosquitoes, sand flies, and sting-rays.

The work is divided into several categories.

1. Practice of travel methods through mangroves—following tidal channels by walking, swimming, use of clothing flotation, rafts (Figures 339 and 340), technic of walking across the mangrove roots
2. Obtaining food in the mangroves—where to look for oysters, stone crabs, fiddler crabs; and how to catch mangrove snappers and what to use for bait. Tasting and recognizing plant foods such as purslane, sea grapes, saltwort

3. Protection both day and night from natural hazards such as mosquitoes, sand flies, sting-rays, snakes. Proper dressing to minimize danger and discomfort from mosquitoes, leeches, ticks and chiggers; use of mosquito repellents.

III. Lunch 1230 to 1330

IV. Work at Tropical Demonstration Area set up in Plant Introduction Garden—1345-1545

The outdoor demonstration area is set up in tropical surroundings and consists of:

1. Various types of shelters and beds constructed from palms
2. A paratepee and parahammock
3. Bird and mammal jungle snares
4. A complete table display of survival articles made from parachutes, plane parts, and plants. A selection of seashore foods.
5. A coconut husking area
6. Cooking fires and improvised cooking utensils.

The men are given instruction in thatching coconut fronds, making fish and snare lines from palm fibers, Hibiscus, and Agave. They are shown and allowed to practice three methods of opening coconuts. Each man is taught how to climb a coconut tree and given an opportunity to do so. They are shown tropical tinders for starting fires, methods of smoking and drying foods, how to prepare candlenuts, breadfruit seeds, palm cabbage, and other plant foods.

V. Bus returns to station—1545

Toward the close of the war, courses in survival instruction combining land and water survival along with the use of the latest survival equipment were well established at many Operational bases beyond the continental limits of the United States.

Salient features of this instruction included 2 or 3 day jungle trips where jungle survival technics already discussed in lectures were put into practice; seashore survival trips emphasizing swimming and rafting in surf; and instruction and practice in the use of emergency equipment (Figs. 344-348).

Special Area or Advanced Base Survival Training

This phase of a progressive and integrated survival training program was just coming into being at the close of World War II. It is designed to supplement the *Basic* and *Intermediate* instruction with specific training for combat areas.

Although basic survival principles and technics can be taught almost anywhere in the United States, the specialized survival training can be given only in regions that similate conditions existing in possible combat areas.

This specific area or advanced base training may be divided into Tropical Seashore, Tropical Jungle, The Sea, and Polar Survival. Others could be added, but experience in World War II indicated that Naval Aviation needs can be met if training in one or more of the above categories is given. Such training should be conducted in areas specifically selected for the purpose, and it is advisable that these locations be established in peace time. Additional centers can be developed in the rear of combat areas to meet expanding needs.

Tropical Seashore Training

Tropical seashore survival includes the knowledge and technics necessary to survive on the small tropical oceanic islands and along the shores of the continents and large island groups. In its simplest form, survival along the tropical seashores narrows down to knowing how to make full use of the coconut and how to get food from the reef.

The following information is largely in addition to that already presented in the text, being specific for the tropical Pacific Area. For more detailed information relative to each island group see *Survival Survey of the Pacific,* prepared by the authors at the instigation of Rear Admiral Thomas J. Hamilton, USN (Ret.).

Tropical Seashore Survival

Often the first aim of a survivor will be to reach sea coasts and beaches. They are in general easier to live along than other regions of the world. Some types of familiar seafoods will be available along all shores. Tropical seashore survival deals with the information and technics that a survivor must know in order to live under emergency conditions along continental and island shores. It varies in detail from place to place, but boils down to knowing how to get seafood from the reef and how to make full use of the coconut and other food plants.

Equipment

A man can survive with very little equipment, but the average airman must have certain articles. They are: a sheath knife or pocket-knife, matches in a waterproof case, and a machete.

Additional equipment that is desirable and will make life more bearable is: underwater goggles, a waterproof flashlight, work gloves, a small file and a sling spear.

Technics of Reaching Shore Safely

The seashore survivor may likely come down in the water. It is important that he should know how to swim and how to handle a rubber raft in surf. On the average, the ability to swim will save a man's life more often than any other survival technic. In addition swimming, particularly underwater swimming, is the key to securing reef foods.

Surf can be dangerous whether traversed by a swimmer or by a man in a raft. Windward reefs should be avoided, if a choice exists. Dangerous surf is usually less formidable at ebb tide, and it is moderated in coves and bays. It pays to pick your time and place for making a landing. Wave cycles are often apparent, and a lull between large waves should be utilized in going through surf. Whether swimming or rafting, approach the surf slowly, look it over, then pick the place and time to catch a wave. Ride the breakers shoreward just back of the wave crest. Don't get too high or you'll drop over the wave front and have the full force of the breaking wave descend on you. After the wave breaks and dumps you in the shallow water of the reef, you are in a vulnerable position to be engulfed by the next wave. Wade or swim rapidly toward shore dragging your raft with you. Wave backwash will tend to draw you seaward.

When large waves are about to break over a swimmer, he should turn, face the incoming wave, and dive into it. If this occurs in shallow water, he should dive to the bottom and grasp a coral formation or a rock or dig his fingers

FIG. 327. Cadets at Iowa Pre-Flight fish through the ice for a meal.

FIG. 328. The Survival Museum, Pensacola, Florida.

into the sand until the wave crest passes. Then let the declining force of the wave carry him shoreward beyond reach of the next one. In such situations goggles enable a swimmer to navigate safely, to see and observe underwater current action, and help to eliminate panic. They may well make the difference between life and death.

Outrunning currents that can carry you beyond the reef should be avoided. They occur during the ebbing tide, where inlets or channels cut through barrier reefs, and are known as rip tides (page 29). Water damned up behind the reef rushes seaward in great force through narrow outlets created by tide action. At the mouth of streams deep inlets are usually cut through the reefs by tide action. From offshore these inlets are indicated by valleys appearing in the shoreline. Along tropical coasts, fresh water prevents the growth of coral, thus forming abruptly deep submarine canyons where the wave action is broken and the water surface is either smooth or choppy. Use such inlets to reach shore on incoming tides, for at such places the task of getting through the surf is greatly simplified. Otherwise avoid them as the currents can be dangerous. If caught in an outgoing rip current, swim diagonally across it to calmer water, not against or with it. It seldom pays to fight any current.

Seashore Travel

Shore or beach travel is generally easier than inland travel and the best time to do it is at low tide. Some of its advantages over jungle travel are cool breezes, little or no vegetation to push through, and greater range of vision. Night travel along the reefs is still cooler, is less tiring, and provides conceal-ment. Travel, foraging, and heavy work should be done during early morn-ing, evening, and at night. During the day it is advisable to immerse fre-quently in the water to prevent heat exhaustion, and undue fatigue. Keep fully clothed to prevent sunburn. Coconut oil is a good sunburn preventive.

Reefs of windward island shores are flat shelves, easy to travel over at low tide, but the beaches are usually higher and rougher than those of lee shores. Sturdy shoes are needed as protection against rock bruises and coral and shell cuts.

Mangrove swamps, or forests, line many tropical shores. When small, they can be circumnavigated by walking or wading around their seaward side at low tide or they can be traversed by following the high-tide mark which divides the mangrove forest from the strand or interior jungle. This is usually a clearly defined belt where vegetation is sparse. In traveling either seaward or shoreward through a mangrove swamp, tidal channels should be followed. Avoid fighting your way through the tangle of roots (Figures 338-340). Swimming may be necessary and must be resorted to whenever muck or water makes wading impossible. A poor swimmer should inflate his shirt by first wetting it and then blowing into the front opening while submerged. An air

Fig. 329. The Tropical Room in the survival museum used for lecturing and demonstrating tropical survival.

Fig. 330. An Arctic or cold weather exhibit illustrating survival technics, Survival Museum.

FIG. 331. An exhibit table illustrating points of tropical survival.

FIG. 332. An overnight survival trip along the seashore at Pensacola, Florida.

bubble will blossom above his shoulders. Trousers tied at the ankles or tucked into boots will provide buoyancy in the same way. (See Swimming and Diving Manual.)

When you encounter freshwater streams cross them where they enter lagoons rather than farther out on the reef where they may be exceptionally deep.

If inter-island travel within an atoll is deemed necessary, the survivor should try to row or sail with the prevailing winds and follow the atoll contour, keeping to the lee side of the reef or bar. When rafting on the lee side of the atoll keep within the lagoon to prevent being blown out to the open sea. On the windward side, keep to the lee side of the islands and reefs. Distances between atoll islands are short and water is shallow. You can often wade from one island to another at low tide (See Chapter 1).

Drinking Water

Drinking water is the limiting factor in tropical seashore survival. Without it food is of little importance and a castaway's days are numbered. Water is available almost everywhere. The trick is knowing where to look for it and how to get it. Fresh or brackish water is usually under the soil back of the debris thrown up by high tides. Select a depression where drainage collects and dig a beach well, preferably in the sand. If wisely located a three to four foot well should reach water. The water may be discolored or brackish, but it is safe and potable.

Where coconut palms line the shore, the green coconut will be the safest and most reliable source of water (Figure 350). The ripe nuts also contain drinkable water and are readily picked off the ground. Their laxative properties have been generally exaggerated. Use ripe nuts, if necessary.

To get green nuts, select a low tree with a good nut crop and walk up the trunk, native style, using old leaf scars as toe-holds. Pressure-grip the side of the pole with your hands. Don't lock your arms or hands around the trunk. Sever the nut by raising and then snapping it downward. Nuts can also be twisted off with a quick spin. Body water and energy can be saved if a good supply of nuts is obtained at each climb. With a sharp machete, slice the rounded end of the nut until a small opening can be cut from which to drink. To carry a water supply, husk the green coconuts, to reduce weight, and string five or six of them together by running a dry leaflet through the fibrous covering at the tip of the nuts. It is not an easy task to climb a coconut tree, nor it is always self-evident how to make use of the food and water it supplies. Training in this is necessary to properly prepare men to survive.

When you get hard up for water, the fresh leaves of seaside purslane (Sesuvium portulacastrum) or common purslane (Portulaca oleracoa) can be chewed and swallowed to relieve thirst. Both may be found growing on the beach or strand (Figures 235 and 107).

In regions of human habitation, all drinking water should be boiled or chemically treated. When you are with natives drink coconut water, water from vines (see Jungle Survival) or boiled water. Don't take a chance with stream water unless you have absolutely no alternative. Stagnant water away from human habitation can be safely drunk.

Food—The Coconut

Coconuts and coconut sap are available the year round (page 157). The nuts can be prepared in many ways. The soft white meat of green or "spoon nuts" is the best and can be spooned out of a split nut by making a "spoon" out of a sharp shoulder slashed off the outside husk. It is more nourishing and digestible than the harder meat of ripe nuts. The meat of ripe nuts can be eaten fresh, grated, and dried to copra; or the milk can be squeezed out of it for food or drink. Oil separates from the milk on standing. Good eating nuts are green and so completely filled with water that they do not rattle when shaken.

Old nuts sprouting beneath trees contain a spongy center that can be eaten raw, but are more tasty and nourishing when cooked. These sprouted nuts should be husked and then baked for 2 hours in a rock oven (Figure 353). When done, the yellow potato-like core tastes somewhat like a boiled yam. To open the husked nuts, strike the three longitudinal ribs successively with a knife handle or rock. The nut casing will split cleanly into equal halves. A large number of such nuts can be cooked at one time and they will keep, unopened, for three to four days. They are not only very nourishing, but are easy to get. Don't pass up sprouted coconuts.

The hearts or growing points of both young and fullgrown coconut trees can be cut out with a machete and eaten raw or cooked. Peel off the outside layers until the tender growth is reached.

Coconut sap is food or drink in the form of a high sugar-content beverage. To get it, tightly bind with twine all but the last few inches of a young flowering spike. Slice off the unbound tip and hang a container beneath it. (A bamboo joint or half a coconut shell will serve.) Collect the sap once a day (preferably morning) and cut a fresh cross-section sliver from the spike to ensure continued sap flow.

A survivor must be able to open a coconut without a machete. Lacking the "know-how," this is not an easy task. The husk will eventually split off if the pointed end of the nut is repeatedly struck on a hard object such as a rock, but it is much easier to use a hard, sharpened "husking stick" firmly anchored in the ground. A hardwood stick 3 feet long and one inch in diameter will suf-

FIG. 333. Living like a castaway, a pilot gathers food and fire wood, then rests in the shade of his raft. He is training for a possible real emergency, Pensacola, Florida.

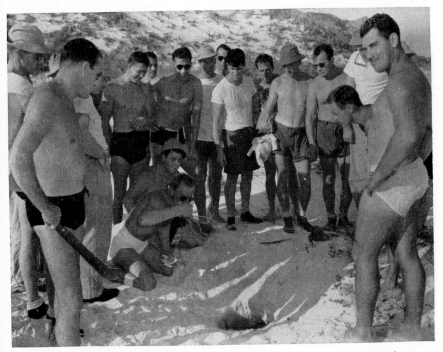

FIG. 334. Receiving instruction in digging a beach well, Pensacola, Florida.

FIG. 335. Instructors demonstrate how to cook crabs in a steam pit, then men divide up in pairs and repeat the process, Pensacola, Florida.

FIG. 336. Setting a snare along the beach for a gull or foraging shore bird, Pensacola, Florida.

fice. The nut should be held by both ends and thrust down on the pointed stick, taking care not to puncture the inside shell. A backward twist of the wrist will pry off a section of the husk and this action is repeated until the nut within comes free of the husk.

Other Plant Foods

In addition to the coconut, numerous other plant foods are available along tropical shores (pages 153-173). At any one time or place they may tip the balance in favor of the castaway. The ones listed, though typical of tropical Pacific shores, are in most cases, found along other tropical coasts. They are arranged in their general order of importance to the survivor.

Pandanus (Pandanus sp.) (Figure 244)—Pandanus fruits ripen and are available throughout the year. On all but the more poorly vegetated islands and shores, some ripe fruits should be available when needed by a survivor. The fibrous succulent tips of the keys or fruit sections contain sugar and starch which can be chewed and sucked out. Edible seeds are also found within the keys. The amount of food obtainable is small in comparison to the other food plants, but is sufficient to keep a man going. The pandanus is important to the survivor because of its wide distribution and general availability. Some fruits may slightly irritate the mouth for a minute or so after eating. This possible stinging is not enough to cause discomfort and does no harm.

Breadfruit (Artocarpus altilis) (Figure 243)—The breadfruit is abundant only on the larger inhabited islands where groves have been planted by natives. The seedless variety must be propagated by shoots and is therefore scarce or lacking on uninhabited islands or coasts. It is seasonal, the fruits being available from June through October. The breadfruit may be eaten boiled, baked, roasted, or fried. The survivor will find roasting the best and easiest method of preparation. This plant will furnish the survivor a great quantity of starchy food, but is limited in its value because of its distribution and seasonal availability.

Taro (Colocasia, Alocasia, Caladium) (Figure 232)—Taro is found inland in low wet areas of rich soil. It is usually planted in patches or gardens and is found only in inhabited or deserted uninhabited areas. The starchy roots, available all year, are its best source of food, but the young leaves and stems can be cooked as greens. The choice preparation for a survivor is to bake the tubers. All forms and all parts of taro must be cooked.

Arrowroot (Tacca leontopetaloides) (Figure 236)—Arrowroot can be found growing wild on both the inhabited and uninhabited tropical Pacific islands. It is found inland on the richer sandy soil and grows best in clearings or beneath trees where the undergrowth is not too heavy. The plant is quite abundant in the Marshall Islands, and the numerous rounded tubers are available throughout the year. They are shallow and easily excavated. The tubers are rich in starch, but must be crushed and washed before being cooked. This leaching process limits the usefulness of this plant to the survivor.

Indian Almond (Terminalia Catappa)—The Indian Almond is most common along island shores, but is also found inland. The yellow or red fibrous covering of the nut can be chewed for its sugar content and the long, cylindrical almond-tasting kernel eaten. The nuts can be split open with a knife or pounded open with rocks.

Seaside Purslane (Sesuvium Portulacastrum) (Figure 235)—This succulent creeping plant grows on both rocky and sandy shores. The leaves and stems are a bit salty, but can be eaten raw or cooked.

Turtle Grass (Thalassia)—Turtle grass grows in patches in lagoons back of the reef on muddy or mixed sandy bottoms. The seed pods contain pea-like seeds that may be eaten raw. They are crisp, tasty, and slightly salty.

Nipa Palm (Nipa fruticans) (Figure 220)—The Nipa palm grows in brackish water at the mouths of streams. The white kernel inside the individual nuts is edible. Young yet fully developed nuts are the best. The meat of old ones are very hard and rather indigestible. The meat has little taste.

Passion Fruits (Passiflora)—Orange passion fruits are quite common on vines along the shore and in open areas. The fruits are small, but will furnish some food value and vitamins.

Thespesia (Thespesia populnea)—Thespesia populnea grows along the shoreline and looks very much like hau or *hibiscus tiliaceus*. The young leaves, flowers, and buds may be eaten raw or cooked.

Morinda citrifolia—This shrub is scattered throughout the tropical Pacific islands and ripe fruits are available the year round. The soft, grayish fruits smell like limburger cheese. A taste must be acquired for them. The young fruits and leaves may be cooked as greens.

Pigweed (Portulaca oleracea) (Figure 107)—This succulent plant grows best along the seashore or in clearings or abandoned land. The leaves and stems may be eaten raw or cooked as a green.

Pemphis acidula—A common tree along the shores of many islands, the leaves may be eaten raw.

Food from the Reef

Reef foods rank a close second to coconuts as a source of emergency food. The seashore survivor must therefore arrange his whole schedule of living around the daily tides. Low tides are the time to hunt lobsters, to spear fish, and to pick up shellfish on the reefs. Fish are active and can be caught on a hook and line on incoming tides, but it is dangerous to get caught far out on strange reefs by rising tides; these usually sweep over a reef forming strong lateral currents.

FIG. 337. A demonstration exhibit of tropical fruits at the Fairchild Tropical Gardens for instruction of pilots at NAS Miami.

FIG. 338. Exercises in traversing Mangrove swamps were given at NAS Miami, Florida, and at operational bases in Panama, the Caribbean Area and Brazil.

FIG. 339. The best way to travel through mangrove swamps is to locate and follow tidal channels, Miami, Florida.

FIG. 340. Where water in mangrove channels is deep, swimming is easier than walking. Inflating shirts is an aid to poor swimmers. Miami, Florida.

Many types of shellfish can be gathered with ease, but obtaining other foods ich as fish, lobsters, and crabs requires both equipment and skill. To tap the st food sources of the reef, a man should be a fairly good swimmer and ive had experience in surf. Diving goggles, a fish spear, gloves, and a water-roof flashlight make reef foraging more efficient. A gill net can be used dvantageously. A hard pointed wooden stick will do for a spear, but a etal rod from a plane fitted with a bungee cord at the rear and barbed at the oint makes a better one and it is elastic-propelled.

Shellfish—Shellfish are in general the easiest source of food for the inex-erienced survivor to obtain. One type or another may be found attached to angrove roots, buried in sand, fastened to the reef, or concealed under rocks.

By looking for breathing holes in the wet sand at low tide it is possible to cate various species of small burrowing clams and to unearth them by dig-ing.

Huge clams such as *Tridacna* are found imbedded in living coral reefs. A wimmer can readily spot their brilliantly colored mantles, which are exposed hen the shells are open. A muscle at the hinge of the shell attaches the *ridacna* to the rock. Sometimes this muscle can be reached with a knife and ie clam freed. The clam will open if a hole is cut between the hinged halves f the shells. More often *Tridacna* cannot be thus removed and the technic then to thrust the knife blade to the bottom of the opened valves and cut ie large adductor muscle which holds the shell shut. The contents can then e removed without freeing the shell. The large valve muscle and a fatty sack, ie size of a tennis ball, are excellent raw.

The giant clam or *Hippopus* is not imbedded in coral, but is found on cky bottoms and in open sandy spots. To open giant clams, bash them in the iell where the valves close and insert a knife to cut the adductor muscle, but e sure to keep fingers out of the valves of live clams; the shells close slowly, ut with great force. You can cook large clams in the shell by placing them on bed of coals. Heating will open them.

Shellfish such as cowries (*Cypraea*), cat-eyes (*Turbo*), and snails can be ound under rocks. Sea urchins likewise lurk in such places. Their spines can flict painful wounds, and though sea urchins have some food value, they re not worth fooling with. Many sea cucumbers are edible, but some contain ckly fluids and other contain poisons sufficiently powerful to kill fish. They hould be considered only as a starvation food.

Lobsters and Crabs—Some crabs are active in the daytime. The fiddler rabs, typical of muddy shores, *Grapsus,* which scoot over rocks at the waters dge, and the land crabs (*Cardisoma*) are examples. None of these contain nough meat to be considered really good foods. Hermit crabs, which make heir homes in old sea shells on the shore, may be removed from their shells y grasping their legs and claws and turning them with the spiral of the shell. Heat in the form of a match or hot coal held against the shell will make them cooperate. Their best use is for baiting fishlines, but they can be roasted in the shell and eaten.

The best crabbing is at night on the reef. In the light of a coconut frond torch or a flashlight, crabs may be seen and speared or may be pinned down and grabbed by their big biting claws. The best results are obtained by crabbing under water, using goggles and a waterproof flashlight.

A coconut frond torch is made by bundling together two or three dried fronds. These are wrapped at intervals with lashings. A longer lasting and brighter torch can be improvised by filling a section of bamboo with coconut cloth soaked in coconut oil.

Spinny lobsters or "languster" are usually abundant on reefs where there are caves and crevices in the coral. They are most active at night during the early hours of the incoming tide, and can be grabbed in shallow water when located by torchlight. The survivor will be much more successful if he uses goggles, a waterproof flashlight, and gloves. He should swim over rocky bottoms in water from one to five feet deep and peer into all nooks and crevices under rocks. When caught in the beam of a light, the lobster will remain motionless for a long enough period to be grabbed or speared.

Lobsters swim backwards, so when grabbing them by hand, hold the light in front and reach them from behind. Once you have grasped the lobster, move him in against your leg and he will grab your trousers and stop struggling. The spines on the lobster can gash your hand, so wear gloves. Swim fully clothed, including shoes, as protection against getting cut by coral. Lobstering, even under emergency conditions is sport, and one goodsized lobster makes both an ample and a delicious meal.

Another delicacy that comes in a large package is the coconut crab or "robber" crab. It is a land crab with tremendous biting claws and a sacklike abdomen. It is active at night and cuts holes into coconuts to get at the meat. Old nuts so cut are a sign of the crab's presence. In daytime the crabs hole-up under rocks, and when located by their well-worn burrow entrances, can be dug up. At night they can be spotted with a light and picked up. Hold them down with a stick and grab hold of the big pinching claws. Be careful; they can crush a finger.

The quickest way to cook lobsters and crabs is to broil them on a bed of coals; however, the meat will remain more moist if they are cooked in a steam pit. Most of the spiny lobster meat is in the tail, while in crabs it is found in the large claws. The sack-like abdomen of the coconut crab contains a sauce-like fat into which the meat can be dipped. Eat all seafoods while hot. They soon spoil in warm climates.

Octopus—Reef octopuses are small and haunt holes and crevices in the reef. They wedge their bodies into such openings until only their eyes may show.

FIG. 341. Instruction in climbing palm trees and in utilizing the coconut.

FIG. 342. A demonstration area at NAS Jacksonville, Florida, showing paratepee, parahammock, palm leaf shelters, firepit, coconut husking stick, and a table exhibit.

FIG. 343. Preparing a bed and shelter during a 2 day survival trip in the Panama jungle
Correct method of splitting palm fronds is illustrated.

FIG. 344. The handling of rubber rafts in surf is combined with overnight seashore trip:

They can be speared and then finished off by turning the body sack inside out through the gill cleft. They will discolor the water with sepia when disturbed. If they grab your arm with their tentacles, run your hand down your arm to break the hold of the suction disks. Don't waste effort trying to pull off the tentacles. Octopus meat, though rubbery, has a delicate flavor similar to lobster. Prior to cooking, sprinkle the octopus lightly with sand and beat gently with a sprig of leaves. This relaxes the muscles and tenderizes the meat. An hour's cooking in a steam pit is sufficient. Before eating, slough off the red skin and disks to reveal the tasty white meat.

Fish—Coral reefs teem with fish, and spear fishing is well worth while if a survivor is equipped with goggles and can improvise a spear. Small school-fish are abundant in shallow water, but are hard to spear. Spend your time looking under rocks and in coral crevices where such fish as sturgeon-fish, butterfly-fish, and rock fish can be easily located and cornered. Look for flounders and small stingrays on sandy bottoms. Small sharks can often be cornered in tidal pools and shallow water and are very good eating. Good sized parrot-fish and sturgeon-fish are abundant just beyond the reef and in tidal channels. Coral heads rising up from sandy bottoms are good fishing spots since fish will seek sanctuary there when a swimmer approaches. When a fish is speared do not move the spear until the fish has been pulled up on the shaft where he cannot wriggle loose. Spear fishing is more successful if conducted at night with an underwater flashlight. Fish "hold" to the light. Carry a line for stringing your catch.

Under the right conditions "chop fishing" produces a big haul. Fish attracted to a light at low tide can be stunned or slashed in shallow water by hitting them with the back of a machete. Needle fish, goat fish, mullet and other school-fish are easily obtained in this manner.

A gill-net used where chop fishing is effective or in shallow channels at changing tide will be productive. Care must be exercised to keep big fish out of the net.

Reef fish such as puffer, trigger, and parrot fish can be poisonous to eat. If natives eat trigger and parrot fish you can eat the same species. Many are delicious. If you are doubtful, cook the fish, eat a few bites, and then wait a few hours; then if no bad results are felt, you can eat more. You can continue to eat a species so tested.

Hook-and-line fishing is usually not profitable on the reef. Practice this method instead in tidal channels, preferably at night, and use hermit crabs as bait. First crush a number of these crabs and throw them into the water to "chum" the fish. With a rubber raft you can successfully bottomfish in lagoons and bays, using hermit crabs or chopped up shellfish for bait. In an hour's time a long fish line can be made from plant fibers (Page 78). Most palm leaves, as well as the inner bark of many plants, contain suitable fibers. Natives use the fibers from dried immature coconut husks to make both line and ropes.

Firemaking, Tinder, and Firewood

Without matches, the best method of making a fire is to use the pyrite on the general issue match cases or a magnifying glass. Use dry coconut husk as tinder. A survivor can, without too much trouble, make fire, using either the native fire saw or the fire plow methods. Both need to be demonstrated and then practiced by airmen if they are to be usable under emergency conditions.

Tinders are too numerous and variable to be listed. A very good and well distributed one is the dry coconut husk. Husks make too slow a fire for cooking, but are made to order for banking a fire. Coconut "cloth," found at the base of the leaf fronds, and dry coconut leaflets serve well as tinder. Soft woods make the best kindling, and hard woods furnish hot, lasting coals. Tropical Pacific island species such as Scaevola and Ochrosia are soft, while Pemphis, Cassuarina, Tournefortia and Callophylum are hard.

Cooking

Most seashore foods such as crabs, fish, lobsters, and even breadfruit and coconut heart, can be cooked on a rock broiler. Rocks first heated in a bed of coals should be arranged so that food can be broiled on their hot, flat surfaces. Broil your fish, ungutted and unscaled, to keep them moist. Peel off skin and remove entrails before eating.

Cooking in a rock oven is another method well suited to the seashore where digging is easy. A fire is built in a pit about two and a half feet wide and a foot deep. After a hot bed of hardwood coals is obtained, a grate of hardwood is placed over the fire and rocks placed on top of it. By the time the grate burns through, the rocks are well heated. The burning brands and coals are raked out and the rocks used to pave the bottom and sides of the pit. A layer of green leaves should be placed on the rocks; next, food such as sprouted coconuts, lobsters, clams, or fish are laid on the leaves. The food is then shingled over with a top layer of leaves. Sand is piled on over the leaves and the food is left to cook. If steaming is desired, an upright stick is placed on the hot rocks before the pit is filled. After the food is covered with sand, the stick is removed and a little water is dropped in the hole before it is closed. Cooking time varies with the food. Let the food cook for at least an hour. If you build and use your pit correctly, you can forage all day and return to find a warm meal ready.

The young whole leaves found on sprouted coconuts are ready-made dishes and can also be used for wrapping food. Coconut flower spathes, empty coconut shells, and large clam shells are serviceable as either cups or plates.

Seafood may be preserved from one meal to another by wrapping it with

FIG. 345. Training with the latest types of survival equipment.

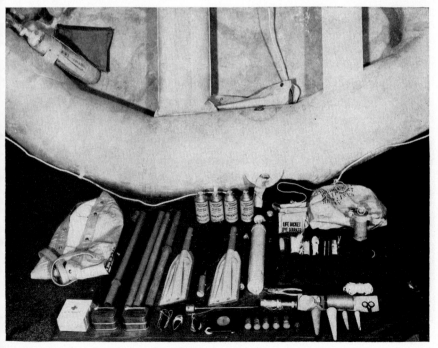

FIG. 346. Emergency equipment contained in the four-man life raft.

FIG. 347. Emergency signalling equipment.

FIG. 348. Emergency equipment in the six-man raft.

leaves while still hot and placing close to a fire or in the hot sun to discourage flies.

Shelter and Beds

The construction of shelters and beds is not as necessary in warm climates as in cold ones. Nevertheless both are more or less essential to any prolonged and comfortable existence. Their main function is to give protection from rain and to ensure rest. If the survivor has sufficient energy, a bed should be made the first night and a shelter constructed later as time and energy dictate.

A comfortable bed can be made by laying down two parallel rows of split coconut fronds (Fig. 343). The leaflets should slightly overlap in the center of the bed. To divide a frond, break or cut at the very tip and pull each side of the leaf so that it splits down the center of the midrib from top to bottom. If a layer of springy leaves such as Scaevola or Tournefortia are used as a base, the bed will be more comfortable. A final topping with a thatch sheet is the ideal (Figs. 176 and 178). The importance of a good night's rest cannot be overemphasized.

When tarps or parachute cloth are not available, a lean-to frame constructed from coconut midribs and shingled with thatch sheets will provide a water repellent and camouflaged shelter. Face the shelter away from the prevailing winds and place it near sources of food and water and in the shade.

Plaiting a coconut frond into a thatch sheet is a simple procedure. Start at the butt end of a half frond and bend the third leaflet back over the second and under the first. Next bend the fifth leaflet back over the fourth and under the first. Continue this check-type weaving until the sheet is completed. The weaving of baskets, eye shades, and other articles can be quickly mastered with this basic technique (Fig. 178).

Lashings for tying together shelters or beds can be stripped from the leaves, bark, and roots of numerous plants. A few examples are: fibers from Pandanus prop roots and the fibers within the midrib of a coconut frond; Hibiscus or hau bark, the dried leaflets of the coconut and Nipa palm; and Pandanus leaves.

A few days of actual tropical seashore survival training will go far toward insuring your safety under emergency conditions. Take the first opportunity to put to practice the information you have just read.

TRAINING SYLLABUS

Lectures on survival both along the seashore and in the tropics have preceded this stage of training. However, a moderate amount of repetition in the teaching of survival facts and technics is desirable.

Field Trips

This advanced phase of training should be imparted almost entirely by means of field trips. The minimum time for such a trip is a day and a half. Three to four days of continuous foraging and instruction is recommended. The following material should be covered in such a way that each man learns by doing:

1. The use of the coconut as food and drink, emphasizing various methods of opening drinking nuts, selection of drinking and "spoon" nuts, preparation of sprouted nuts, procurement and use of the palm heart and coconut sap, the use of ripe nuts, and the rendering of coconut oil

2. Technics of climbing coconut trees and breaking off the nuts, as well as husking both ripe and green nuts on a husking stick, and opening nuts with a machete

3. Instruction in methods of making a rock oven and steam pit, and cooking such foods as coconuts, breadfruit, fish, and crabs; the use of various tinders, including the coconut husk; fire making with a magnifying glass and fire plow

4. The splitting and thatching of coconut palm fronds to make beds, shelters, and baskets; preparation of utensils and cordage from the coconut palm, and similar uses of other plants such as the Pandanus

5. Obtaining drinking water from green coconut, from a beach well, and by collecting rain water—the latter including the channelling of runoff from coconut trees

6. All possible methods of getting food from the reef, including various fishing methods; use of hook and line, chop fishing, spearing of fish and lobsters, making tidal traps, poisoning fish; various technics of locating and foraging for clams, crabs, and lobsters, and the recognition of dangerous reef foods; the use of goggles in underwater foraging

7. Methods of approaching, swimming, and rafting in surf, tides, and rip currents; the use of goggles in surf, and methods of protecting the body from coral cuts.

SEA SURVIVAL TRAINING

Information for surviving at sea is included in the text and outlined under the lectures (See page 255). The most noteworthy advances in sea survival have taken place in the design and use of emergency equipment. Instruction in this phase of training falls more appropriately under Water Survival and is treated in the *Swimming and Diving Manual* prepared by the V-Five Physical Education Organization. The use of emergency foods, drinking water equipment, signalling gear, cold water exposure suits, various types of rafts, and practice in ditching procedures are included in this training. Where possible, a day and night should be spent afloat on a raft, simulating emergency conditions.

FIG. 349. Approaching the lee shore of an uninhabited coral island in the Marshall Island group, a typical area for tropical seashore survival.

FIG. 350. Preparing coconuts for food and drink: (*Left*) drinking the water of a green nut; (*Right*) eating the soft white meat of a spoon nut.

FIG. 351. (*Left*) coconut hearts; (*Right*) sprouted nuts.

FIG. 352. Ripping off the husks with the aid of a coconut husking stick, a vital technic for the castaway to know. Marshall Islands.

Jungle Survival

The information and techniques that will enable a lone individual or an aircrew to survive in the jungle areas of the world are basically: the ability to obtain food and water; to improvise shelters, make fires and cook foods; to travel; and to overcome or avoid the physical and biological hazards encountered. The general problem of meeting man's essential needs is no different from that in other regions of the earth; the details, however, vary considerably. Nevertheless, a good woodsman from the temperate regions can make out in a strange tropical environment, and can soon master the use of new materials as well as improvise odd techniques to meet unfamiliar conditions.

The jungle areas of Brazil, the Belgian Congo, and Asia are so tremendous in expanse that a downed airman might have to travel thousands of miles, requiring months of primitive living, before reaching civilization. The problem of surviving in the jungle is comparable in magnitude to the task confronting a castaway at sea or a man downed in polar regions. It requires physical stamina, survival know-how, high morale, and at least a minimum of equipment. During World War II many airmen made their way safely through the jungles of the Pacific Area. *You can do what others have done.*

The Jungle

Almost any heavily vegetated area in tropical regions is referred to as "jungle." For survival purposes we can classify the jungle into mangrove forests, secondary forests and primary forests, but it is not feasible to treat them separately; in fact it is impossible here to discuss jungle areas of the world except in a general way. Wherever jungle regions occur, be they in Africa, Asia, South America, or in the Pacific islands, they will appear much the same to a survivor and will contain some similar types of plants and animals. In other words, survival procedures do not differ greatly from one jungle area of the world to another.

In order that we can cover some specific details as well as general principles of jungle survival, we will confine the discussion to the task of surviving in the tropical forest of the Pacific Area. Much of the information can be applied to other jungle areas of the world.

The mangrove forests lining many tropical seashores, coconut plantations, and the rank secondary vegetation occurring in the vicinity of villages where man has disturbed the virgin forests, will not be considered here, since survival in such areas is intimately associated with tropical seashore survival and will be presented in a separate lecture.

Primary jungles are generally characterized by great trees and a network of vines or lianas. The species of trees and vines that make up such forests vary considerably throughout the world, but in general jungle areas look much alike. The interior forest floor is often relatively open, but the forest margins are dense thickets of trees and vines. Thus the most difficult travel problems are at the periphery of the jungle rather than in the interior. The forest canopy may be 200 feet above the ground and so dense that little direct sunlight strikes the earth.

Both birds and mammals may be relatively scarce, and thus the survivor must depend heavily on plant life for food. In the tropics, edible plants assume a far more important role in survival than in polar or temperate regions.

Equipment

To survive in the jungle, the average American requires the following as minimum equipment:

Lightweight clothing
Knife and machete
Compass
Rifle and Ammunition
Gill net, fish hooks, and line

Magnifying glass and waterproof matches
Lightweight poncho and jungle hammock
Malaria drugs and mosquito head net

A good machete is an absolute necessity. The possession of an accurate small-caliber rifle will be a tremendous advantage over the .38 and .45 sidearms and the carbine of World War II. The lightweight Army jungle hammock with mosquito net sidewalls is an ideal shelter and bed. The parahammock will substitute, but does not fill the need of this practical and well designed piece of equipment.

Travel

Various regions of the earth present their own unique obstacles to travel. In the far north, low temperatures and deep snow are factors limiting travel; in the mountains it is rough terrain that exacts a heavy toll on human energy; in swamp land it is the fight against poor footing and rank vegetation; while in the jungle, the oppressive heat and the mass of thick vegetation are major obstacles confronting a traveler.

Whether jungle travel be through mangrove forests, thick secondary jungle, primary jungle, or high mountain forests, there is seldom any extent of view; there are few, if any, landmarks for fixes; and there is a monotonous sameness that hems in the traveler and quickly confuses him if he has neither a trail or a stream to follow. Following a compass course cross-country is difficult. When such a course is undertaken, the compass must be read frequently and no detours made in route-finding except those that are absolutely necessary.

FIG. 353. Preparing an earth oven. A fire is built in the pit, then a grate of green sticks is laid across it. Rocks are piled on top of the grate and heated before dropping them into pit. Sprouted coconuts (*Right*) should be baked for about two hours in such an oven.

FIG. 354. The simple leaf of a sprouted coconut utilized as a dish.

FIG. 355. A bed and shelter made from the split fronds of the coconut tree will protec a castaway from rain and sun. Marshall Islands.

FIG. 356. Once a few of the simple weaving technics are learned, useful articles such as baskets and sun shades can be made. The easiest way to master weaving technics is to watch a native or an instructor, and then practice a few times.

In general, maintaining a course is more important than ease of travel. In other words, effort should be directed toward following a compass sight rather than selecting an easy route of travel. This holds true in unfamiliar country where vision is strictly limited.

A compass should always be worn, as it is possible to get completely turned around in a matter of minutes after leaving a known landmark. Rain squalls are numerous and the jungle canopy is dense, so that even on a sunny day it is often impossible to get your bearings from the sun. A map is a big help in traveling, but once a man is oriented, he must continually keep track of his whereabout through the use of the compass, and must concentrate on memorizing landmarks and terrain. Whenever possible, it is wise to establish a base line (See pages 9-17).

In all jungle travel, better results are generally obtained by following rivers and streams (Fig. 364). Native or game trails usually follow the banks of large rivers. You can afford to travel many extra miles on a trail to avoid a single mile cross-country. In the absence of trails the best traveling is via small stream beds, while large streams and rivers are best navigated by rafting. Bamboo, being hollow, is ideal for raft construction and can be used green.

Mountain jungle streams are fast running, and flood quickly. It may be necessary to cross such streams frequently in a day's travel. A knowledge of swimming in rapids, selecting fording sites, and wading swift currents is of great practical value (Pages 20-29).

In most types of country it is easier to travel the ridges and divides than the valleys. In general, however, ridges should be avoided in jungle country as they are often crammed with dense thickets of rattan bamboo and scrub growth. At high altitudes they may be matted with coarse ferns. The view is usually no better than along stream beds, and a stream offers a more definite course to follow. Even with the aid of a compass, branching spur ridges can completely confuse a traveler in dense vegetation.

Hurrying accentuates the discomfort of heat and humidity and brings on fatigue more quickly. A steady pace adjusted to a man's physical condition will take him farthest with the least effort.

The greatest annoyances to travel in the Pacific jungles are thorny rattans and small animal pests such as mosquitoes, ants, and leeches. Rattans are trailing, climbing palms with recurved thorny stems and tendrils that rip and tear skin and clothing. The smooth rattans form unyielding networks of vines that hinder a traveler at every turn. It is next to impossible to work through some thickets of rattan without becoming entangled in the thorns. A machete is useful only if it is sharp. You cannot tear yourself free by force, as you will only set the thorns deeper. It is far wiser to stop and carefully unfasten each thorn, or, if caught by one tendril, to make a slow spin away from it.

The best defense against mosquitoes and leeches is proper clothing. Trousers should be long, lightweight, and tucked into boot tops. The shirt should be mosquito proof, and the hat, water repellent. Nylon top boots, 8 to 10 inches high, with instep vents to allow water to run out, are a light, cool, quickly dried footgear. Wool socks are preferable to cotton. Where leeches or ticks are abundant, frequent stripping to examine the body will be necessary. A lighted cigarette or match held close to the body of an imbedded tick or leech will cause it to loosen its grip and it can then be removed.

Concealment

If a man can live off the land and knows how to take care of himself, he can hide out and evade enemies in the jungle for an indefinite period. The best way to lose a pursuer or to avoid an enemy is to get off the trails. This entails difficult traveling, to be resorted to only when the necessity of concealment is more imperative than ease of movement or conservation of energy. It is difficult to stalk an alerted man in the jungle, as it is necessary to get within a few yards to make sure of a shot. On the other hand it is simple to ambush an enemy following a trail. If a group is traveling together it is well to spread out along the trail, each person keeping within sight of the man ahead.

Few civilized men are capable of tracking down a man in jungle country, or are sufficiently trained to observe tell-tale marks left by a traveler. On the other hand, primitive natives are uncanny in their ability to track a man, and they can move through the jungle much faster than persons who have not spent their lives there. When natives are employed by an enemy for such tasks, the utmost care must be exercised to evade them. Hiding places in bamboo and rattan thickets, banyan trunks, and rocky outcrops are plentiful. The jungle is predominantly dark; a man wearing dark green clothing blends in with the surroundings and is unlikely to be detected by a passing enemy as long as he remains motionless. Lack of movement is more important than camouflage.

Smoke from a small cooking fire can seldom be seen for more than a few hundred feet, and a similar fire at night cannot be detected through dense jungle growth for any greater distance. An enemy approaching at night can be heard before he is within sight of a small fire, as it is extremely difficult to move through thick jungle at night without making considerable noise.

Caution must be exercised to prevent silhouetting yourself against a fire at night. You can do this by determining the most difficult approach for an enemy and putting your back to this approach, with a tree or bush backrest as camouflage. If watches are kept, the sentinel should select his post a short distance out of the circle of firelight so that his eyes adjust to the darkness. Camps should be as simple as possible, and all signs of their use should be removed before the site is abandoned.

Fig. 357. Small octopus can be caught on the reef, and they are surprisingly good to eat.

Fig. 358. The Languster or spiny lobster makes a delicious meal, and can be speared in shallow water at night or caught as pictured.

Fig. 359. A coconut crab trussed up with Pandanus leaves and awaiting the rock broiler.

Fig. 360. Making fire with the bamboo fire saw on the Island of Palawan.

Water

Water is a basic necessity, and even in the tropical rain forests it can be a problem to the survivor. Some types of jungles are quite dry, others have a wet and dry season, while high mountain forests are almost continually wet. Primary jungles are well supplied with streams and rivers, and rainwater is generally available. Rainwater collected as it falls, or trapped in pockets on the jungle floor, is safe to drink, but many serious diseases can be contracted by drinking from streams or rivers in the vicinity of native camps or villages. Such water, even if clear and inviting, should not be considered safe until boiled or treated with halazone.

Securing water will be a serious problem during the dry season even in the primary jungle, and is always a problem in the thorn forests and other arid-type jungles. But in all jungles there are some kinds of water yielding plants that will provide pure, potable water, often in unlimited quantities. The large jungle vines or lianas are the most widely available of such plants and offer the best drinking water. It is safe to assume that any of the innumerable jungle vines that do not yield a bitter or colored sap will furnish water safe to drink. The best vines yield a clear water with a slight acid or mineral flavor. In general, large diameter vines yield more water than small ones, and since this water is being pulled up the vine to be transpired through the leaves, more water is present during the heat of the day than at any other time. This water will be many degrees cooler than the air temperature.

To tap a vine, sever it as high as you can reach, or cut a deep notch; then cut off the vine at knee level to give you a water tube six or seven feet long. Water will start flowing from the lower end (Page 45). A single section of a large, rough-barked vine will yield a pint to a quart of water.

The slender, smooth rattan vines are a particularly good source of water in some areas. To obtain a large quantity of water from them, several vines should be cut into 6-foot lengths and then held horizontally until a bundle has been obtained (Fig. 363). All are then turned vertically at once and allowed to flow into a container. When the flow ceases, cut a foot off the top of the vines and more water will drain. Continue this process until no water flows.

In securing water from any type of vine it is important to make the top cut first, otherwise the water will ascend and much or all of it will be lost.

Some species of bamboo contain water in the green stalks and this water is usually good to drink, though in some cases it is quite bitter. Old stalks that have dried and split often catch and hold rainwater between the nodes. Water trapped in this manner during the wet season is available during the dry season. Most of the climbing bamboos contain good water. To get a drink, cut

FIG. 362. Such delicacies as monitors (large lizards) should not be overlooked by the survivor. Palawan Island in the Philippines.

FIG. 361. Cutting the edible heart out of the growing tip of a rattan palm or vine. The heart can be eaten raw but is better roasted. Palawan Island.

a section for a container and then cut and drain the contents of each succeeding section (node and internode) into the container.

Bromeliads are pineapple-like plants whose up-curved leaves form natural cups that catch and hold rainwater. These air plants affix themselves to jungle trees or they may grow out of the ground. They are found in both wet and dry jungle areas. In the latter regions they catch the dew and the little rain that falls, holding it deep in the heavy leaf bases where it does not evaporate. During the driest periods, an apparently empty bromeliad will yield some water if it is cut and held upside down to drain. In the primary jungle these air plants are filled with water that is frequently laden with decayed vegetable matter and small insects. It is pure, however, and can be sucked or siphoned off with a hollow reed so as to leave the sediment undisturbed.

Keep in mind that water from plants is pure, and except in wilderness areas it will save time and insure your health to utilize such sources. In some jungle areas plants may be the only readily available source of water.

Water-borne diseases are major hazards of tropical and subtropical regions. In the vicinity of native populations, amoebic and bacillary dysentaries are the most common of these diseases. They are highly debilitating and can be fatal. Cholera, typhoid, blood flukes transmitting schistosomias and other diseases, worms, and leeches can be picked up by drinking impure water. A good rule is to boil or chlorinate all surface water except in primitive areas. Special care must be taken in this respect when living or traveling with natives since this direct contact increases disease hazards many fold (See Chap. 3).

Plant Foods

Plant foods in the jungle are widely distributed and generally are more available than animal foods. To make full use of the many edible plants, they must be specifically identified and should be learned and recognized before an emergency occurs. It is not practical for military personnel to learn a great many plants, but there are a few common jungle plants of the Pacific area that are almost always available and there are some general principles that will serve a man well in any type of jungle.

Fruits and nuts that are being utilized as food by monkeys are usually safe for a man to eat but should be sampled in small quantities until their edibility is established.

Various species of palms are found throughout the tropics. They are, as a group, conspicuous, readily recognized, and many of them are excellent sources of food. A great many species yield edible fruits, inflorescences, terminal buds, sugary sap, or stored starch within the trunk.

The fruits of some of the Old World palms are not edible as they contain irritating crystals, but most of the New World palms are edible or can at least be safely tested.

Some groups of edible plants found in the United States are widespread throughout the world. Such plants have characteristics that will appear familiar, and many of them can be used in the same manner as those at home (See Chap. 4).

Jungle fruits are frequently borne at the tops of high trees and can only be harvested on the ground. The most useful plants in the primary jungle are rattan palms, bamboo shoots, ferns, and the fruits, nuts, and leaves of various jungle trees (Pages 153-173).

Rattan Palms (Calamus).—Rattans are vine-like palms that look like climbing bamboos. These plants are common throughout the Pacific jungles. Their growing tips are edible just as is the coconut heart, and are obtained in the same manner. To obtain the edible portion, cut the vine and gradually pull it down through the jungle canopy. The thorny sheath about the stem of some species can be removed to facilitate pulling. The 6 to 8 foot growing tip should be cut off and the spiny outer sheath removed. This section of rattan can then be cut in short lengths and placed on a bed of coals to cook. When the outer covering is well charred, the tender inner heart will be cooked. Some species taste as good as "coconut heart" and others are slightly bitter, especially when cooked in the sheath. Most are edible raw, but are more palatable and nourishing when cooked.

Bamboos.—There are many species of bamboo, some of them climbing vines like the rattans. Their stems are hollow and divided into nodes. The new shoots of these bamboos, or the buds often found along the stems, can be cooked and eaten in the same manner as described for the rattans.

Ferns.—Ferns of almost every description are found in the jungle. The young fronds of all of them can be boiled as greens. Some may be too bitter for your taste, but often a change of water will eliminate this. The better ones can be sorted out by trial and error.

Bago (Gnetum gnemon).—The seeds and young leaves of this small forest tree may be eaten. The seeds may be eaten raw or cooked, and the leaves cooked as greens.

Pillinut (Canarium).—There are numerous species of this large nut tree in the jungles. The single, more or less triangular seeds of the fruit are edible raw or roasted.

Bread Fruit (Artocarpus).—Various species of Artocarpus are found in the primary and secondary jungles. The pulp of the round, spiny fruit of the Artocarpus rotunda is very tasty raw. The seeds should be boiled or roasted.

In cut-over jungle and abandoned garden areas, fruits such as bananas, papayas, mangos, custard apples, sour sops, jac fruit, limes, plantains, guavas, cashews, and antidesma will be found.

Yams are plentiful in both the secondary and the primary jungles, but some of them, such as the wild yam (Dioscorea hispida), are poisonous unless properly prepared. The natives do not use the wild yam except in time of famine. It is abundant in the jungles and contains numerous tubers, some as large as a man's head.

The number of jungle trees whose fruits are edible are scarce. Some furnish young leaves that make excellent greens. Most of these edible and useful plants are known to the natives, who have spent either all or part of their lives in the jungles. A few hours spent learning edible plants from the natives of a region will pay large dividends in an emergency (See *Plants of the Pacific World*, E. D. Merrill).

Animal Foods

The plant and animal foods found in jungle areas of the world are so great in number that we can treat them only in a very general way lest we lose sight of basic applicable knowledge in a mass of detail. Streams and rivers should be considered the best source for securing animal food, as here aquatic animal life is concentrated into relatively small areas and the immediate terrestrial environment is nearly always more heavily populated with birds and mammals than is the surrounding country. A survivor should, in general, plan to keep traveling until he strikes a stream, and then make camp until a supply of food can be obtained.

Wilderness streams are well supplied with fish, and a survivor possessing a gill net should experience little trouble in securing enough fish to sustain him. A gill net (12 by 3 feet, with 1½ inch mesh,) can be effectively used by stretching it across a small stream and then driving fish into it by throwing stones into the water or by wading netward, herding the fish ahead. The lower side of the net should be well weighted so as to rest on the bottom. Several dozen fish can be netted at one time. Care should be taken not to tear the delicate net.

Remember that fishing methods that work at home are very likely to be successful. The hook and line is a good standby when baited with crushed snails, wood grubs, or insects. Trot lines for turtles or eels and other fish are always good. Improvised hooks can be made from rattan thorns (Page 77). Under the right conditions you can catch fish with your hands, or can noose, snag, spear, or gig them. Improvised nets and seines will yield results where minnows and small fish abound. You need to have no concern about poisonous fish, but be sure to thoroughly cook all freshwater animal life before eating it.

Obtaining bait is often a greater problem than catching the fish. Crustaceans, mollusks, and aquatic insects and larvae are present in jungle streams, and are found in the same types of habitats as in temperate waters. Even if you have no fishing equipment, bark and fiber line can be made from plant materials (Pages 78-79), and you can improvise toggle or gorge hooks from bamboo or other hardwoods, or can utilize rattan thorns as snell hooks. Fishing techniques are too varied to discuss in detail, but a survivor's results will be in direct proportion to his previous fishing experience.

The numerous species of birds and mammals found in the jungle are available to a man equipped with firearms. Although traps and snares are useful (Pages 92-101), no primitive method of catching or killing game, when used by inexperienced men, can compare with the modern rifle.

A man does not need to know how to recognize the many species of birds and mammals, since all of them are edible. A knowledge of the habits of specific species is a great advantage, but such knowledge is gained only by long experience, and most survivors must make out without this advantage. It is well to remember that a good hunter in temperate regions can do well in jungle country by following basic procedures and techniques.

1. A cardinal rule when hunting unfamiliar game is to proceed at all times so that you are not heard, seen, or scented.

2. Look for animal signs such as tracks, feces beds, runways, trails, and feeding marks, and do your hunting where such indicators of game are conspicuous and fresh.

3. Many jungle animals have highly developed senses of hearing and smell. You will see more animal life by stillhunting at a trail, water hole, or feeding area than by hours of walking. Seldom will you be able to locate and stalk game, but you must wait for it to come to you. Select a spot downwind from the most likely approach, and remain silent.

4. Jungle life is most active during early morning and late evening, and is generally quiet and inactive during the heat of the day. You must hunt when the animal life is active.

5. In regard to bird life, it is best to hunt in early morning and late evening, and in general, it is a waste of time and effort to hunt during showers or stormy days.

6. Many species of birds are attracted to trees bearing fruit, and the noise they make in feeding can be heard for a long distance in the jungle.

7. Jungle edges and openings support larger populations of birds than the unbroken interior forest.

A few jungle foods are worthy of specific attention.

Monkeys are conspicuous and numerous in some jungle areas, and can be shot with relative ease. Monkey meat is excellent, tasting somewhat like veal. Wild pigs are common in many areas, their tracks and rootings being conspicuous in moist places. Pigs are difficult to stalk, but can be shot by waiting at a feeding area in early morning or late evening. Natives kill them by means

FIG. 363. Draining drinking water from sections of rattan. Palawan Jungles.

FIG. 364. The easiest traveling in dense jungle country is often to follow up or down the stream beds. This necessitates wading and sometimes swimming. Philippines.

of the spear trap. The large monitors, iguanas, and lizards found throughout the tropics are all excellent eating. They must be skinned and gutted. The long cylindrical tail muscle is best baked or roasted. Snakes are not to be overlooked, for they too are far better eating than their appearance would indicate. The crocodile is also a good bet. Large ones should be left alone, but small ones can be shot on the bank or in shallow water where they can be retrieved. They can also be caught with large steel hooks or improvised toggle or gorge hooks, baited and suspended from bushes overhanging the water. A dead or wounded crocodile will sink to the bottom, so don't shoot them in deep water.

If things get really tough, the survivor can always resort to termite larvae and beetle grubs, which are abundant in rotten stumps. Large termite nests in open grassland or along the jungle fringes are easily spotted.

Shelters and Beds

The construction of some type of shelter and bed will insure a better night's sleep and will protect you from cold and rain, thus increasing your chances of surviving.

Try to determine what factors are most likely to prevent a good night's rest and then prepare against them. Often a bed to keep you off the ground is all you need; at other times a waterproof shelter is essential, while protection from mosquitoes, leeches, fire ants, or other jungle insects may be of more concern than either a bed or a shelter.

Examine a camp site before setting up camp and consider its desirability with regard to bedding and shelter material, firewood, available food and water, air movement, a level spot for sleeping, absence of insect pests, concealment, and protection from storms, falling trees, floods, and the like.

If a natural shelter exists, use it. A key to surviving is conserving energy whenever possible. The fronds of the various species of palm trees and rattan vines can be easily split and shingled to form a waterproof roofing. In heavy jungle, rain comes straight down and a roof is all that is necessary to give protection. A teepee or leanto made from parachute silk is an adequate shelter under many conditions. More practical for jungle camping is the parahammock. When covered with a waterproof roof of palm fronds it makes an ideal bed and shelter.

Sleeping platforms should be constructed 1 to 3 feet off the ground and then blanketed with palm fronds or other vegetation. The types of beds and shelters that can be constructed from jungle vegetation are limited only by the ingenuity of the survivor (Figs. 343 and 355). Remember that a good general rule is to make a bed off the ground, construct some type of roofing over it, and rig a mosquito net or use a head net. This will meet most jungle requirements.

Many jungle areas get cold at night, and you will have to dry your clothing or keep a small fire going to keep warm. Don't sleep on damp ground or in wet clothing, unless there is no alternative (See Chapter 7).

Firemaking and Cooking

The trick of making a fire in wet jungles is to secure enough dry wood or tinder to get it started. The wet exterior of dead limbs can be cut away to reach dry wood. Generally, the inside of dead bamboo stalks is dry, and the fine, membranous-like skin adhering to the inner wall will ignite when most other tinders fail. Gather wood that is not on the ground. Wet wood will burn, once you get a good fire going. The fibrous leaf sheaths and dried fruit stalks of palm trees, the dead leaves of pandanas, and the fine fuzz covering on the growing tip of tree ferns make good tinder. Keep dry tinder on hand at your camp and carry some with you when on the move.

The fire saw (Fig. 360), and fire thong are emergency firemaking methods that evolved in jungle country. They are very effective, but should be mastered before an emergency (Pages 109-110).

Wild game can be simply and effectively broiled over hot coals or roasted on a spit or in an earth oven. Fish can be similarly prepared, but are best roasted on hot stones. Many types of food can be boiled in bamboo or leaf containers. Excess meat, fish, and fruit should be sun dried or smoked to preserve it for future use (Pages 111-119).

Living off the land in strange jungle country is a science; it is the practical application of biological facts and principles. Native peoples the world over have perfected this science, each in their own environment. You can learn to live primitively in the jungle, but to do so you must observe, and think and act with every faculty. Above all, you must constantly observe and interpret what you see in terms of food, water, and shelter, the basic necessities of life.

TRAINING SYLLABUS

Jungle survival training should be imparted entirely through the media of field trips. The minimum time necessary for such a trip is two days. The following material should be worked into the trips:

1. Travel in the jungle, laying a course so as to intersect varied topography and vegetation conditions. An excellent exercise is to hike landward through mangrove swamps into the primary jungle and return by way of river or stream.

2. Obtaining water from vines, bamboo, bromeliads, and other water-catching plants. Purification of surface water.

3. Selection of a camp site, construction of improvised shelters and beds.

4. The collection and preparation of bamboo shoots and hearts of rattan vines, and of other plant foods that may be available in quantity.

5. Emphasis on freshwater fishing techniques. Set-lines should be put out at night. One or two trapping methods should be demonstrated and sets made during the night. It is best to confine hunting to a few experienced individuals, but all members of the group should receive instruction in stalking and specific hunting techniques for the vicinity.

6. Building a fire under wet jungle conditions; practice fire-making with bamboo fire saw, fire thong, and fire plow. The use of various jungle tinders. Cooking of food in green bamboo utensils, and in a rock or earth oven. Various broiling methods should be particularly stressed.

7. Discussion of biological hazards, demonstrating proper precautions against insect-transmitted diseases, flukes, leeches, ticks, snakes, and crocodiles; unfamiliar jungle noises should be identified. As many physical hazards as possible should be encountered in the course of the trip, and means devised for surmounting them.

8. Improvised signalling methods demonstrated, as well as the use of standard signaling devices.

FIG. 365. Trapping a snowshoe rabbit with a wire noose. A small coil of copper wire will prove of great value to the man forced to survive in the Arctic or far north.

Polar and Subpolar Survival

The basic skills and knowledge that will enable a man to travel safely, to make a fire and shelter, and to rustle his food from the land and cook it, apply in the cold regions of the world as they do elsewhere. The major difference is that survival is more difficult in snow and under low temperatures, and that the right thing must be done *the first time*. Cold allows no time for trial and error experimentation. *Thus the basic survival problem in polar regions is keeping warm.*

To keep warm under emergency conditions in sub-zero temperatures requires specialized clothing and equipment, and a knowledge of controlling heat loss from the body. Many types of clothing have been tested and approved for cold weather use. A discussion of their relative merits is outside the scope of this work. However, minimum cold weather equipment should consist of the following:

1. Heavy underwear (50% wool, 50% cotton)
2. Intermediate trousers and jacket
3. Two to three pairs of wool socks
4. Felt insoles
5. Shoepacs, felt boots or mukluks
6. Fingered gloves and mittens
7. Outer trousers, and parka with hood
8. Dark glasses, matches, and field glasses
9. Sleeping bag
10. Machete
11. Gasoline stove and emergency rations
12. Snowshoes, rifle and ammunition

With these items and the ability to improvise, a man will have confidence that he can successfully cope with most emergency conditions in cold regions of the world until aid arrives.

It should be an ironclad rule among pilots and aircrewmen never to take off without clothing and foot gear that will serve well in an emergency, and to carry a down sleeping bag, *always*.

Keeping Warm with Clothing

The body tends to maintain an average temperature of 98° F. When the environment is warmer than this, heat is absorbed; when it is colder, heat is lost. The range of thermal adjustment in man is very limited, and thus, in cold climates, clothing functions to hold the heat generated by the body by insulating against the cold outside air. Cold weather clothing, such as fur, wool, fiber glass, and down, consist of thousands of tiny, dead airpockets that trap air warmed by the body and hold it close to the skin. It is this narrow zone of warm air, not the clothing itself, that makes you "feel warm." Thus several layers of medium-weight clothing are warmer than one heavy garment; and loose, porous clothing covered by a light windbreaker is warmer than a great bulk of clothing. The layers of insulating clothing hold warm air in, while wind-resistant fabric keeps the cold air out.

The insulating effect of clothing is greatly reduced when it gets damp or wet, when it is not worn loosely, or when the windbreaker is not adequate to stop outside air movement. A windy day always feels colder than a still day of equal temperature, because the warm air next to the body is being constantly blown away and replaced with cold air. The result is that the microclimate next to the skin, which determines whether the body is hot or cold, is actually lower on the windy day.

Overheating should be avoided, for when you get hot you sweat. Sweat dampens clothes, and wet clothes conduct heat from the body and reduce the air spaces which act as insulators. Also, as sweat evaporates, it cools you. Sweating can be held at a minimum by opening the clothing at the neck, wrists, and front closure, or by removing layers of clothing. Moist air may be removed from the parka by loosening it at the neck and pumping the bottom of the garment like a bellows. Clothing should not be tight. Tight clothing reduces the zone of still air and also prevents free circulation of the blood.

Clothing must be kept dry inside and out. Heat from the body will melt snow and frost; therefore, don't sit or kneel in snow for long periods. And be sure to remove snow from boots and clothing when standing around a fire or entering any heated shelter.

If you chill any part of the body, other parts also become chilled. Since the extremities of the body cool more quickly than other parts, the hands and feet should be given special attention. Hands should be kept under cover as much as possible. When they get cold they can be warmed by placing them next to warm flesh under the armpits, between the thighs, or against the ribs. A footgear sufficiently warm for sub-zero weather should be worn at all times. However, keeping the feet warm is difficult because they sweat more readily than other parts of the body and because when they get damp they get cold. Exercise will warm cold feet but it produces perspiration. Insoles and socks will absorb some of this sweat, but unless these are periodically dried, much of their insulating effect is lost. It is not practical nor advisable to remove footwear for ventilating or cooling purposes. Freezing of the feet is serious; and since it is difficult to tell when the feet are approaching the freezing point, a good rule is to overdress rather than underdress your feet, but always avoiding tight socks or boots.

FIG. 366. A bough shelter, and makeshift snowshoes constructed from willow bushes and parachute silk.

FIG. 367. A snow cave can accommodate one or many men.

FIG. 368. Winter travel in mountainous country is often best and safest along the ridges. Care must be taken to avoid snow cornices. (Fig. 369)

FIG. 369. Breaking through over a snow cornice.

Keeping warm in your clothing, in a sleeping bag, in a snow cave, or in other shelter is basically the same. Air movement must be reduced to a minimum so that it can be warmed by body heat or fire; and all garments must be kept as dry as possible to prevent heat loss through conduction and through reduced insulating air space. (See page 187).

Keeping Warm with Fire and Improvised Shelter

Cold, not food or water, is the critical factor in the far north. The prime consideration of a man stranded under polar conditions is how to supplement the protection afforded by arctic clothing until help arrives. This can be done by creating a dead air space such as a snow cave, snow house, or bough shelter; and by the use of fire. These technics have been fully discussed in Chapters 6 and 7.

In open country, a camp or shelter should not be built in a lee, as it may get covered with snow. However, in mountain or forested country a safe camp can and should be made in a lee, as such a site is generally warmer and snow does not pile up by drifting. If at all possible, make camp below timber line in mountain country even though you must cope with the problem of deep, soft snow. Timber breaks the wind, and wind is a major factor in keeping you cold. The contour and depth of the snow which lies on the ground is the best indicator of whether a lee will be safe from heavy drifting. In timbered country, find a sheltered spot out of the wind (see page 188), then construct the type of shelter most suitable to the occasion. The snow cave (Fig. 367) is an extremely effective, easily constructed type of one-man shelter. A small fire or even a candle will raise the air temperature many degrees above the outside air. The floor should be lined with boughs or other vegetation; and if no fire is used, the entrance should be closed. The dome and sides can be glazed with a candle or firebrand to prevent the snow from flaking down. The snow cave is cramped and uncomfortable, but, with a sleeping bag, it makes one of the best cold weather shelters with the least expenditure of energy. A more permanent shelter (Fig. 366), constructed of boughs and heated with a fire and snowbank reflector, is readily constructed in forested sub-polar regions.

Windbreaks of snow blocks or boughs increase the comfort of a camp, and protect a fire, and will even serve as emergency sleeping shelters. A windbreak 2 or 3 feet high placed about 2 feet to windward of a shelter in exposed country is generally quite effective. Windbreaks at a distance of 5 to 10 feet will cause a snowdrift to form that will bury such a camp.

The snowhouse is the ideal cold-weather shelter, and the technic of its construction should be included in any polar survival training (Fig. 371). It is

FIG. 370. Makeshift goggles to prevent snow blindness can be made from the bark of aspen or birch trees or from canvas cloth or other suitable material.

FIG. 371. A snow house makes an ideal shelter for a group of men.

generally not practical for a lone individual; however, with a little experience, some modification of it can be utilized to advantage. It is best adapted for a permanent camp for a crew of 4 or 5 men. Its construction, advantages, and practicability are discussed by Stefansson in his *Arctic Manual*.

A parachute makes an excellent tepee, and this type of shelter (Fig. 342), is, according to Stefansson, unexcelled for Arctic summer camping. It is equally useful in temperate and tropic climes.

For additional information on fire making, shelter, and cooking, see Chapters 6 and 7.

The Sleeping Bag

The sleeping bag is as essential to the man stranded in polar regions as the life raft is to the castaway. When properly used and cared for, the down bag will keep a man from freezing, regardless of whether he has fire or shelter. The bag should be kept dry and loosely fluffed, and should have a water-repellent cover. Do not use it directly on the snow if insulating material such as boughs, grass, or outer-garments are available.

Beneath the bag is where you need extra protection. The weight of the body compresses the down thus enabling heat to escape. In general it is best to remove your outer garments before getting into your sleeping bag. Each day the bag should be turned inside-out to allow the sun and wind to dry the moist air that collects inside.

Remember that if you have a down sleeping bag with you in an emergency, nine-tenths of your worries are over.

The Dangers of Cold

The dangers associated with cold, frostbite, snow blindness, and carbon monoxide poisoning must be anticipated, for they are dangers that creep up on a man unnoticed. In very cold weather you must anticipate frostbite, detect it early, and remedy it. The face is most likely to be frostbitten. When stiffness is detected by grimacing, remove a hand from the mitten and hold it to the frozen part until the stiffness and accompanying whiteness are gone. Frozen, cold, or wet feet should not be undressed unless there is a fire or a warm shelter or sleeping bag handy. Exposure to cold air will only aggravate the situation (See page 187).

To prevent snowblindness, protect the eyes with dark amber glasses or makeshift goggles (Fig. 370). (See page 185.)

Carbon monoxide is a potential danger in any closed shelter that is warmed by fuel such as gasoline, kerosene, fuel oil, or alcohol. Proper ventilation is the only preventive. Generally there are no warning symptoms. But if you have a headache, or experience dizziness, weariness, and nausea, you can sus-

FIG. 372. The paratepee makes an excellent winter shelter. It consists of 14 panels stretched around nine (9) tepee poles, and is pegged to the ground where the shroud lines meet the fabric. A fire warms the interior. This excellent survival shelter was devised following basic Indian tepee design by Mr. Belmore Browne.

FIG. 373. A tarp can be extremely *useful* to a survivor. Erected in this manner, with a fire pit and snowbank windbreak, the interior warms up many degrees. The open front enables a survivor to camp in comfort and at the same time watch for game or enemy patrols.

SHOWING STEPS IN CONVERTING
PARACHUTE INTO PARATEPEE

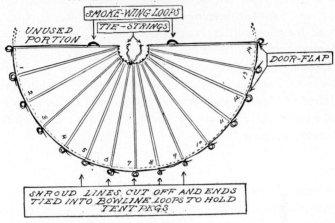

SHOWING CONSTRUCTION OF INDIAN SMOKE-WINGS
AND PARATEPEE COMPROMISE

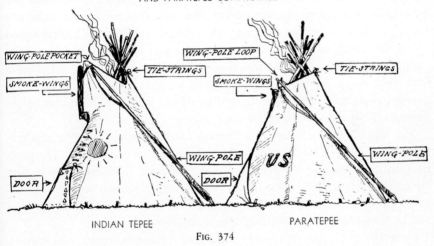

INDIAN TEPEE   PARATEPEE

FIG. 374

pect carbon monoxide poisoning and should get to fresh air immediately. If you have suffered from such poisoning, do not exercise, as this further reduces the oxygen supply in the blood. Rest in your sleeping bag in the fresh air, even if this requires going outside the shelter.

Food and Water

Emergency subsistence in the far north has been treated in Chapter 8, pages 173-182, and various useful technics have been discussed throughout the text. Snares (Fig. 365) are particularly useful in the sub-polar regions, and a good rifle should be basic equipment. Food is the fuel for generating body heat, and, as pointed out earlier, the conservation of this heat close to the body is the basic factor in keeping warm. Obtaining food in polar regions is not difficult for men with experience; however, you should always make certain that rations are included in your emergency equipment.

Obtaining the body's water requirements each day is important, and generally is not a serious problem. Snow should be eaten quite frequently and is preferred to drinking water at cold temperatures. When fire is available, snow should be melted and warmed for drinking. Cold water chills the stomach and causes shivering.

Travel

The polar and sub-polar regions are vast expanses of relatively unexplored territory. Distances alone make travel a major problem. In general the best bet is to stay with a downed plane unless fully equipped for polar travel. Both Wilkins and Stefansson indicate that they believe an experienced polar traveler could walk to the nearest settlement from anywhere in the Polar Sea if he had one good companion, good clothes, an adequate hunting outfit, and a sled or the means of constructing a sled. The journey from a central region of the Arctic pack might require 2 years, or 2 winter seasons. Stefansson states, "For men skilled in hunting and properly equipped, the Arctic sea is safer than most Arctic lands, so far as securing food and fuel is concerned." A downed pilot can live by hunting, and he should be so equipped that he can depend on big game as the major food source.

The hazards and problems that a traveler will encounter in polar and sub-polar travel are so varied that they can only be treated briefly here. The problems on polar seas are different from those on polar land, and these in turn are quite different from those in the forested and mountain regions. For detailed travel technics, the reader is referred to Stefansson's, *Arctic Manual* and to Henderson's *Handbook of American Mountaineering.*

Generally speaking, spring is the worst season for traveling in polar regions, as the snow becomes soft, heavy, and wet. Ice melts, opening streams, bays, and seas. Circuitous routes of travel are necessary, depending upon the terrain. The traveler may encounter such hazards as flooded streams, quicksand, muskeg, ice break-up, snow avalanches, and tormenting insects. For a properly equipped individual, winter is the time to cover distances in the polar regions.

Deep snow and cold present serious obstacles to winter travel anywhere in the polar and sub-polar regions, and specialized gear such as snowshoes, skis, and sleds are necessary. Do not attempt to travel any distance in deep snow without snowshoes or skis; it is exhausting work and your energy is better

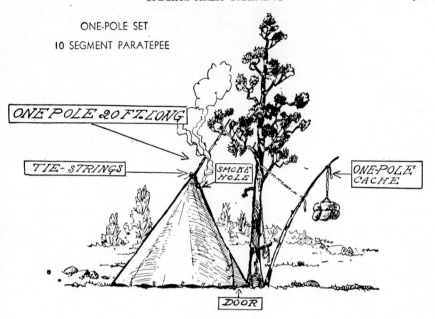

ONE-POLE SET
10 SEGMENT PARATEPEE

ONE POLE 20 FT. LONG

TIE-STRINGS

SMOKE HOLE

ONE-POLE CACHE

DOOR

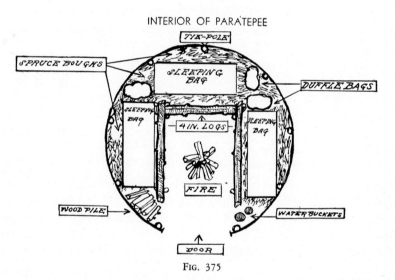

INTERIOR OF PARATEPEE

TIE-POLE

SPRUCE BOUGHS

SLEEPING BAG

DUFFLE BAGS

SLEEPING BAG

4 IN. LOGS

SLEEPING BAG

FIRE

WOOD PILE

WATER BUCKETS

DOOR

FIG. 375

utilized for improvising a camp. Crude snowshoes can be made from willow and other woody vegetation, but in general this task should not be attempted until a camp has been established. Parachute cord or stripped clothing (Fig. 366) makes usable webbing for snowshoes.

It is generally wiser to remain in camp than to travel into a cold wind. Wait for a shift in the wind or a rise in temperature before venturing forth. If you must head into a cold wind, try to lay your course so that you hit the lee side of timber, hills, ridges, or escarpments. The protection afforded usually more than compensates for a longer trek.

The use of snowshoes can be mastered much faster than skis, and it is not necessary to have specialized footgear to snowshoe. For these reasons snowshoes are better emergency traveling equipment than skis.

In mountains, snow above timberline is generally hard-packed along the ridges, but in the timber it is deep and soft, making travel without skis or snowshoes frequently impossible. The best traveling is generally on the windswept ridges (Fig. 368).

When traveling above timberline, try to avoid steep southern exposures where the snow may avalanche. In such places a cracked, crumpled appearance indicates that the snow has already avalanched and that the slope can be negotiated with safety. On any slope, danger of avalanche is greatest during the warmest part of the day, or on a day following several days of relatively high temperature or heavy snowfall, the greatest danger occurring in early spring (See Chapter 1, pages 31-39).

When fording polar or high mountain streams (See Chapter 1, pages 20-28), remember that the water is ice-cold. Your ability to swim, wade, or hold on is greatly reduced in cold water, and cold, wet clothes are to be avoided at all cost; therefore proceed with utmost caution.

Crossing deep, snow-covered streams is particularly dangerous. Snow itself is an excellent insulator. If a heavy fall has occurred before safe ice has formed, the blanket of snow will frequently prevent further ice formation. Small streams wind-protected by high banks or heavy vegetation are more apt to have thin ice beneath deep snow than large windswept bays or rivers. A probing stick is useful in such cases.

If a lone man falls into water, he should make a fire before attempting to change to dry garments. Stefansson states that "When the right snow is available, the first thing to do after falling into water is to roll in a deep, soft bank. The snow acts as a blotter, abstracting some of the water from the clothing."

The problems and technics of travel on sea ice are peculiar to the polar regions and are described in detail in Stefansson's *Arctic Manual*.

Survival in Polar Waters

Ocean survival is treated in Chapter 8, pages 132-144. In polar waters, exposure rather than food and water is the critical factor. The Mae-West, antiexposure suit, and rubber raft are essential. An unprotected swimmer can survive only a short time in freezing waters. Surviving is not a matter of ingenuity or physical fitness, it is primarily a case of having the proper equipment and knowing exactly how to use it. Other things are secondary, therefore special emphasis should be placed on equipment drills, bailing out, and ditching procedures.

Training

Military strategists realize that if another war occurs in the near future, it may be fought largely in and over the cold regions of the earth. Realistic training programs for instructing airmen to meet emergency situations in cold regions will be essential. The health, safety, and morale of airmen will to a large extent depend upon how thoroughly they have been grounded in polar experience, technics, and knowledge.

Emphasis should be placed on the necessity for having proper survival equipment. Large bombers can, and should be, equipped with sufficient gear to allow the crew to set up a permanent-type camp, to obtain food by hunting, and to travel long distances afoot if necessary. The problem of adequately equipping the small fighter and interceptors is greater, and the airmen that fly such planes must be thoroughly trained in survival "know-how" so as to substitute knowledge and experience for a dearth of equipment.

Training Syllabus

Time is always a limiting factor in war; therefore the ensuing syllabus is based on minimum basic requirements.

1. Two hours of lecture on polar climate, topography, and the problems of polar survival, with special emphasis placed on the principles of keeping warm.

> References—*How to Survive on Land and Sea*
> *Cold Facts for Keeping Warm,* Office of the Quartermaster General, Washington, D.C.
> *Operation Zero,* Boy Scouts of America
> *Arctic Manual,* Stefansson

2. Two-hour demonstration on the use and care of clothing and equipment. (Demonstration Exhibit Room.)
3. One-hour demonstration on the use of rubber rafts, exposure suits, and other emergency water survival gear.
4. One-hour lecture on polar travel and snow characteristics.

> References—1. *Arctic Manual,* Stefansson
> 2. *How to Survive on Land and Sea*
> 3. *Handbook of American Mountaineering,* Henderson.

5. Two half-day field trips for instruction and practice in:
    A. The use of snowshoes, skis, and sleds, and the application of various traveling and signaling devices and technics.

B. The construction of a snow cave, snow house, and windbreaks.
  References—*How to Survive on Land and Sea*
  Arctic Manual, Stefansson

6. Overnight excursion using basic emergency equipment and snow caves and snow houses as shelters. The trip should be planned to impart a maximum of information through actual experience. Technics such as fire-building, cooking, ice fishing, snaring and hunting (taught in basic training) should be refreshed through practice and applied to polar conditions.

7. Additional training aids as time permits, such as films and restricted references not listed.

The training course outlined covers only the minimum training requirements. During peacetime, the course should be extended to include:

1. Additional instruction and practice in the use of skis and snowshoes.
2. Oversnow marches and setting up bivouac, with emphasis on orientation.
3. First aid and methods of caring for wounded in extreme cold.
4. Practical work in construction of improvised sleds, skis, snowshoes, clothing, and shelter.
5. Introduction to Polar and Sub-polar flora and fauna.
6. Hunting and fishing expeditions rigidly supervised.

Organizational Problems

Method of Instruction

Field experience and actual participation by the individual in performing useful survival technics is the crux of all survival training. Lectures, movies, and demonstrations, although useful, are far inferior as a means of communicating survival "know-how."

Future training should seriously consider the fact that actual participation in performing survival technics under realistic conditions is necessary if such training is to succeed thoroughly. Likewise sufficient time must be allotted to allow for such work. It cannot be individually experienced in a matter of a few hours.

The greatest value of the survival films used for training during World War II was to introduce men to the problems of survival and to awaken an interest in learning. They were of only secondary importance as a means for imparting useful survival information; however, it is possible to produce a series of movies that would be of great educational value in depicting survival procedures and facts. Such films should parallel field training, should be correlated with the various training stages, and should be so produced that they impart specific information on special areas and problems.

Permanent survival exhibits such as those set up at Pensacola, Jacksonville, Bishop Museum, and other places are definitely useful in refreshing the student with survival facts and technics, and they serve as reliable reference sources. They supplement but cannot take the place of field trips for imparting survival knowledge.

Teaching Personnel

Throughout the survival training program there was a scarcity of trained men qualified to organize and teach a wellrounded course. Training courses for officers helped remedy this situation. However, at the end of the war, personnel was still a bottleneck. Officers in charge of survival training at any large activity should have at least the following specialized qualifications:

(a) Mastery of swimming and all phases of water survival work.

(b) A firsthand knowledge of outdoor living supplemented with actual survival work in several climatic regions.

(c) Training in the use of all up-to-date survival and rescue equipment.

(d) A knowledge of Air-Sea Rescue functions.

The last two qualifications can be mastered relatively quickly in training courses. The first two are a result of long experience, practice, and study. Men with a background of work in this line should be selected for training positions.

Training Areas

The success of any survival training program depends largely on three factors: the ability of the officer in charge, the cooperation he gets in securing sufficient time for the work, and the physical conditions of the area in which the training must be given. The latter is very important in regard to the special area of advanced base training. Tropical survival cannot be taught satisfactorily in temperate regions, nor can Pacific Island work be duplicated along the New England coast. It is therefore necessary that training centers be set up in regions that simulate conditions of possible combat areas. Basic survival principles can be taught almost anywhere in the States. Survival courses adequate for the tropical Pacific Islands can be given in the Hawaiian, Marshall, Mariana, or Philippine Islands. This would be a typical course in reef, seashore, and coconut belt survival. Jungle survival, typical of large tropical islands and mainland, can be given in the Philippines, the Panama Canal Zone, and a fair substitute can be given on the Islands of Hawaii and Guam.

Centers of cold weather and Arctic survival training can be established in our western mountains or in Alaska. Cold weather survival research and training stations could be profitably organized in peacetime in such states as Wyoming, Colorado, Idaho, or Montana.

Coordination Between Training and Operational Units

To be fully effective, any training program should be based on needs, and should be adjusted as these needs change. The needs in this case are the survival problems that are encountered in current theatres of operation, and those anticipated in future theaters. It should be the responsibility of operational units to convey this information to training units. The latter should see to it that student pilots are given the type of training necessary to enable them to cope with these problems.

Similar cooperation is called for in the matter of survival equipment. Obviously the operating units that are using this equipment every day are best qualified to recommend changes in its design. Training units are not concerned with such mechanical problems, but they are responsible for instructing aviation personnel in the use of survival gear. They should therefore be kept informed of changes in equipment that have been approved for the Fleet, and should be furnished with samples of new gear for teaching and testing purposes. By this means, and by standardizing all survival equipment, student pilots can be checked out on equipment that they will see and use when they reach the Fleet, and not have to waste time learning to use gear that may already be obsolete.

Early in World War II the Army, Navy, and Marine Corps each maintained separate survival establishments. Later the various services achieved a fair degree of coordination in the field of emergency equipment, and in rescue operations, but unfortunately not in the field of training.

The training set-ups of each branch of the Service contained many excellent features and in general the training objectives of all branches were similar. It is highly desirable that better liaison be maintained among these various training units, so that Army pilots will be familiar with Navy and Coast Guard equipment and rescue procedures, and so that pilots of all the services may receive the benefit of features of training that formerly were limited to individual branches.

Survival training records are important, since they indicate just what instruction the pilot has received. The practice of keeping the training records for an entire squadron on the key sheet was advantageous in that it showed at a glance the training status of the unit. In practice, however, many of these records were lost, or, when a squadron was broken up, its pilots arrived at their new bases with no record whatsoever. An individual record that can be entered in the pilot's record jacket would be a satisfactory solution to this problem.

In a future war, survival "know-how" will prove of even greater value than it did in World War II. Such information will benefit both civilian and military personnel. Under the leadership of Mr. Fred Mills, the Boy Scouts of America have developed an excellent survival training program. Modified courses of instruction in outdoor living should be available to grade school, high school, and college students. It should be a policy of the Armed Forces to encourage such training among our youth at civilian institutions, since men who had had experiences in outdoor living during their youth learned the essentials of global survival in a shorter time and fared better in emergencies than did inexperienced men. The training of our youth in survival principles and technics will be of immeasurable value to both the individual and to military organizations responsible for war-time training.

Glossary and Scientific Terminology

African puff adder—*Bitis arientans*

African walnut or gabon—*Coula*

Air plants, epiphyte—a plant attached above ground to another plant

Alder—*Alnus*

Amanita—a group or genus of poisonous mushrooms

Amphibians—animals such as frogs, toads, newts and salamanders

Anaconda, water boa—*Eunectes*

Archipelago—sea or large body of water interspersed with islands

Aroids—a group of plants generally containing stinging crystals of calcium oxalate and belonging to the calla lily family (*Araceae*)

Aspen—*Populus*

Atabrine—drug used in treating malaria

Australasia—Australia and adjacent islands

Australian black snake—*Pseudechis porphyriacus*

Australian needle bush—*Hakea leucoptera*

Australian nut trees—*Macadamia*

Badu, Coco—*Xanthosoma violaceum*

Bamboo snakes—*Trimeresurus*

Baobab tree—*Adansonia*

Barrel cactus—*Echinocactus*

Basswood—*Tilia*

Beaded lizard—*Heloderma horridum*

Beech family—*Fagaceae*

Betel nuts—*Areca catechu*

Bitter manioc—*Manihot esculenta*

Bivalve—an animal with a two-value shell like an oyster

Black birch—*Betula lenta*

Black snake—*Coluber*

Black widow spider—*Latrodectes*

Bloodwood—*Eucalyptus terminalis*

Boas and pythons—*Boidae*

Bottle tree—*Brachychiton*

Brake fern—*Pteridium*

Bushmaster—*Lachesis mutus*

Butternuts—*Juglans*

Calla lily—*Calla palustris*

Cape viper—*Causus rhombeautus*

Carnivores—mammals that feed chiefly on meat such as tigers, wolves, bears

Caster oil plant—*Ricinus*

Cheetal—Indian spotted deer

Chinese lacquer tree—*Rhus verniciflua*

Climbing hemp weed—*Mikania scandens*

Copperhead—*Agkistrodon*

Coral snake—*Micrurus*

Coulter pine—*Pinus coulteri*

Death adder—*Acanthophis antarcticus*

Desert oak—*Casuarina decaisneana*

Elephant ear—*Alocasia macrorhiza*

Emodi pine—*Pinus longifolia*

Euphorbias—spurges

Feces—animal excrement

Fer-de-lance—*Bothrops atrox*

Frond—the leaf of ferns

Fig trees—*Ficus*

Fireweed (northern)—*Epilobium latifolium*

Flukes—parasitic flat worms

Garter snake—*Thamnophis*

Genus—a related group of plants or animals containing one or more species that are structurally similar

Genera—plural of genus

Gila monster—*Heloderma suspectum*

Goatsuckers—*Caprimulgus*—Whippoorwill-like bird

Great white shark—*Carcharodon carcharias*

Gray nurse shark—*Carcharias*

Hardwoods—hickory, oaks, ironwoods, locust, birches, sugar maple, ash, holly, etc.

Heath—*Ericaceae*

Hemlock—*Tsuga*

Herbaceous—green succulent plants as compared with woody ones

Herbivorous—feeding on plants—animals such as deer, antelope, buffalo

Humus—black or brown organic soil formed from the partial decomposition of vegetable and animal matter

Iguanas—large lizards found in Tropical America

Jack-in-the-pulpit, Indian turnip—*Arisaema triphyllum*

King cobra, hamadryad—*Naja hannah*

Korean pine—*Pinus koraiensis*

Labrador tea—*Ledum latifolium*

Lemming—small mouse-like rodents

Lianas—tropical vines

Limber pine—*Pinus flexilis*

Lodgepole pine—*Pinus contorta*

Lymphatics—vessels within the body containing or conveying lymph

Machete—a large heavy knife

Malay Archipelago—Malay Peninsula and adjacent islands

Mangrove trees—*Rhizophora*—one of the more common of many genera

Millets—*Setaria*

Mints—plants belonging to the *Labiatae* family—usually have square stems and opposite aromatic leaves

Monitors—large Old World lizards

Morels—*Morchella*

Mountain sorrel—*Oxyria digyna*

Nepal nut pine—*Pinus gerardiana*

Omnivorous—eating a wide variety of plant and animal food

Osage orange—*Maclura*

Palmate—leaflets of leaf radiate out from stem like fingers on a hand

Palm Vipers—*Bothrops*

Papain—a protein splitting enzyme

Parching—(corn)—to dry or scorch over a fire until brown and brittle

Pemmican—a concentrated ration of dried, ground meat mixed with melted fat

Poplars—*Populus*

Pine Family—*Pinaceae*

Pinnate—leaf with leaflets arranged on each side of stem like walnut leaf. (See fig. 67)

Pinon pine—*Pinus edulis*

Poisonous long fanged snakes—*Viperidae* and *Crotalidae*

Poisonous short fanged snakes—*Elapidae*

Poke weed—*Phytolacca*

Portugese-men-of-war—*Physalia*

Prawns—shrimp-like crustaceans

Prickly pears—*Opuntia*

Quinine—drug used in treating malaria

Regal python—*Python reticulatus*

Rengas trees—trees belonging to the genera *Gluta, Melanochyla, Melanorrhea, Semecarpus and Swintonia*

Russell's viper—*Vipera russellii*

Sambar—Indian deer

Sand grouse—*Pterocles*

Sand shark—*Carcharias*

Sapodilla tree—*Achras sapota*

Sassafras—*Sassafras officinale*

Scotch pine—*Pinus sylvestris*

Sea snakes—*Hydridae*

Single leaf pine—*Pinus monophylla*

Skunk cabbage—*Symplocarpus foetidus*

Softwoods—examples—most pines, willows, spruce, basswood, yellow poplar, aspen, red cedar, alder, etc.

Sorghums—a genus of grasses

Species—a plant or animal with characteristics that distinguish it from all other members of a group or genus. In a scientific name the species name follows the genus name as in *Typha latifolia.* The species name is *latifolia*

Spicebush—*Benzoin*

Spruce—*Picea*

Spurge family—*Euphorbiaceae*

Star apple—*Chrysophyllum africanum*

Stinging plants—examples—*Tragia, Mucana, Jatropha, Ortega,* fruits and leaves of various palms

Strychnine trees—*Strychnos*

Sugar pine—*Pinus lambertiana*

Sumach—*Rhus*

Swiss stone pine—*Pinus cembra*

Tamarack—*Larix*

Tiger shark—*Galeocerdo articus*

Tiger snake—*Notechis scutatus*

Traveler's tree—*Ravenala madagascariensis*

Tree nettles—*Laportea*

Tubers—thick, roundish underground stems that store food for the plant

Umbrella tree—*Musanga Smithii*

Upas or Ipoh tree—*Antiaris toxicaria*

Voles—field mice

Walnuts—*Juglans*

Water hemlock—*Cicuta maculata*

Water moccasin—*Agkistrodon Piscivorus*

Water tree or vine—*Tetracera potatoria*

Water trees—various species of Eucalyptus called "Mallees."

> *Eucalyptus microtheca, E. incrassata, E. oleosa, E. paniculata, E. populifolia*

> Other species of Eucalyptus known as Tasmanian Cider trees (*E. Gunni*) (*E. resinifera*) (*E. mannifera*) yield a refreshing liquid in the spring from cuts made in the bark.

White heather—*Cassiope tetragona*

Wild oats—*Avena*

Willows—*Salix*

Wintergreen—*Gaultheria*

Selected Bibliography

GENERAL

ABRAHAM, G. D. 1907. *The Complete Mountaineer.* Methuen and Co., London. 493 p.

Army Air Forces, ADTIC. 1943. *Army Air Forces Emergency Kits and Equipment.* Elgin Field, Fla. 6 p.

Army Air Forces, Headquarters. 1945. *Emergency Uses of the Parachute.* No. 60-1. 24 p.

Army Air Forces, ADTIC. *Survival.* Elgin Field, Fla. 74 p.

COCHRAN, D. M. 1943. *Poisonous Reptiles of the World,* a Wartime Handbook, Smithsonian War Background Series, No. 10. Smithsonian Institution, Washington, D.C. 37 p.

Ethnogeographic Board & Smithsonian Institution. 1943. *Survival on Land and Sea.* ONI., United States Navy. 187 p.

FERNALD, M. L. and KINSEY, A. C. 1943. *Edible Wild Plants of Eastern North America.* Idlewild Press, Cornwall-on-Hudson, N.Y. 452 p.

GRAHAM, S. A. and O'ROKE, E. C. 1943. *On Your Own.* Lund Press, Inc., Minneapolis, Minn. 150 p.

HANSON, E. P. 1942. *Reconnaissance Report on Concentrated Rations of Primitive Peoples.* OQMG., Washington, D.C. 115 p.

HEDRICK, V. P. 1919. *Sturtevant's Notes on Edible Plants.* G. B. Lyon Co., Albany, N.Y. 686 p.

KEPHART, H. 1936. *Camping and Woodcraft.* The Macmillan Co., New York. 883 p.

MARGAREY, A. T. 1895. *Aborigines Water Quest in Arid Australia.* Aust. Ass. for Advancement of Science Proceedings, Sec. F VY 6.

MATHESON, R. 1932. *Medical Entomology.* Charles C Thomas, Springfield, Illinois. 488 p.

MEDSGER, O. P. 1939. *Edible Wild Plants.* Macmillan Co., N.Y. 323 p.

MUENSCHER, W. C. 1940. *Poisonous Plants of the United States.* Macmillan Co., New York.

REYNOLDS, O. 1946. *70,000 to 1.* Random House, Inc., N.Y. 217 p.

RICKETTS, F. E. and CALVIN, J. 1939. *Between Pacific Tides.* Stanford Univ. Press, Calif., 320 p.

U. S. Naval Air Station, Pensacola, Fla. 1944. *Survival Training Exhibit,* 29 p.

VAN DYKE, T. S. 1913. *The Still Hunter.* The Macmillan Co. 390 p.

WATSON, W. N. 1939. *Early Fire-Making Methods and Devices.* Gibson Bros., Ind. 75 p.

WHITLEY, G. P. 1943. *Poisonous and Harmful Fishes.* Bul. 159, Council for Scientific and Industrial Research, Commonwealth of Australia, Melbourne. 28 p.

WULFF, L. 1939. *Lee Wulff's Handbook of Freshwater Fishing.* Frederick A. Stokes, N.Y. 263 p.

TROPICAL

Army Air Forces, ADTIC. 1944. *Living Off the American Tropics.* Information Bul. No. 10, Training Headquarters, Army Air Forces. 62 p.

Auckland Institute and Museum. 1943. *Food Is Where you Find It.* Auckland, New Zealand. 72 p.

BROWN, W. H. and MERRILL, E. D. 1919. *Philippine Palm and Palm Products.* Bul. No. 18, Manila Bureau of Printing. 129 p.

BROWN, W. H. 1921. *Wild Food Plants of the Philippines, Minor Products of Philippine Forests.* Vol. 2, Bul. No. 21, Manila Bureau of Printing. 165 p.

CARTES, T. D. and HILL, J. E. and TATE, G. H. 1944. "Animals of the Pacific World," *The Infantry Journal,* Washington, D.C. 195 p.

CRAIGHEAD, J., CRAIGHEAD, F., LYNCH, J., and STITT, M. 1946. *Survival Survey of the Pacific.* Aviation Training Div., Office of the Chief of Naval Operations. U. S. Navy.

CRAIGHEAD, J. and CRAIGHEAD, F. January, 1947. "We Survive on a Pacific Atoll," *Nat'l Geog. Magazine,* Washington, D.C. 21 p.

CURRAN, C. H. 1946. "Insects of the Pacific World," *The Infantry Journal,* Washington, D.C. 281 p.

DAHLGREN, B. E. and STANDLEY, P. C. 1944. *Edible and Poisonous Plants of the Caribbean Region.* Bureau of Medicine and Surgery, Navy Dept., U. S. Gov. Printing Office, Washington, D.C. 102 p.

EMORY, P. K. 1943. *South Sea Lore.* Bernice P. Bishop Museum, Honolulu, Hawaii. 75 p.

General Staff, L. H. Q. Australia. 1943. *Friendly Fruits and Vegetables.* Arbuckle Waddell Pty. Ltd., Melbourne, Australia. 71 p.

GODSHALL, A. B. 1942. *Edible, Poisonous and Medicinal Fruits of Central America.* The Panama Canal Zone. 47 p.

HOSE, C. and McDOUGALL, W. 1912. *The Pagan Tribes of Borneo.* Macmillan and Co., Ltd. 283 p. Vol. 1.

LOVERIDGE, A. 1945. "Reptiles of the Pacific World, *The Infantry Journal,* Washington, D.C. 236 p.

MERRILL, E. D. 1943. *Emergency Food Plants and Poisonous Plants of the Islands of the Pacific.* TM 10-420, War Department, Washington, D.C. 149 p.

MERRILL, E. D. 1945. *"Plant Life of the Pacific World,"* The Infantry Journal, Washington, D.C. 298 p.

MILLER, C. D., and BAZORE, K. 1945. *Fruits of Hawaii. Univ. of Hawaii Agr.* Exp. Sta. Bul. No. 96. Honolulu, Hawaii. 129 p.

MOWAY, H., TOY, L. R., and WOLFE, H. S. 1936. *Miscellaneous Tropical and Sub-Tropical Florida Fruits.* Agr. Ext. Service., Univ. of Florida. Bul. 85. 91 p.

Naval Medical School. 1943. (Restricted). *Notes on Tropical and Exotic Diseases of Naval Importance.* Medical Center, Bethesda, Maryland. 82 p.

Naval Medical School. 1945. (Restricted). *Laboratory Guide to Medical Entomology with Special Reference to Malaria Control.* Medical Center, Bethesda, Maryland. 225 p.

NICHOLS, J. T. and BARTSCH, P. 1945. *"Fishes and Shells of the Pacific World,"* The Infantry Journal, Washington, D.C. 192 p.

OSBORN, F. 1944. *"The Pacific World,"* The Infantry Journal, Washington, D.C. 156 p.

ROUGHLY, T. C. 1936. *Wonders of the Great Barrier Reef.* Angus and Robertson, Ltd., Sydney, Australia. 282 p.

SAFFORD, W. E. 1905. *The Useful Plants of the Island of Guam.* Smithsonian Institution, Gov. Printing Office, Washington, D.C. 416 p.

VERDOORN, I. C. 1938. *Edible Wild Fruits of the Transvaal.* Dept. of Agr. for South Africa, Bul. No. 185.

WALLACE, A. R. and VOORST, J. V. 1853. *Palm Trees of the Amazon and Their Uses.* London. 124 p.

POLAR

Army Air Forces, ADTIC. 1943. *Notes on Arctic Living.* Eglin Field, Fla. 17 p.

Boy Scouts of America—(Lawrence, E. W.) 1947. *Operations Zero.* Boy Scouts of America. New York. 30 p.

British Ministry Training Pamphlet No. 90. 1945. *Snow and Mountain Warfare.*

G-2, Alaskan Department. 1944, *Emergency Foods in the Aleutians.* 11 p.

GOULD, L. M. 1931. *Cold.* Brewer Warren and Co. 275 p.

HENDERSON, A. K. 1942. *Handbook of American Mountaineering.* Houghton Mifflin Co. 239 p.

O Q M G. Pamphlet. 1948. *Cold Facts for Keeping Warm.* 68 p.

PORSILD, A. E. 1937. *Edible Roots and Berries of Northern Canada.* J. O. Patenuade. I.S.O. 17 p.

R.C.A.F. 1942. *Manual of Winter Operations.* Special Series No. 18 (Restricted). 141 p.

SIPLE, A. P. *General Principles Governing Selection of Clothing for Cold Climates.* U. S. Antarctic Service.

STANDLEY, P. C. 1943. *Edible Plants of the Arctic Region.* Bureau of Medicine and Surgery, Navy Department. 49 p.

STEFANSSON, V. 1913. *My Life with the Eskimos.* The Macmillan Co. 538 p.

STEFANSSON, V. 1943. *The Friendly Arctic.* The Macmillan Co. 812 p.

STEFANSSON, V. 1944. *Arctic Manual.* The Macmillan Co. 556 p.

STEFANSSON, V. 1945. *The Arctic in Fact and Fable.* Headline Series, Foreign Policy Association. No. 51, 96 p.

War Department. 1943. Special Series No. 18 (Restricted). *German Winter Warfare.* 215 p.

War Department. 1944. F.M. 70-15. *Operations in Snow and Extreme Cold.*

War Department. 1944. T.M. 1-240. *Arctic Manual.* 131 p.

War Department. 1944. T.M. 10-275. *Principles of Cold Weather Clothing and Equipment.* 82 p.

War Department. 1944. F.M. 70-10. *Mountain Operations.*

OCEAN

Air Sea Rescue Agency. *Air Sea Rescue Bulletin.* (Numerous Monthly Issues) U. S. Coast Guard, Washington, D.C.

Army Air Forces, ADTIC. 1943. *Ocean Survival,* Elgin Field, Fla. 17 p.

BLACKMAN, T. M. 1944. *Birds of the Central Pacific Ocean.* Tongg Publishing Co. Honolulu, Hawaii. 70 p.

GATTY, H. 1943. *The Raft Book. George Grady Press.* New York, N.Y. 152 p.

HARBY, S. F. May 1945. *They Survived at Sea.* Nat'l. Geog. Mag. Washington, D.C.

JONES, G. P. 1942. *Two Survived*. Penquin Books Inc. New York. 189 p.

RICHARDS, P. and BANIGAN, J. J. 1942. *How to Abandon Ship*. Cornell Maritime Press, New York. 152 p.

RUSSELL, R. S. and YONGE, C. M. 1928. *The Seas*. Frederick Warne and Co. Ltd., London and New York. 379 p.

Index

TRIMMED SIZE: 6 x 9
TYPE PAGE: 28 x 46 picas
TYPE FACE: Linotype Garamond
TYPE SIZE: 10 point on 12
CHAPTER TITLE: 18 point Garamond Light
PAPER: 50 lb. White Modern Gloss